How Philosophy
Can Save Your Life

ALSO BY MARIETTA MCCARTY

Little Big Minds

How Philosophy

Can Save Your Life

10 Ideas That Matter Most

~

MARIETTA McCARTY

JEREMY P. TARCHER/PENGUIN
a member of Penguin Group (USA) Inc.
New York

JEREMY P. TARCHER/PENGUIN
Published by the Penguin Group
Penguin Group (USA) Inc., 375 Hudson Street, New York, New York 10014, USA •
Penguin Group (Canada), 90 Eglinton Avenue East, Suite 700, Toronto, Ontario
M4P 2Y3, Canada (a division of Pearson Penguin Canada Inc.) • Penguin Books Ltd,
80 Strand, London WC2R 0RL, England • Penguin Ireland, 25 St Stephen's Green,
Dublin 2, Ireland (a division of Penguin Books Ltd) • Penguin Group (Australia),
250 Camberwell Road, Camberwell, Victoria 3124, Australia (a division of Pearson
Australia Group Pty Ltd) • Penguin Books India Pvt Ltd, 11 Community Centre,
Panchsheel Park, New Delhi–110 017, India • Penguin Group (NZ),
67 Apollo Drive, Rosedale, North Shore 0632, New Zealand (a division of Pearson
New Zealand Ltd) • Penguin Books (South Africa) (Pty) Ltd, 24 Sturdee Avenue,
Rosebank, Johannesburg 2196, South Africa

Penguin Books Ltd, Registered Offices: 80 Strand, London WC2R 0RL, England

Most Tarcher/Penguin books are available at special quantity discounts
for bulk purchase for sales promotions, premiums, fund-raising, and
educational needs. Special books or book excerpts also can be created to
fit specific needs. For details, write Penguin Group (USA) Inc.
Special Markets, 375 Hudson Street, New York, NY 10014.

Library of Congress Cataloging-in-Publication Data

McCarty, Marietta, date.
How philosophy can save your life : 10 ideas that matter most / Marietta McCarty.
        p.   cm.
ISBN 978-1-58542-746-8
1. Conduct of life.   2. Philosophy.   I. Title.
BJ1581.2.M4168   2009   2009036615
170'.44—dc22

Printed in the United States of America
7   9   10   8   6

BOOK DESIGN BY AMANDA DEWEY

While the author has made every effort to provide accurate telephone numbers and
Internet addresses at the time of publication, neither the publisher nor the author
assumes any responsibility for errors, or for changes that occur after publication. Further, the publisher does not have any control over and does not assume any responsibility for author or third-party websites or their content.

FOR JUNE

my mother and hands-up favorite philosopher

Contents

Welcome

"What is the good life?" For more than twenty years I have been asking philosophers of all ages and in every imaginable setting this question. The answer so poignantly given by Joe, one of my fatigued and bedraggled college students, sums up the most common response as well as my motivation to write *How Philosophy Can Save Your Life*. "Good living for me means having the time to actually think and make my ideas coherent, instead of feeling forced to react on impulse—quickly and not very intelligently—to everything in my life."

Wherever my philosophical travels take me, I sense a similar eagerness. So many of us are longing for richer, more vibrant emotional and mental lives. We're tired of running in circles, flitting from one barely finished task to another in the pursuit of things that likely don't matter all that much. Sadly, while we're busy spinning, curiosity and awe are cast aside. All too often, we do not take the time to *think* and therefore have little idea what it is that we *need* for the good life.

Ideas are the building blocks of our lives—they help us find our way and know what really matters. The good news is that the prospect of slowing down to discover the lasting benefits of clear thinking, quiet introspection, and, of course, good conversation is drawing more and more new philosophers together in living rooms, on back porches, around picnic tables, and at libraries and community centers every day. This book is an invitation to join them.

In thinking about writing *How Philosophy Can Save Your Life*, I quickly understood that my first task presented the biggest challenge. What ten ideas, if clearly understood and integrated into daily life, can weave together the threads for good living? In a world brimming with ideas, where should I begin? End?! I walked with human and canine friends, talked and pondered, and walked some more. Of all the possible ideas to consider, which ones are absolutely essential for us to understand? Not surprisingly, questions, the calling cards of philosophy, served as my trusted guides. I asked a lot of questions and listened to many more. I recalled the concerns that surface year after year in my philosophizing circles. I could hear the echo of certain thoughts, whether in mixing with my college students, sitting in tiny chairs with child philosophers around the country, or participating in philosophy clubs from Olympia, Washington, to Marblehead, Massachusetts, to Fairfax, Virginia. What simple pleasures in life am I neglecting? Why is honest communication so hard for me? When will I learn not to give in to the crowd? Where did I lose my youthful spontaneity? How can I flow better with changing circumstances? At last, I was satisfied; I picked my top ten.

Philosophy, the art of clear thinking, is not, at least at first, a call to action. It is a wake-up call to think. Philosophy announces that it is spring-cleaning time for our mental and emotional houses.

Intimidated by the expertise of professional "experts," we often, unnecessarily and unfortunately, lose the confidence that we can recite a poem and then interpret it in our own way, listen to classical music and appreciate it just as it sounds to us, talk about a landscape painting without the correct terminology. . . . Be bold and up for adventure! The ability to "philosophize" may seem the most daunting of intellectual pursuits. The truth: it's not. If you can carve out the time and space, philosophy is yours for the asking.

Much good comes from private reflection and cultivating one's sense of wonder in solitude. But there is something uniquely energizing in launching a lunchtime conversation about Camus' belief in human solidarity, or reciting an intriguing lyric from a Led Zeppelin tune to instigate casual musings that can light the spark of philosophy at a party. Dialogue is central to the practice of philosophy. We rely on one another to challenge our assumptions; we grow as we share our discoveries. And, while the solitary reader can dig deep into the ten ideas and benefit from introspection through reading *How Philosophy Can Save Your Life*, this book is perfect for group philosophizing. So gather round. It's time to enter the *real* chat room and reap the rewards of minds and hearts opened and expanded by asking good questions, by sharing personal experiences, and ultimately by using your findings day by day.

One aspect of philosophizing that many find refreshing and appealing is that it does not lay blame, tell you what to do, or make demands. In this spirit, *How Philosophy Can Save Your Life* spreads before you a banquet of ideas and approaches, ancient and modern, Eastern and Western, and leaves you with all the necessary utensils to sample every dish. Where you return for a second helping, what you want to take home with you, and which new tastes were hard to swallow—it's up to you. Are *you* one of the prisoners in Plato's Cave? Do *you* accept Simone de Beauvoir's challenge to map out the future you desire? Have *you* intentionally manufactured drama and difficulty in your life as Charlotte Joko Beck hints? See what fits and wear it well.

I know full well what's in store for you because it is what happened happily for me while writing *How Philosophy Can Save Your*

Life. What a pleasure it was to talk through ideas at a leisurely pace and share with my friends some ways that we might put our new insights to good use. I reread favorite books and dove into ones that had been waiting on the shelf. I scavenged for much-loved poems and was pleased all over again, reading them aloud in return for friends' recitation of their treasured verses. Oh, and the fun we had listening to music of all kinds and chatting about its unique way of imparting soulful wisdom.

Certain themes recurred with insistent force throughout the book. The sheer beauty of the natural world, the silliness of self-importance, the danger of unchecked materialism, the priority of self-improvement, the necessity for gratitude, the hunger for relationship, the desire for a less fearful life. . . . Lifelong and first-time philosophers concur: we know some things to be true. And if we trade in our mental and emotional baggage for clear thinking, we can earn more loving and more fulfilling days.

Yes, the good life is yours for the asking. When asked by my mother what he had learned in my philosophy classes, another one of my college students, Mick, smiled and then worded his answer with care: "It's the sort of thing that doesn't hit you right away. Then you realize it's working big-time." I hope it hits you sooner! I want for you what philosophy continues to feed me: a mind full of ideas that light the path to good living.

USING THE BOOK

This book consists of ten chapters, one for each of the ten ideas. In every chapter, we first explore the given topic and its significance, and then we meet two philosophers whose work lends itself especially well to an investigation of the concept. Discussion questions follow— what I hope to be a lifetime's supply!—guaranteed to stimulate

immediate conversation. Next, you dive, well prepared, into the fun
of "homework assignments" unlike any you endured in school. These
quite enjoyable activities include samplings of engaging prose, poetry,
music, theater, and film that will continue to broaden your conversation about the concept in a new way. Suggestions for individual and
group activities and a list of resources complete each chapter.

Enjoy the book alone in your favorite curling-up spot if you
choose—my guess is that soon you will be asking questions and talking with others about new ideas. Because I can attest to the merriment
and the ongoing benefits of membership in a philosophy club, I urge
you to create one. Whether on your own or with your philosophical
mates, decide how to use the book to best suit your interests. You can
move along with me in the order in which I present the material, but
feel free to vary at will. For example, mix in some of your personal
favorites in music, film, and written works with special relevance to
the topic at hand. If yours is a group particularly drawn to poetry or
music, or a book club focused on prose works, you can devote the
evening to philosophizing through that one genre. Start anywhere in
the chapter: watching a documentary and fielding discussion questions; creating an artistic work suggested in the activities; adding your
stories to those told in the opening section; reflecting on one quote
from each of the two philosophers. . . . This paperback bends easily.

Make or purchase your very own philosophy journal. Bring it to
group gatherings and use it to record your private reflections, sketch
a drawing, create a poem, compose spontaneous lyrics, write a letter.
As years pass, these tattered notebooks appreciate in value.

GETTING STARTED

JUST GET STARTED! Form your own group. Choose four people to
join you, and each of the founding four can invite two more; or

you can ask one person, who then asks another, until you've gotten to your magic number. There is no right way. Twelve philosophers make for good conversation that gives everyone full opportunity to talk, but I've enjoyed fine evenings in smaller and larger gatherings. My college classes of forty prove that good conversation can be enjoyed in large groups. A company can host a meeting for the entire business organization to gain an overview of a topic chosen and introduced by a volunteer employee, and then rendezvous in smaller groups for more personal chats about community or simple pleasures or spontaneity. For future discussions, rotate the members of the smaller groups for variety, keep them intact for familiarity, or use a mix of both.

WHO? The more diverse the group, the more you'll learn. Neighbors, family, colleagues; parents, volunteers, team members or classmates. Mix it up: ages, backgrounds, interests, circumstances.

How OFTEN? At a minimum, once a month. It's good if it's at a consistent time—say, the third Thursday of every month? Possibly supplement this meeting with one or two get-togethers in smaller groups. Regardless of the details, the important thing is to make a commitment of your time and energy to the other members and to the life of your group. Believe me, once you start, it won't be difficult. You will soon count on the grounding supplied by your regular meetings and the practice of philosophy.

HOUSE RULES

Choose an Inviting Setting

If at all possible, avoid the harsh glare of fluorescent lights. Natural light is best; soft lighting and candles in particular call for conversation. Outdoors is perfect if no allergies or other physical limitations pose problems. Sit close together because the wind carries away even the strongest voices. Rotate your meeting place among group members. Be consistent yet flexible.

Sit in a Circle

Make sure that eye contact is easy all around. No backs turned, so that everyone feels a sense of belonging. Our faces and our eyes in particular express truths as well as, and sometimes better than, words. Include all members in your comments, even when speaking directly to one person with a specific question or response.

Start with Quiet Time

Give the first five minutes of every meeting to sitting quietly. The mind clears as you settle and this stillness restores and energizes. You'll look forward to these minutes. Five minutes will grow to ten. . . .

Do Not

1. Talk when someone else is speaking.
2. Make fun of what someone says.

While these golden tenets work beautifully in philosophizing with children, they are even more important for grown-ups. Trust me. Revel in mayhem from time to time, but basic good manners are requirements for meaningful conversation. Interruption usually comes from excitement; making fun often masks discomfort.

Food Matters

Breaking bread together fortifies the body as it buoys spirits. Keep it coming.

Welcome Laughter and Tears

Philosophizing reaps its best rewards when accompanied by laughter. Examining your life, rearranging priorities, and changing your mind is hard; tears spring naturally from honest reflection. Be comfortable, roll, and breathe.

The Moderator

I recommend a rotating moderator for each meeting. This person's charge is to move the dialogue along and bring derailed conversations back on track with a gentle touch. Honing the skill to lead a discussion without dominating it will prove useful in all sorts of situations: at dinner tables, in meetings, in classrooms. Honor the moderator (your turn is coming)!

Watch Yourself

Good conversations ask a lot of the participants. Tone of voice makes or breaks the group dynamic. Listen to your tone and modulate, strictly, as needed. Many times it is *how* you say something that makes all the difference. Animated voices and gestures mark heartfelt dialogue; let lively be. But a good discussion is not the same as an argument. Recognize too much heat and turn it down. Drop your guard and develop the willingness to be challenged. Questions are not attacks. Relax. Asking questions is the business of philosophy. Do not dominate the dialogue; resist the temptation to prove your point. What point?! Learn to sit back; practice pivoting and asking someone, "What do you think?"

Be Ready

Do your homework. Bring your A game.

Make a Plan for the Next Meeting

There is never enough time to talk about it all. As the evening ends in a flurry, be sure that everyone is clear on the specifics for the next meeting. Decide on the best way to include all members in any communication between gatherings: e-mail, holler over the fence, sticky notes on the door. . . .

Simplicity

Life is actually a very simple matter.
—CHARLOTTE JOKO BECK, *Everyday Zen*

THE TOPIC

I can count on it the moment the topic is introduced: the faint breeze of a group exhale wafts through the room. Just the thought of leaving behind complicated lives to savor a life spent enjoying the "simple pleasures" invites the participants to drop their tense and tired shoulders.

Isn't it curious? Caught by a trap we set for ourselves, we want out. Over and over I witness members of a group express their fervent desire for a simpler, happier life with the rest of the audience nodding in agreement. So many of us are moving too fast, and even when we determine to slow down and unpack our consumer bags, just taking a first small step feels nearly impossible. "I need to hurry up and slow down." What?

We are mired in a thicket of *things*, dulled by the noise of advertising and the fury of acquisition. Fads, trinkets, gadgets, name brands only . . . are toys us? Hectic lives overflow the brims of oversized mugs. Debt conquers peace of mind. Many pride themselves on their ability to do many things at once even though none are done especially well, neither thoroughly nor attentively. "Multitasker" is a badge worn by those who maneuver their way through life's traffic jam holding phones, steering wheels, and conversations simultaneously. This race through life comes with a steep price, however. We pay for the whirlwind physically, mentally, and emotionally. We are not in the center of our lives. Energy is scattered and depleted. We are *missing in action.*

Here's one example. Think of the audiovisual attack on the senses that casts its spell on spectators at sporting events—the video screen commercials, blaring music, and on-field entertainment, all competing for a fan's attention to the game. I remember too well my experience last summer at a Mariners game in Seattle. In the row in front of me an excited mother and son sat huddled over the scorecard cradled between them. Alas, the "scorecard" receiving their smiling, undivided attention was a handheld video game. In the row behind me, a party of friends laughed and chatted together . . . on cell phones in separate "conversations." I know, I should have been watching the baseball game! The fans' distractions, however, are snapshots of our times.

Concerning this race to nowhere, philosophers throughout time and across cultures join hands and issue a dramatic warning: unchecked desire is never satisfied. Further, the philosophers are encouraging in their insistence that we do not need much to satisfy our material needs. The underlying heartbeat of philosophy is the firm conviction that our first priority is mental and spiritual well-being. Devotion to material possessions robs the mind and heart of the time we owe to our inner development. Thinking trumps things. But is it possible to ignore advertising? Can we be wisely modern? What really matters? Here we are and it is time to take a stand. What to do?

We can begin by paying attention to the attraction that simplicity still holds for us. Open spaces beckon—a park, a garden, a field, a porch—and invite us to linger. Similarly, unassuming people draw us to their company—direct, open, natural; they make us feel at home. Just a taste of plain living can stay with us no matter how busy we are. What touches us when we catch a glimpse of a solitary figure resting with outstretched legs on the bank of a flowing river? Just the river and its lone admirer, so *simple* . . .

What is simplicity? What is a *simple* way of living? Words come quickly to mind: plain, pure, uncomplicated, basic, modest, essential. Essential . . . that's it. A simple lifestyle is complete in the essentials needed to live well. We can uncover or rediscover these essentials for satisfied living by streamlining our lives. What are the basics that we must have for good living?

It is clear now that philosophy's insistent caution against attachment to material possessions is sound, practical advice. Once our physical needs are met, and philosophy reminds us that they are few, the basic desires of the mind and heart remain. Simple pleasures feed our essential selves: listening to music, being outdoors, seeing a loved face at the door, laughing all the way, knowing we did our best work, wearing clothes softened by age, reading all day, watching a flight of wild geese, running for home, and breathing deeply. . . . Such soul food has been at our fingertips all along. We overlook "ordinary" joys completely when we overextend our reach into the world of things. It is time to use a paring knife to peel away unnecessary concerns; it is time to take the pruning shears to preoccupations that sap the spirit from our lives.

Now your work begins to explore and define the meaning of simplicity. Sitting around the table with you as part of your group, here is my contribution. Simplicity is living close to the marrow of life. I imagine nibbling at life's essence while being surrounded by it. The breath of simple living feels clear and crisp. Simplicity's promise is that it will make me rich: I will have plenty of time to spend, some to give away, and even more in the bank. I can be involved in my life and savor each experience because my priorities are in keeping with lasting happiness. A simple life includes difficulty and heartache, of course, but newfound calm and clarity will be great assets. The knot of pointless pursuits loosens. Space appears, giving me room to meet my responsibilities. There is something oddly grand about the prospect of living life at its juicy core.

By far the number-one problem brought up in philosophical discussions over the years—in bookstores, business seminars, book clubs, classrooms—is the dead end of materialism and the anxiety and sadness that is the real cost of acquiring "stuff." The frustration for so many of understanding the need for simplicity yet failing to act accordingly magnifies the problem. Often I ask fledgling philosophers to imagine being alive in the thrill of the invention of the printing press. Copying manuscripts by hand was hard work and access to the written word was limited to a select few. The printing press made the process of reproducing texts easier and books became available to regular folks, but the press did not take over people's lives. Again, it must have been quite startling when a telephone clanged for the first time in a quiet home, yet it was easier than running to fetch the physician or driving the wagon to tell your sister the good news. But can you imagine an immediate desire to take that phone everywhere, always? We can be smart about what constitutes progress and dismiss the frills that complicate.

Simplicity is the concept that comes first in our lives and in this book. Clear thinking is impossible if material concerns remain our priorities and our goals. A good grasp of simplicity is a prerequisite for thinking clearly about communication, perspective, possibility— all our topics. Simplicity serves as a dust cloth for the mind, and as the mind brightens, anything is possible.

Epicurus (eh-pih-KYOOR-us) brings good tidings from ancient Greece. Opt for the good life. Live well. Thrive on life's simple pleasures. Charlotte Joko Beck agrees with Epicurus thousands of years later. Slow down and stop. Sit. Enjoy.

THE PHILOSOPHERS

Pleasure is the end . . . . freedom from pain
in the body and trouble in the mind.
—EPICURUS, *"Letter to Menoeceus"*

Imagine that you are enjoying a walk on the outskirts of ancient Athens. You come upon a house with a garden and move closer to see what's going on. The house is plain and the garden inviting in its simplicity; contentment hangs in the air. Barefoot men and women stroll through the garden alone and in pairs, some with hands clasped behind their backs, others gesturing toward a field of wheat or birds gathered in a treetop. Occasionally the strollers stop for a drink of water and break bread together, continuing their conversations or solitary contemplation. Slight smiles crinkle the corners of their mouths and eyes. You must wonder what secret way of life breeds such obvious satisfaction. You see no evidence of wine and cheese or olives and fruit and absolutely no indication of luxury. What kind of commune is this?!

Epicurus was born a citizen of Athens on the island of Samos in 341 BCE. His family was uprooted by the political turmoil of the day, and Epicurus's resultant disdain for political life never wavered. He decided that public life in general and politics in particular made tranquillity impossible. His house and garden served as a secure retreat for his friends/followers, an egalitarian mix of slaves and free citizens, women and men.

Epicurus's philosophy evolved from his life experience. A practical, commonsense approach to living, it recognizes that pleasure is the main ingredient of a good life and that simplicity is the key to obtaining pleasure and minimizing pain. Epicurus's brand of enjoyment does not consist of immediate and intense gratification; his goal was abiding satisfaction unaltered by circumstances spread over a lifetime. He chose to live his beliefs in his house and garden, celebrating the wealth of simple pleasures available to those who turn their backs on extravagance and its consequences. A spare diet, good conversation, lasting friendships, shelter, a soft rain, the sun on your back, time spent recalling happy times—all are free and the rewards last a lifetime. Epicurus begs us to discover the freedom that comes from needing little.

Alas, few of us can retire with our friends to a house and garden of simple delights. Can Epicurus speak to the consumer age? Can he help us realize simplicity in *our* everyday lives? I watch year after year as he equips grateful philosophers of all ages with rich appreciation for life's bounties. His philosophy seduces many to give simple living a try.

Prudence

Epicurus's central virtue, prudence, requires a no-*nonsense*, rigorous examination of the circumstances of our lives. Prudence determines that while pleasure is the goal of life, we must be very smart in how we go about achieving it. Many pleasures come with painful consequences that override the original enjoyment. "And since pleasure is the first good and natural to us, for this very reason we do not choose every pleasure, but sometimes we pass over many pleasures, when greater discomfort accrues to us as the result of them . . ." (Epicurus, "Letter to Menoeceus" [meh-NEE-see-us]). We must first be vigilant in recognizing the ingredients of a happy life and then experience pure pleasures unaccompanied by misery. Taking the time to write a letter to express your joy in a friend's happiness is time well spent. A drink of pure water is utterly gratifying. Also, temporary, short-term pain can buy a multitude of future simple pleasures. Be smart. It may be temporarily unpleasant, for example, to take a prudent look at a few credit card statements, but the short-term pain of recognizing excess can provide many simple pleasures in the future. Look hard at your purchases, Epicurus whispers. Did you actually purchase anxiety, fitful sleep, and more work at the expense of unnecessary items? Prudence suggests trading the name-brand sneakers for a first-class nap. Curbing the desire to spend can buy peace of mind and time to relax.

Desire is powerful fuel. Prudence can keep desire in check with its sensible detection of the true needs in our lives.

The Difference Between Need and Want

Epicurus spent a lifetime dissecting desire, and his insights retain great relevance for contemporary living. He pointed out the critical distinction between needs and wants while insisting that we must get better at recognizing the difference between the two. Epicurus categorized some desires as natural, other desires as vain. For example, it is natural to want to move from place to place. Prudence suggests we first try our feet and legs, maybe a bike, perhaps public transportation or a car pool. Vanity suggests a big car with all the fancy accessories, one to be traded in for a new model every year. The desire for friends is natural, while clinging to the hope of friendship with an "important" person is vain. Epicurus continued his careful dissection. Among natural desires, some are essential while others are trivial. The desire for food is essential. You can picture Epicurus at a farmer's market, buying what is produced locally while encouraging his neighbors to grow fruit and vegetables on a shared plot of land. Leftovers are welcome. Eat the potato and the apple, skin and all. In stark contrast, buying processed food, eating out as the norm, making caviar a staple of your diet—all of these practices reduce the essential desire for sustenance to a triviality. Shopping at a "convenience store" for food calls the meaning of both "convenience" and "food" into question!

One can learn to discriminate between natural and vain desires. It's *simple*, Epicurus concluded: "The wealth demanded by nature is both limited and easily procured; that demanded by idle imaginings stretches on to infinity" ("Principal Doctrines"). Easy, actually, does it.

Independence from Desire

You have the power of discernment. You can figure out what is essential for a pleasurable life and what is not. You can do this, Epicurus encourages us today, but first you must, to some extent, leave behind the swirling pace set by those around you. Frequent the company of those who believe as you do that "independence of desire we think a great good" ("Letter to Menoeceus"). Just as Epicurus departed from public life in Athens, you must shift—not necessarily physically, but surely mentally and spiritually—away from the roar of mainstream culture's advertising and media glitz. According to Epicurus, society's determination of the good life is surely meaningless. Why hand over your good judgment to corporate sponsors? Priorities begin to shift with the powerful decision to recapture our lives. Simplicity takes us back to the past and moves us forward into the future.

Be Wide Open

The more one reads Epicurus, the clearer it becomes: simple joys are both abundant and easily gotten. We are surrounded by them. Be open to sensory pleasure: the taste once again of a favorite food from childhood and the warm memory that comes with it; sitting on the porch as day slips into night and feeling on your skin the beginning of the shift of seasons; the smell of damp earth and fresh-cut grass;

watching a lonely person begin to make friends; thinking a much-loved song is over and all of a sudden there's another verse! Epicurus is still correct: the "limit of good things is easy to fulfill and easy to attain" ("Letter to Menoeceus").

Finally, he was optimistic that we have the ability to deal with mental disturbance. Using sound reasoning we can get to the root of anxiety and adjust our lives accordingly. He elevates mental pleasures in general over physical pleasures. Mental pleasures are more numerous, more easily controlled, and rarely have painful consequences: countless stars come out at night, addiction to stargazing is rare, and looking at the sky at night is free and harmless. And while some physical pain cannot be avoided, we have the mental power to minimize its effect. Epicurus suffered from chronic pain and diminished its power by recalling the joys of friendship.

BUT, BUT, BUT, BUT . . . Do you have reservations about the benefits and even the possibility of finding a simpler way? Epicurus is ready to listen.

"*But*, I have a lot of responsibilities in my life that are real. I take care of my mother, have two children and a job." The response from ancient Greece: I understand. Use good common sense to distinguish between your responsibilities and all the extras that are not your obligations. Meetings, clubs, hosting, joining, parties—decide what is necessary. What about all those planned activities for your children?

"*But* I will be ridiculed for changing my lifestyle. I will be judged a failure if I scale back my possessions and commitments. People will think there is something wrong with me and I'll be an outcast." Epicurus cautions us to think about it. Be your own measure of success. Grow strong and confident in your conviction that an unadorned life is full of pleasure and lasting satisfaction. Now, is your brow less furrowed and your jaw unclenched? Yes? Simplicity becomes you.

"*But*, I can't do it. I want things and I love to look at the clothes in my closet. Shoes are my passion." Practice the virtue of temperance, Epicurus patiently recommends. You can temper desire, chipping away at it so that it loses its stranglehold. It is possible to discipline yourself to need less. Every day at a certain time you can open a book instead of your closet. You can live more simply if you *choose* to do so. How expensive are those clothes and shoes? Think hard. "No pleasure is a bad thing in itself: but the means which produce some pleasures bring with them disturbances many times greater than the pleasures" ("Principal Doctrines"). Whoever you are, whatever your circumstances, you can take the urgency out of want.

"*But*, are you asking me to give away all my possessions? C'mon, do you expect me to live on bread and water like you? Are you telling me it's wrong to enjoy sitting on my patio in a comfortable chair while enjoying a fine meal?" "Those have the sweetest pleasure in luxury who least need it. . . . To grow accustomed therefore to simple and not luxurious diet gives us health to the full, and makes a man alert for the needful employments of life, and when after long intervals we approach luxuries, disposes us better towards them, and fits us to be fearless of fortune" ("Letter to Menoeceus"). Lean back and savor that meal! You can be active and involved in the world, doing this and that, and still be prudent about your priorities. Meet essential needs. Simplify wisely, and enjoy thoroughly, the gardener from Athens concludes.

Epicurus knew that there was only so much room in his community. Most people live in the world. The question is how best to do so. "Wherefore both when young and old a man must study philosophy, that as he grows old he may be young in blessings through the grateful recollection of what has been, and that in youth he may be old as well, since he will know no fear of what is to come" ("Letter to Menoeceus").

We're all looking for an ideal life.

—CHARLOTTE JOKO BECK, *Everyday Zen*

"I did it to myself." "It's all in my mind." "I have no idea why I did that again." These common refrains make it clear that our minds need work.

Charlotte Joko Beck studied at the Oberlin Conservatory of Music and is a gifted pianist and teacher. An American woman who has worked a variety of jobs while assuming the responsibilities of a divorced mother of four children, she was in her forties when she delved into the study of Zen Buddhism, later founding the Ordinary Mind School of Zen, and in 1983 opening a Zen Center in San Diego. She directed the center until 2006 and now teaches part-time in Prescott, Arizona.

Her informal conversations with her students, recorded in *Everyday Zen*, are remarkable in their razor-sharp simplicity. Beck clear-cuts her way through the tangle of modern life and takes her students with her. She deals with universal concerns—expectations, choices, fears, feelings, dreams—and discusses her weaknesses with refreshing candor. Beck keeps it simple for her students and for us as she returns at the end of each conversation to her central point: live life as it is from the center of your being. We must stitch ourselves together and engage fully in each moment of our lives.

The realization that desire causes suffering is at the heart of Buddhist teaching. We can diminish suffering significantly as we gradually reduce the clinging, grasping addiction to our wants. A big effort of will is called for once we acknowledge the power that desire holds over our lives. We must be willing to work hard, bit by bit, to grow less attached. While it is a step to keep walking past the shop window, it is important to know deep down that the purchase was indeed unnecessary. Walking past the store, putting down the catalog, and ignoring the advertisement . . . this constant practice in little things matters.

Letting Go of Ego

According to Beck, the number-one project is to work on our mischievous minds. And it is no easy task to move the mind from confused, frantic jumble to calm, clear simplicity. Seeking restlessly after an imagined ideal life must stop. We create complication, manufacturing confusion as we try, hopelessly, to manipulate life to suit *our* expectations. We use our endless desires, binding attachments, and strong sense of ego to create our own version of reality. Things get fuzzy. The more we impose our needs on the world, the more hidden the real world becomes. The ego is *the* problem, a broken compass that uses our own perspective as the reference point for everything. "Stop being mean to me," the loud ego shouts. "*I* like, that's *mine*, get out of *my* way." "Life is a second-by-second miracle, but dreaming our *I*-dreams we miss it" (*Everyday Zen*). Of course we want the best vantage point at a concert or sporting event, the place that will give us the best view of the event. In our own lives, unfortunately, it turns out that we have been in the rafters behind a big post only imagining what is going on.

It is so easy to assume that *our* view is *the* view and that the world conforms exactly to our perception of it. To highlight the ego's trickery with an analogy, I ask my students to imagine a self-centered photographer. She stands on a hillside admiring vibrant autumn colors in the distance framed by the backdrop of a stunning sunset. She really wants this photograph. But she can't bring the landscape into focus no matter how hard she tries; the lens distorts the picture at every turn. What is creating the distortion? What is the problem with the lens? The photographer's ego, in my example, is blurring the lens with its self-centered perspective. "I am imposing *my* needs, *my* opinions, *my* emotions on the landscape," she realizes. Letting go of her limited viewpoint, the picture grows sharper and more precise in detail. "Through living each moment as it is, the ego gradually drops away, revealing the wonder of everyday life" (*Everyday Zen*). Ahh . . . The fall foliage and the colors of the sunset appear as they are and our photographer experiences the landscape as part of it. Beck proposes just such a merger. We can join with the world as it is as we become whole in our lives again. Just one single, simple reality: the world and us *within* it.

Let's take a hard look at ways in which we expertly complicate our lives, and Beck's simple, though not always easy, remedies.

Playing at a Cinema Near You

We make of our lives a dramatic production, serving as both director and star of a film that is always some version of *Big, Big Me*. What about this "Me"? Listen to him: "Everybody is against me and you would not believe how hard my life is. Nobody has time for me and I have so much to offer. I had a bad experience at the bank and some fool banged into my fender. I have too much to do and no one cares." Who wants to see *this* movie?! It is worth watching, however, because everyone suffers mental agitation and emotional obsession to some extent. "It's interesting to me that people don't see any connection between their misery and their complaints—their feeling of being a victim; the feeling that everyone is doing something *to* them" (*Everyday Zen*). We can't let go of a conversation, an event, a past wrong, or a future worry. Emotion-riddled thought patterns build upon themselves. Beck warns against "add-ons"—the layers of confusion that we pile on top of life *as it is*. This mistaken investment in time and energy makes us physically and mentally sick. It is really hard work for our filmmaker to construct a reality designed to suit his needs only, but it's his career. Perversely, perched on a low branch as an outside observer of his life, he enjoys the drama he's created, taking peculiar pleasure in his poorly made fiction rather than living *his* life. "The secret is, we like that unreal structure a lot better than we like our real life" (*Everyday Zen*).

Beck has a suggestion for the filmmaker in all of us: remember the empty rowboat. If you were enjoying the day in a boat on a lake and were suddenly rammed by a rowboat, you would be furious! But the rowboat is empty. . . . With no way to personalize the event, with no target for your agitation and anger, complete attention zeroes in on the repair job. Our "add-ons" can complicate any event, but we can learn to concentrate on the situation rather than directing emotion at a particular person. Our minds keep us attached to drama but they can also serve as part of the solution. We can work on ourselves and refuse to give in to the obsessive attachment to "big, big me." Our question shifts from "How can *you* do that to *me?*" to "How can I best deal with this *event?*" "Ninety percent of the thoughts spinning around in our heads have no essential reality. And we go from birth to death, unless we wake up, wasting most of our life with them" (*Everyday Zen*). Empty the rowboat until only life preservers remain.

The Endless If

We are crafty, always able to find new ways to complicate our lives. "If only, if only, if only . . . if only I had a bigger house, if only I could meet the right person to get me in the door, if only I had a stock portfolio, if only I had the money to join the club, if only I could get a better paying job, if only I . . . my problems would be solved and my life would be great, if only." Wrapped and wired by dreams of a better life, we miss this one. We desperately "seek a solution outside ourselves" (*Everyday Zen*). Fancying this and itching for that, we wander. The belief that we can find the good life externally ruins our lives.

What is Beck's thought on a life of *if onlys*? Stop it. A pleasant, comfortable life consists in living the circumstances of your life as they are as only you can. We really want a natural life, a stripped-down life that does not focus on competition and achievement.

Dreams of people and things that will make us happy always end in frustration and disappointment. Look within. It's all there. And you know it.

Just Sit

Finally, let's eavesdrop on one last effort to accept and even embrace complicated living. Imagine that you are one of Beck's students and, oh, yes, you are going to set her straight. "Have you forgotten how hectic our lives really are? There is no way to escape society's scrutiny. How many of us can retire to a garden like Epicurus or spend time in a monastery? I don't know anyone without anxiety, and the many sources of stress in our lives spiral exponentially. I do want to empty my rowboats and I know my endless list of *if only*s is foolish, but it seems hopeless to me. My lifestyle is essentially distracted and it's too far gone to fix." Beck has heard it all before and answers: "If we don't simplify the situation the chance of taking a good look at ourselves is very small—because what we tend to look at isn't ourselves, but everything else" (*Everyday Zen*).

Just sit. How many times have those two words been Beck's answer, lesson, solution, and plea? Oh, come on, is it as simple as "just sit"? Yes, Beck encourages; though not easy, it is just that simple. Sitting in silence allows the self to settle. "Most people who sit for years find their lives considerably simplified—not because of some virtue but because, needing less, desires naturally drift away . . . years ago I never could go to work without nail polish and lipstick (all matching). . . . But as you practice . . . your central concern about what you really want for your life changes" (*Everyday Zen*). Sitting returns the sitter's life to its essential unity. Breathing, inhaling and exhaling, deep and rhythmic, pulls the pieces together. Sitting is a most practical approach to simplifying our lives. This practice gives us the space and the time to open to a centered, satisfying life. The wonder of being alive awakens; myriad simple joys abound. Alone and quiet, allowing thoughts and emotions to course freely through the mind and then letting them go . . . eventually the sitter becomes still. Fragments of a scattered life melt together like ice cream. Sitting soothes and restores gently. Confusion and difficulty are no match for stillness. An inner life of the spirit is our basic nature. Sitting awakens simplicity. There is a sanctuary at our core that is simple, clear, and peaceful.

Think of the periodic table of elements in chemistry. Such elements—iron and sodium, for example—are the purest, simplest, physical unity. Made up of one type of atom only, each element is complete and whole in itself. Oxygen is oxygen. Basic human nature is complete much like these elements. There is solid integrity at the core of every human being. Each of us is one energetic whole. In essence we are safe, stable, secure beings. It is the goal of sitting to put this calm, simple center in charge of our lives.

Meditation and relaxation are ways of "sitting." Traditional Buddhist meditation emphasizes posture, focus, and breathing. Imagine a string at the top of your head softly lifting slumped shoulders and tight muscles. A healthy, slow inhale that expands the diaphragm and a slow, releasing exhale whose push opens the body. When you focus on breathing, the breath takes over. The internal world rouses as external forces fade. *Relaxation* is a less fancy word than *meditation* and one with which we are all familiar. Relaxation, however, as a way to practice "just sitting" is not a vacation in an imagined future. It is an everyday retreat that refreshes the body and clears the mind. Concentrated relaxation serves as a tune-up that ignites the connection between the mind and the body. Our natural biological response to "shutting down" is rather miraculous. With fifteen to twenty minutes of "time-out," the body's autonomic response kicks in. Head spinning ceases in the comfort of the same daily repeated activity. Playing games, reading a book, watching TV are not examples of doing nothing. In contrast, concentration on one object—knitting, or walking in a consistent, rhythmic pattern of movement—constitutes relaxing rehabilitation.

Beck helps us find a place in our hearts for Epicurus's garden. The simple self, recovered through sitting, finds uncommon delight in "ordinary" joys that have been concealed by the mind's shenanigans. Each moment has its own measure of amazement: the air is cold and the sun is warm on my face. The drama ends and contentment is the new show. "If only" becomes "look at this!" Keep sitting. Sitting grounds us and brings us home to our true nature and restores the simple unity of one life. We can carry this simple rhythm within us in our work, play, interactions—in the midst of all of it, as best we can. Holding fast to the center is the effort of a lifetime. "Remember also that a little humor about all this isn't a bad idea" (*Everyday Zen*).

Yes, Humpty Dumpty had a great fall, but look at him now! All the pieces *are* back together again. Like Humpty, we can become whole. "When we aren't into our personal mischief, life is a seamless whole in which we are so embedded that there is no problem" (*Everyday Zen*). Sure, our minds' finagling will always cover the pure center of our lives with some extra stuff, but we can make this dusting paper-thin. Breathing helps us remember that life is a simple matter. We can practice life as we practice piano. Practice the scales every day, without fail. Be still and practice relaxation every day, or else. It is possible to be in the world yet not be molded by it, possible to love it all without attachment. Remember the meaning of "enough."

Enough.

DISCUSSION QUESTIONS

- What is simplicity? (Use as few words as possible.)
- What does it mean to live simply?

- What are the ingredients of a good life?
- What are five realizations about your life that you will remember from your look at Epicurus?
- What are five personal insights from Beck that you will remember and use?
- What are some of life's many simple pleasures? Why do we forget them?
- What are some things in your life that you can deposit in your "unnecessary" file? What assumptions and opinions can be added to the file? Emotions? Worries? Fears?
- Do you confuse what you need with what you want?
- In what ways has indulgence hurt your life? Give some examples. What are the consequences of extravagance?
- Why don't we slow down? What is difficult about "pruning back" our lives?
- How do we work hard to complicate our lives? Be specific. Why do we do this?
- If we know that it's too much, too fast, too often, why don't we stop? If we are doing it to ourselves, is it in our power to change?
- Describe what you need for a satisfying life. Are you surprised at the things that you do not include?
- What does it mean to be "too busy"?
- How can we be lonely and restless if we possess every possible material comfort?
- Steadily mindful of simplicity, how do you imagine your life changing . . . slowly, surely?
- When you look back on your life—let's say one hundred years from now—can you picture the memories pressed close to your heart?

HOMEWORK

Listen and Hum

Sound is simple. There are so many ways to experience simplicity by listening to music. Just listen. Now listen again. How does simplicity reveal itself in the notes and the spaces between the notes, in the interplay between instruments, through voice and the pauses between words? Everyone choose at least one musician and his or her work from *each* of the following groups. Make sure every artist is covered so that you can share snippets and comments.

Set 1

- Alison Brown is a girl in love with her banjo. Defying neat description, her quartet's instrumental music is a tapestry of bluegrass, jazz, and folk. Eavesdrop on a five-minute conversation between the banjo and the mandolin on "Musette for a Palindrome." One reviewer remarks about Brown's recordings: "Like the best acoustic music, these are exquisite celebrations of simple pleasures." How does acoustic music embody simplicity?

- Aaron Copland's "Old American Songs" returns us to days gone by through the delicate baritone of Thomas Hampson, including his moving rendition of "Simple Gifts." Dawn Upshaw's struck-crystal soprano celebrates Copland's "Eight Poems of Emily Dickinson." Copland's composition is straightforward and uncomplicated, and the two vocalists dive directly to the heart of each note. What can you learn from yesteryear?

- Thelonious Monk creates solitude while inviting the listener to share it in his quiet, spacious compositions. Imagine that you slip unnoticed beside him at the piano bench and watch his fingers, especially as he plays "Ask Me Now." How does Monk's sound, with so few keys touched, create a place to rest?

Set 2

- Benjamin Britten's *Simple Symphony*, composed when he was twenty-one, is the product of music he wrote between nine and twelve years of age. The four parts of this symphony are termed Boisterous, Playful, Sentimental, and Frolicsome. How do string instruments convey those descriptions exactly? Why would a child's composition likely be simple?

- Dianne Reeves, the first Creative Chair for Jazz with the L.A. Philharmonic, has a voice that knows instinctively how to find the pitch of each note perfectly. Without frills or drama, her rendition of "Morning Has Broken" welcomes a new day; simply, she promises that "There'll Be Another Spring." Reeves meshes with the music in a way that invites the listener to be part of the song, as well. How does it feel to be drawn into the music?

- Climbing up three notes and climbing back down, this riff has moved feet, hips, and shoulders for generations. It's really hard to get any "Satisfaction," especially "when I'm drivin' in my car / and that man comes on the radio . . ." The Rolling Stones, in 1965, take an unflinching, critical look at information overload and advertising's endless nagging. The relevance of the lyrics and the lure of the irresistible beat endure. How can you weed out the unending influx of "useless information"? Is it possible to experience "the health of the body and the soul's freedom from disturbance" (Epicurus, "Letter to Menoeceus")?

Set 3

- "I got cotton in the bottom land" and I'll "get new shoes come Pickin' Time." Johnny Cash, with his simple yet elegant guitar style, sings about life's basic necessities and the joys of family, a good crop, and a wagon that keeps rolling. "But the only people who live comfortably are those who learn not to dream their lives away, but to be with what's right-here-now, no matter what it is" (Beck, *Everyday Zen*). As you listen you can imagine a world in which satisfaction comes from relishing the essential ingredients of a good life. What would give you joy come "Pickin' Time"?

- You can hear each pluck of the strings of the cuatro, the small Venezuelan guitar played by Marta Topferova. Her voice is strong and direct, emotive and relaxing. Harp and drums complement the cuatro beautifully on "Grano de Arena." Instrumental and vocal sections highlight each other, giving Topferova's music the power to calm and comfort. Practice enjoyment.

- A man slaps a plank of wood and motions for you to join him on the "Dock of the Bay." Otis Redding is "watching the tide roll away" and he'll be "sittin' when the evenin' comes." The movement of the water at the song's opening and his whistle when the song fades away soothe. Just sittin'. Resting. Idling. Describe the experience at the dock with Otis and Beck.

- "Twinkle, Twinkle, Little Star"! Mozart finds much to do with this simple folk tune known in many cultures. Enjoy the variety contained within simplicity in *Twelve Variations in C on "Ah! Vous Dirai-je, Maman."* It seems that you can do a lot with a little. A simple life is open to infinite possibilities. Do you agree?

Set 4

- From the first notes exchanged between Charlie Haden and Hank Jones, the duo's interpretations of spirituals, hymns, and folk songs invite you to do just as the title of this collection suggests: *Steal Away*. The beautiful, respectful interplay between the bassist and pianist creates a mesmerizing, satisfying sound in which every note counts. Sometimes the music does just as Beck suggests: it "just sits." Listening to "Nobody Knows the Trouble I've Seen" is so uplifting that you can find pleasure in thinking about what trouble you have *not* seen. Name some troubles that haven't come your way. Similarly, "We Shall Overcome" has no trace of obstacle or hardship about it and seems a simple statement of fact.

- What is it about a lullaby? What ingredients are *not* found in a lullaby and what qualities remain? Listen to Gustav Mahler's lullaby-like "Adagietto." Listen again. How do you feel? Can you explain why?

- "Don't have to buy me diamonds or pearls," assures Kitty Kallen in her signature tune "Little Things Mean a Lot." The song sings for itself. With a kick and a twist Doc Watson lends his legendary voice and guitar to his version of the song. Name some "little things" that are big for you.

Recite and Write

Take turns reading aloud these poems several times, pausing sufficiently between readings to absorb the ways in which the poem touches you. With each recitation the poem has a chance to seep into another space in your heart. In your philosophy journal, write your own poem in direct response to at least two poems.

- Behold in color and verse William Wordsworth's "The Daffodils" from Caroline Kennedy's collection of her favorite poetry for children. The painted daffodils accompanying the poem leap from the page. What pleasure a simple flower can bring! "And then my heart with pleasure fills, / And dances with the daffodils." Wordsworth exclaims that just picturing a daffodil fills his heart. What one simple pleasure moves you in this way?

- "may my heart always be open to little / birds who are the secrets of living." e. e. cummings begins this poetic celebration of life's simple pleasures with a reminder to be attentive to the birds overhead. cummings takes no pride in being somehow useful to society and smiles at the thought of pulling the sky over him like a blanket. If your heart remains open to _____, then _____?

- "Poem Without a Category" invites you into the poet's world. Gensei takes a seventeenth-century walk by a garden, stops for tea, and crosses a small stream. His walk inspires him to write poem after poem with a joy reminiscent of that shared by Epicurus and friends. "The point in life is to know what's enough." What is your response to Gensei's proclamation? How did he know about "enough" centuries ago? "Meditate therefore on these things and things akin to them night and day by yourself, and with a companion like to yourself, and never shall you be disturbed waking or asleep" (Epicurus, "Letters to Menoeceus"). Gensei suggests, as well, that infinite happiness would not even begin to fill the human heart. What expands your heart and keeps expanding it?

- After you read Emily Dickinson's "Nature, The Gentlest Mother," stretch your legs and listen as Dawn Upshaw sings Aaron Copland's musical rendition. "Her golden finger on her lip / Wills silence everywhere." In clear and simple language Dickinson presents Mother Nature as the caretaker of us all. Nature's affection is infinite, extending to the squirrel, the lichen, and the fallen tree. What happens to the poet's words when Upshaw's voice carries them? What carries your heart in the most basic way?

- In tenth-century Japan, Izumi Shikibu writes crackling-sharp poems that capture a moment in only a few lines. She understands herself perfectly as she gazes alone at the moon as night slips into day. "Watching the Moon" conveys a world in five short lines. How can looking at the moon in solitude teach you basic truths about yourself? What do plum trees and snow, the wind and the grass teach you? Paint a picture with words by limiting your response to "Watching the Moon" to five short lines.

- Mary Oliver asks "How Would You Live Then?" Were you startled when "the mockingbird came into the house with you and / became your advisor"? If we were open to the magnificence of the world and awe took hold, how would we live? How busy would we be? What would our priorities be? What if we realized that the silver shade of water is brighter than silver coins? What if we knew in our bones that sunflowers were more valuable than gold? Tell Oliver how you would live then.

Read and Talk

- "Every person needs to take one day away." Maya Angelou's "A Day Away" is an invitation that is hard to refuse. Angelou entices the reader with images of park benches, comfortable shoes, and no clock to alarm the body. "The most unalloyed source of protection from men . . . is in fact the immunity which results from a quiet life and the retirement from the world" (Epicurus, "Principal Doctrines"). She presents a day away as a delight for the escapee and a boon to all when the refreshed person returns to the world. Angelou's very short personal essays are earthy and plain-spoken. Share other essays from her collection that model simplicity.

- "Touch the earth, love the earth, honour the earth, her plains, her valleys, her hills, and her seas; rest your spirit in her solitary places. For the gifts of life are the earth's and they are given to all, and they are the songs of birds at daybreak, Orion and the Bear, and dawn seen over ocean from the beach." Henry Beston spends a year on the beach of Cape Cod and records his love affair with the world in *The Outermost House*. The dunes and moors may have changed since its publication in 1928, but the joy of experiencing nature's simple pleasures remains. What happened to Beston during this year? What happens to you when you become immersed in nature?

- Bobbie Ann Mason celebrates the art of short-story telling in *Shiloh and Other Stories*. She takes us home with her to rural western Kentucky and makes us a part of the collision between modern life and simpler times. "Granny's teeth no longer fit, and she has to bite sideways, like a cat." Take pleasure in Mason's tales, the humor and poignancy in her loving detail of country living. Cleo insists, "I could tell you things that would sizzle your tail feathers." Sizzling in simpler days reminds you of . . . ?

- What are the benefits of the use of simple, direct language? How can uncomplicated words make meaning clear? Edith Wharton cuts to the heart of language, and the vibrancy that comes from her pure way with words strikes the reader in *Ethan Frome*. Some examples: "rigid gooseberry bushes," "intensely blue shadows of hemlocks on sunlit snow," "something bleak and unapproachable in his face . . . the red gash across Ethan Frome's forehead." It is a simple, gut-wrenching tale told with spare language. You can feel the cold of the air and the lives of the townsfolk in Starkfield. Why is it hard to speak and write in a clear, articulate way? Does mental confusion twist the tongue? How can we work on ourselves to think and to speak without "add-ons" and on and on? Select passages from *Ethan Frome* that elicit emotion and paint a vivid picture in but a few words. For me: "After another interval he added, turning to the figure in the armchair: 'And this is Miss Mattie Silver . . .'"

- What happens when we slow down and pay attention? Lang Elliott and Wil Hershberger invite your group to a concert of "insect musicians." Katydids and crickets are performing in the backyard for free. The photographs in *The Songs of Insects* are a delight, and the accompanying compact disc is an excursion into a relaxing world all too easy to ignore. Discuss ways in which the cicadas and their friends embody simplicity as you listen to their music and look at the photographs. Notice the intricacy of their simple beings. Such sophisticated simplicity!

- How is it possible that in 2004, the three major networks gave twenty-six minutes to the unthinkable tragedy in Darfur and 130 minutes to Martha Stewart? In *Fame Junkies*, Jake Halpern looks in depth at the obsession in the United States with celebrity. He calls this obsession "America's Favorite Addiction," and Halpern takes us to the "International Model and Talent Association" convention where the best in "kiddie talent" will be determined. What in the world? Why do so many children and adults count on future fame as the solution to their problems? What problems? What is missing from *our* lives that we want nothing more than to live the lives of *others*?

Discuss the allure of living outside one's own life and inside imagined glitz and glamour. "What we want to do is to find some way of working with the basic insanity that exists because of our blindness" (Beck, *Everyday Zen*).

Watch and Reflect

- Watch *The Wild Parrots of Telegraph Hill*. A street musician, Mark Bittner, learns to love his life through his simple, intimate relationship with red and green parrots in San Francisco. He and the parrot Mingus sing about "peace of mind." Judy Irving's film *is* simplicity celebrated in countless ways. The camera lingers so that you can absorb the vision of that first parrot glimpsed amid the white blossoms. Chat casually about your reactions. What is your favorite image or scene? Watch the movie again. What did you miss the first time? Which parrot taught you something new? I picture Connor, especially, making friends in Epicurus's garden. Bittner's pure devotion to the parrots and Irving's effortless entry into their world are primers on the rewards of simply living.

- Grover's Corners, New Hampshire, could be any sleepy community of two thousand townsfolk satisfied with their local interests and everyday routines. Thornton Wilder's *Our Town*, written in 1938, captures the shared joys and sorrows of the Webb and Gibbs families between 1900 and 1913. This very popular, very American play is performed in settings ranging from school auditoriums to Broadway stages. Its simple production ensures that viewers never forget they are watching a play whose focus is the importance of enjoying precious, commonplace treasures. An all-knowing character called the "stage manager" tells the story to the audience, speckled with his personal observations, and as he forecasts the characters' futures, their daily lives take on urgency for viewers but unfortunately not for the characters. Emily, the central character, makes her ghostly return back in time to her twelfth birthday, poignantly realizing the significance of all the little things she took for granted. She asks the stage manager, "Doesn't anyone ever realize life while they live it? Every, every minute?" Now that it is too late, Emily is overwhelmed by all the beauty that she overlooked in her youth, and laments that "we don't even have time to look at one another." At the play's end, the stage manager gives his audience its charge with his announcement that tomorrow brings a new day full of precious moments. "This is the way we were," he says. Must this lack of awareness be the way we are? How can we avoid Emily's regret and savor the lovely details of our lives? How can we learn to appreciate the little big things?

Get Up and Do
- Look out the window. Nothing else.
- Just sit.
- Slowly . . . deliberately prepare the ingredients and make soup. Do one thing (washing rice or peeling parsnips) at a time. Allow the soup and yourself to simmer. Taste each ingredient as you eat and appreciate the whole that these ingredients became. Wash dishes.
- Choose one object and give it your undivided attention for a period of time; five minutes is good and ten is better. Perhaps a leaf, a rock, a candle, a sleeping cat, a cloud, a hand . . . What details did you notice about the object? What did you realize about yourself during your observation of the object?

- Choose a quiet spot and arrange your body in a comfortable position. Stay there. Let thoughts come and go, in and out, up and down. Breathe deeply. Settle.
- Sketch spontaneously. Black pencil lines on white paper.
- Pick up any harmonica and breathe into it. The basic diatonic harmonica in the key of C major is great for starters. Just play. Listen to yourself! If you purchase a box of diatonic harmonicas, each one is in a different key.
- Take a walk. As you walk, be mindful of simple pleasures along the way. What do you see, smell, taste, hear, and touch? Walk again, this time with a dog. Do you notice additional simple pleasures with your canine companion? Walk yet again, this time with a human companion and enjoy friendship, Epicurus's dearest simple pleasure.
- Work a crossword puzzle as you sip a cup of tea. Color in the spaces left empty.
- Get out your calendar for a month-long math assignment. Each day subtract two "add-ons" from your life. Write each dismissed "add-on" on the calendar. Start with the most obvious baggage and it gets easier. Take baby steps.
- Learn, gradually, to say "NO" more often. It is not hard if you begin with things that are not your responsibility.
- Dismiss the industrial revolution for a day. No electronics. Jump into the silence.
- Simplifying your life gives you more time to _____. Enjoy one of these new/old opportunities today.
- Think about people without access to some simple pleasures for whatever reason. What do you have to offer to someone who is homebound, blind, suffering from poor health? Can you think of a group project? Acquiring material goods is not a possibility for many in American

society, making luxurious lifestyles that much harder to understand. Some people endure desperate lives on the edge, barely making it. Survival, not simplicity, is their goal. How can you make simple pleasures become reality in some of these lives?

- From nineteenth-century Germany Friedrich Nietzsche (NEE-chuh) passionately insists that we examine the ways in which we busy our lives. He chides us that we have made our lives "furious work and unrest." He issues this challenge: "your industry is escape and the will to forget yourselves." Is this true? Can we endure "idleness"? Why has it become so difficult to fuel restorative juices by *doing nothing*? Wear your hard hat as you read Nietzsche; he tries to incite a response so give it to him. Work on a definition of idleness as a group.

Resources

Music
- *The Fabulous Johnny Cash* by Johnny Cash: "Pickin' Time."
- *Out of Our Heads* by the Rolling Stones: "Satisfaction."
- *La Marea* by Marta Topferova: "Mañana Nevada," "Grano de Arena," "Ensueño."
- *American Songs* by Aaron Copland: "Old American Songs" with Thomas Hampson; "Eight Poems of Emily Dickinson," with Dawn Upshaw; St. Paul Chamber Orchestra, Hugh Wolff conducting.
- *Good Night and Good Luck*, soundtrack by Dianne Reeves: "Straighten Up and Fly Right" and "There'll Be Another Spring."
- *In the Moment: Live in Concert* by Dianne Reeves: "Morning Has Broken."
- *The Dock of the Bay* by Otis Redding: "Dock of the Bay."
- *Stolen Moments* by Alison Brown: "The Sound of Summer Running" and "Musette for a Palindrome."
- *Replay* by Alison Brown: "Mambo Banjo," "Red Balloon," and "The Promise of Spring."

- *Monk Alone: The Complete Solo Studio Recordings of Thelonious Monk* by Thelonious Monk: "Ask Me Now," "'Round Midnight," and "Body and Soul."
- *Steal Away—Spirituals, Hymns and Folk Songs* by Charlie Haden and Hank Jones: "Nobody Knows the Trouble I've Seen" and "We Shall Overcome."
- *Docabilly* by Doc Watson: "Little Things Mean a Lot."
- *The Kitty Kallen Story* by Kitty Kallen: "Little Things Mean a Lot."
- *Andras Schiff Plays Mozart: Twelve Variations in C, on "Ah! Vous Dirai-je, Maman"* by Wolfgang Amadeus Mozart, Andras Schiff, piano.
- *Mozart: "Ah! Vous Dirai-je, Maman,"* Catherine Perrin, harpsichord.
- *Young Person's Guide to the Orchestra Op.34; Simple Symphony Op.4,* composed and conducted by Benjamin Britten, London Symphony; English Chamber Orchestra.
- *Mahler Symphony No. 5,* Chicago Symphony Orchestra, Georg Solti conducting: "Adagietto."

Poetry

- *A Family of Poems* by Caroline Kennedy: "Daffodils" by William Wordsworth, illustrated by Jon J. Muth.
- *The Ink Dark Moon* by Ono No Komachi and Izumi Shikibu, translated by Jane Hirshfield: "Watching the Moon" by Izumi Shikibu.
- *The Enlightened Heart,* edited by Stephen Mitchell: "Poem Without a Category" by Gensei.
- *Blue Iris* by Mary Oliver: "How Would You Live Then?"
- *100 Poems* by e. e. cummings: "may my heart always be open to little."
- *The Poems of Emily Dickinson,* edited by R. W. Franklin: "Nature, The Gentlest Mother."

Prose

- *Everyday Zen* by Charlotte Joko Beck.
- "Letter to Menoeceus" by Epicurus.
- "Principal Doctrines" by Epicurus.
- *Wouldn't Take Nothing for My Journey Now* by Maya Angelou: "A Day Away," "New Directions," "Living Well. Living Good," "Style."
- *The Outermost House* by Henry Beston.
- *The Songs of Insects* (CD included) by Lang Elliott and Wil Hershberger.

- *Ethan Frome* by Edith Wharton.
- *Thus Spoke Zarathustra: First Part*, "On the Preachers of Death" by Friedrich Nietzsche, translated by Walter Kaufmann.
- *Shiloh and Other Stories* by Bobbie Ann Mason.
- *Fame Junkies* by Jake Halpern.

Drama
- *Our Town* by Thornton Wilder, directed by James Naughton (DVD).

Documentary
- *The Wild Parrots of Telegraph Hill*, directed by Judy Irving (DVD).

Communication

We must learn to talk with each other,
and we mutually must understand and accept one another
in our extraordinary differences.
—KARL JASPERS, *The Question of German Guilt*

THE TOPIC

How well I remember one particular class of first-graders who detailed for me their frustration that adults seldom listened to their stories. "Give me a try," I invited, and they jumped at the chance. One after the other they told tales, asked questions, and welcomed a gentle peppering of comments from their classmates and me. An opening appeared and I asked the children how they could be sure that someone was not listening. "Maybe the person is paying attention and you can't tell. How do you know when someone doesn't hear you?" They looked surprised and a bit disappointed that I would need to ask such a question. Finally, with a sigh, a child philosopher explained so that I could understand: "They don't answer."

This youthful longing for self-expression is confirmed wherever I rove with my philosopher's kit. People are hungry for conversation.

"What do you think?" I ask, and backs straighten and throats clear. Most relish the opportunity to speak up and out and to win a response from their audience. Such sharing of ideas and feelings in the back-and-forth of a good chat is fun. Often I see a new philosopher's initial reticence mingled perhaps with a touch of fear quickly melt into friendly camaraderie. The word "stranger" quickly loses its meaning. Good conversation reassures us that we can know ourselves and one another better. Failure to communicate, on the other hand, leaves a void. A couple of descriptions that speak to this breakdown in communication: "I felt incomplete and frustrated," or "I felt at odds with others . . . and myself." While it is hard to verbalize such emptiness, frequently I see satisfaction in communicating this recognition of loss.

It is instinctive for human beings to reach for a connection, to long to know and to make ourselves known. Drawings etched on cave walls, papyrus transformed into paper, countless languages developed, both spoken and signed—all point to our basic need for relationship. The arts in general and music in particular unite sculptor with viewer and composer with listener. What is the purpose of language itself if not to connect? Words pulsing in the speaker's throat vibrate in the listener's ear and we are pulled into each other's world. It is the same world, after all.

Despite our great reliance upon it, could we have forgotten the central place of communication in our lives? Do our lifestyles encourage it? Do I use my voice to the best of my abilities and do I truly listen to yours? Have I lost my taste for rich conversation and settled for substitutes without knowing it? A text message? Any skill suffers from lack of practice. If I were clearer about the meaning of communication, would that awareness place communication at the heart of my life? Communication . . .

What *is* communication? Communication is the synchronized,

sincere exchange of ideas and feelings. Verbal, written, or wordless, it wraps us together. It is the hinge that joins seemingly separate lives. I picture you and me . . . leaning in toward each other, digging deep into conversation on an equal footing. Explorers without a map or a predetermined goal, we are open and appreciative of the various ways in which we view the world and our places within it. Counting on honesty, our defenses naturally drop and trust grows. Good communication takes time, patience, and the willingness to try again. We all need to take turns paying the tab.

As philosophers we must be especially precise and clear in our communications. Putting your mind and heart on a page is hard; Friedrich Nietzsche claimed he wrote with blood rather than ink! While philosophical thinking is recorded permanently in books, philosophy comes alive through dialogue. From strolling Socrates (SAH-kruh-teez) in ancient Athens to animated Simone de Beauvoir (see-MONE duh boh-VWAHR) in a Parisian café, from dedicated Confucius (kon-FYU-shuss) traveling with students in China to Joko Beck's piano-playing "lectures" in California, philosophers hang out in lively chat rooms. Conversation is the swinging door through which wonder, ideas, questions, and experience pass back and forth. No concept has more relevance to the philosopher than communication. Language, written and spoken, is our (that means you!) tool for conveying our mental and emotional lives.

Many Eastern philosophers, and some Western thinkers, as well, agree that at times our minds and hearts outrun words. Words, albeit powerful, remain only symbols that we use to express what lies inside us. Once words are stretched and pushed to their limit in full-bodied and full-minded communication, sometimes wordless, immediate communion graces human life. Its language is silence and its truth inexpressible. A quiet metronome comes to mind.

Karl Jaspers (YAH-spurs) and Gloria Anzaldúa (ahn-sahl-

DOO-uh) come from very different worlds and experiences, yet this Chicana woman and German man speak the same language. "Listen to me," Anzaldúa insists. "Talk with me," Jaspers invites.

THE PHILOSOPHERS

In this world the task remains: to come closer and closer to each other in an ever-widening perimeter of communication.

—KARL JASPERS, *Basic Philosophical Writings*

Karl Jaspers was a German professor, lecturer, and author, and his professional and personal life revolved around communication. As lifelong friend and confidante Hannah Arendt attested, "Jaspers exemplified in himself, as it were, a fusion of freedom, reason, and communication" (*Correspondence*). He witnessed the First World War spiral into the Second, and, married to a Jewish woman, he grappled with the collective responsibility shared by all Germans for the rise of the Third Reich. Emerging from this excruciating experience, the central focus of his philosophy was never more clear: his conviction that successful, ongoing communication is critical for the survival of the human race at all times.

Jaspers was adamant. We must learn, as if for the first time, to talk together and bridge our differences through strong relationships. It can be done. Communication between two genuine beings ennobles their humanity and unveils truths impossible for them to understand alone. Connection helps us cope with the tension, perplexity, and doubt that come with the human condition. Jaspers envisioned the bond forged in soulful dialogue multiplying from two to four, and expanding ever-outward. These widening circles of connection create community; strong communities make peace possible.

Further, Jaspers pleaded not only with his students but with all

Germans to face with him without flinching the question of German guilt after the war. He labored to convince his countrymen that dialogue is vital in coming to terms with the past so that robust living is possible once more. Jaspers's worry extended to every individual as well. Note his grim assessment: stagnation mars personal lives and interpersonal relationships. Sunk in the noise of nationalism and technology, people are intellectually and emotionally stifled, stuck. The crowd rules. Slogans and rhetoric pass for meaningful conversation.

"Man is always something more than what he knows of himself" (*Basic Philosophical Writings*). The human horizon knows no limits. Realize your promise! An infinite spark burns at our core and we are open to unimaginable possibility. "One who has genuine courage is one who, inspired by the anxiety of sensing the possible, takes hold in the knowledge that he alone who wills the impossible can attain the possible" (*Basic Philosophical Writings*). This true center of our humanity, "existenz," is real, valuable, and authentic. Live from this essential core and thrust perceived barriers aside. Evolve bravely into an unknown future. Solitude will restore your strength; communication will return you to yourself, to your community, and to your world. Regardless of the darkened past and an uncertain future, Jaspers was able to say of the world that "I am transported by its grandeur" (*Basic Philosophical Writings*).

Loving Struggle

Jaspers presents communication and its rewards in compelling fashion. He dares us with the problems inherent in true communication yet dangles its gifts alluringly. Wrestling first *against* inner complacency and fear is necessary. Choosing to wrestle *with* another in "loving struggle" is beauty.

"Loving struggle" is Jaspers's term for dynamic communication between two well-intentioned, genuine individuals. Two intermingled lives, each rooted in a secure sense of self, come together, intimate self-expression the tight thread that ties *two* as *one*. "When we talk aloud to each other, we merely continue what and how each individual inwardly talks to himself" (*The Question of German Guilt*). Personal independence and integrity flower in heartfelt exchange with a conversational partner.

Solitude is the training ground for this lovely strife because time spent alone strengthens the spirit and prevents loss of one's identity in another. "Either I continuously risk solitude anew in order to achieve self-being in communication, or I have suspended myself with finality in another being" (*Basic Philosophical Writings*). Paradoxically, what both wrestlers know is that, without the awareness illuminated by their communication, they would lose themselves in the end. Rediscovery of "old" insights and glimpses of "new" truths are impossible alone. The "combat" never ends; the conversation is never "over." It is bold, nothing-hidden, no-manipulation communication, a soulful meeting in which both parties open themselves to questions and welcome tender investigation into their lives as they experience "being-through-each-other" (*Basic Philosophical Writings*). According to Jaspers, communicating from the heart is not easy, but it *is* the way to a more true, a more full life.

Communicating the Unspeakable

Jaspers tackled a mighty burden after the Second World War when he demanded that all German citizens open the lines of communication and face their recent past in all its horror. Who would want to look at *that*? Which individuals would choose to accept responsibility for their actions and/or inaction in the midst of numbing dreadfulness? Not surprisingly, many asked what possible good could come from this gut-wrenching dialogue? Could the benefits of "loving struggle" extend to an entire country? Jaspers's faith in the human capacity for connection never weakened.

Imagine Jaspers's inner tension and the misery that subdued every audience as he publicly confronted the question of shared German guilt. Picture him as he moved slowly to a podium night after night. "Everyone must deal in his own way with the thoughts I expound. He is not simply to accept as valid but to weigh, nor simply to oppose but to test, visualize and examine" (*The Question of German Guilt*). Even as he asked people to consider his words, he acknowledged that no two responses would be identical. Far from preventing dialogue, however, human differences provide the strongest motivation for us to join together; he urged his audiences to persist in addressing as a community the unthinkable mistakes and unforgivable omissions of the past. We must talk, he repeated incessantly; every voice must be heard, every question asked, nothing taken for granted.

I think of Jaspers warming to his conclusion. Resist skepticism, he warns wisely. Despair comes easily. Communication is *the* challenge of our lifetimes. We *can* live together. Mindless self-assurance *can* give way to humility. Summon your courage. Let's nurture our innate goodwill and use the power of silence. "Then, amidst discussion, that silence is possible in which men listen together and hear the truth" (*The Question of German Guilt*). We are all "co-responsible"—for ourselves, for Germany, and for the world.

A Message for Philosophers Everywhere

Jaspers was disheartened and fearful as he watched philosophy lose its zest and its relevance when it had the potential to invigorate minds and incite change. In his world of academic philosophy, he observed stale husks of accepted, unquestioned "learning" handed down as tired relics to bored students. Philosophy was withering without vigor or practical application to a world in desperate need of fresh ideas. Jaspers labored ceaselessly to give academic philosophy wings to fly and to breathe life into depleted spirits. His challenge remains for all of us engaged in the practice of philosophy.

And just as it was true for Jaspers and his beloved German citi-

zenry then, it is true for us today. It is now, as well, time to start over
in our country, to initiate conversations without fear, and to resolve,
as Jaspers hoped, never to part in stubborn silence again. "It is easy
to seize an opinion and hold on to it, dispensing with further cogita-
tion; it is difficult to advance step by step and never to bar further
questioning" (*The Question of German Guilt*). Minds are hungry for
stimulation and our hearts long to trust and be trusted again. True
communication can identify and dismiss the irrational passions that,
Jaspers admitted, anyone can adopt ignorantly, blindly.

Over the years I watch as Jaspers touches philosophers of all ages
despite his hard look at shared responsibility, the perils of modern
society, and our sometime tendency to sabotage communication. His
appeal lies in the promise of self-discovery through hearty conversation. The possibility that lives linked through "loving struggle" can
create dynamic communities is comforting. One of my students,
reflecting on the value of caring dialogue after our examination of
Jaspers's philosophy, gave an animated testimonial sure to have
pleased him. She wrote about the continuing power of an intimate
conversation long after it ends. The talk does not stop when the two
people part. Both people think about their exchange and indepen-
dently add to it and uncover new truths. The original conversation
expands in this "afterglow." Embers burn. "Communication, or the
readiness to communicate, becomes the instance of the birth of
the 'I myself'" (*Basic Philosophical Writings*).

Jaspers was a prolific letter-writer, and his ongoing correspondence with his former student Hannah Arendt takes us with candor
into their personal lives and vividly imparts the larger history of these
tumultuous times. This Jewish woman and German man exude mutual gratitude for a friendship sustained and enhanced through these
notes. As Jaspers's pupils, what might we expect to read in a letter
from him today?

Get real. Find yourself. Drop your sense of superiority. Trust. Communicate. Experience the fullest life. Strive to sustain active communities. Deal with difference. Take a hard look at your country. Talk together. No more hide-and-seek. Go to the mat and wrestle, lovingly.

> *This book, then, speaks of my existence . . . and with*
> *my almost instinctive urge to communicate, to speak, to*
> *write about life on the borders, life in the shadows.*
> —GLORIA ANZALDÚA, *Borderlands /*
> *La Frontera: The New Mestiza*

Take a look around her office as we wait to meet Gloria Anzaldúa. Imagine a room arranged for conversation: chairs facing one another, the desk in a corner strewn with sources for her upcoming work on a Chicano dictionary. Literature and poetry from many cultures mix with Chicano works on her bookshelves. Smiling faces in family photographs decorate the walls, many of her as a little girl with her father, Urbano, and grandmothers Eloisa and Ramona. Migrant workers surround their teacher in some photographs; her high school students laugh with Anzaldúa in others. A poster of César Chávez marching with farmworkers hangs by an open window. She greets us warmly, in Chicano Spanish and in English.

Gloria Anzaldúa, Chicana writer and poet, historical analyst and cultural theorist, was born in 1942 in Jesus Maria of the Valley, Texas, and died in 2004. This borderland between Texas and Mexico, sandwiched in the valley between the Nueces and Rio Grande, was her home both geographically and spiritually. This unique culture is a living mix of generations of shared experiences and traditions, numerous languages and legends, and is marked by an ongoing struggle for acceptance. Anzaldúa's major work, *Borderlands/La Frontera: The*

New Mestiza, is a bravely personal rendering of her story as well as a challenging invitation for the reader to tear down the psychological borders that divide people everywhere.

Chicano Spanish identifies a group bound by a common past in the "Valley of South Texas." Physically separated for centuries from other Spanish-speaking groups, the people who called the valley home merged a variety of linguistic influences into a blend that belongs to this group alone. Even though its members may be scattered geographically, as many now dwell in the midwestern and eastern parts of the United States, this living language makes a Chicano/a at home anywhere. It is an evolving and fluid tongue that adapts day by day to the changing circumstances of people on the move. Her language was born of the borderland experience, which absorbs diverse cultural traits, and for Anzaldúa the spoken and written word was vital to her identity; its legitimacy was central to her sense of self. Reading her books, her desperate need for self-expression, a brand of communication only possible between equals, is palpable. Beginning in childhood, Anzaldúa felt the silencing of her voice, the utter disregard for her language and its history. It is not surprising that speaking her voice and presenting her language for all to read became her life's work. Living with pride, without apology, was her hope for herself, Chicanas/os, and anyone caught in the vise of taught and learned inferiority.

Imagining a Life

Let's listen to Anzaldúa's story. Contradictions tug at her from all directions. In the borderlands there is "chile in borscht/Tex/Mex with a Brooklyn accent" (*Borderlands/La Frontera*). That gender expectations fulfill the stereotype of male dominance repulses her; she loves her brothers and her father. Her mother was ashamed that her young daughter spoke English with a Spanish accent; she loves her mother. She is the first in her family to leave the Valley and receive a formal education; the Valley never loses its place at the center of who she is. "To separate from my culture (as from my family) I had to feel competent enough on the outside and secure enough inside to live life on my own. Yet in leaving home I did not lose touch with my origins because *lo mexicano* is in my system. I am a turtle, wherever I go I carry 'home' on my back" (*Borderlands/La Frontera*). She revels in the sound of her language; she speaks eight versions of her "native tongue." Memories from childhood, smells from her grandmother's kitchen, and Tejano music stir her still; her own culture taught her to be quiet. Nothing is easy in the borderlands. Communication is the answer.

As her story continues, we must remember that Anzaldúa has no voice *unless* we listen without judgment. She asks that we allow her to take us into *her* world without reservation, that we accept her invitation to transport us into *her* life with *her* voice in her lilting language. The willingness to refrain from interpreting another's experience in a way that makes us feel comfortable, the refusal to stack that "other" life up against our own in comparison, are requirements for communication. Anzaldúa rarely finds these prerequisites met.

She recalls the dentist trying to control her tongue, symbolic of so many instances of imposed silence. "And I think, how do you tame a wild tongue, train it to be quiet, how do you bridle and saddle it? How do you make it lie down?" (*Borderlands/La Frontera*) Pressure weighs her down in early childhood. Raps on the knuckles with a ruler are the price paid for speaking Spanish at recess. Asking her teacher to pronounce her name properly, young Gloria finds herself banished to a corner of the classroom with the parting admonition to speak "American" or go back to Mexico. How odd for a girl born in Texas . . . As her education continues, both in academics and in her second-rate status in society, Anzaldúa struggles to include Chicano literature in her studies, her requests consistently rebuffed because *that* is not *real* literature. She sits in speech classes with other Chicano students in college, working hard and sadly to lose any trace of accent. The high school principal scolds the motivated new teacher when she risks the suggestion that she include a few Chicano works for her class of Chicano students. Her job is to teach American and English literature. How odd, "American . . ." She sneaks a play, some poems and short stories into the classroom. Her students, sworn to secrecy, take that humiliating vow of silence so familiar to their teacher. When it is her turn to speak in her writers' group, this Chicana scholar finds her sentences completed for her and listens as others clarify what she surely means and thinks. The color of her skin as well as her sexual orientation become relevant factors in her professional life. "They were not willing to be open to my own presentation of myself and to accept that I might be different from what they had thought of me so far" (Borderlands/La Frontera). How odd.

"Who am I?" Anzaldúa ponders. A whole person, she believes, without any confirmation of her identity in a life fraught with border divisions. She is a speaker with a voice seeking reception. She is a writer needing to believe in her language so that she can create images and communicate with the exact words she chooses. "I write in red. Ink. Intimately knowing the smooth touch of paper, its speechlessness before I spill myself on the insides of trees. . . . When I write it feels like I'm carving bone. It feels like I'm creating my own face, my own heart . . ." (Borderlands/La Frontera). Her passion for communication tugs at her readers. What is it like to have a mouth but no voice? "They don't answer," the child philosopher reminds us. To have an alphabet and a dialect but no language? To have your words echo and bounce back in your face? Why does she tell her story? What does Anzaldúa want?

She longs for what Jaspers celebrates: "loving struggle." But loving struggle requires both parties' willingness to enter fully into the world of their conversational partner—to imagine a life perhaps quite unlike one's own and welcome an introduction. With mounting confidence, Anzaldúa demanded just this: that we recognize the dangerous psychological borders that separate us, threatening to proclaim domination. These borders quiet the different voice and cement superiority. Borders kill communication. We must learn to speak one another's languages. "If you want to really hurt me, talk badly about my language. Ethnic identity is twin skin to linguistic identity—I am my language. Until I can take pride in my language, I cannot take pride in myself. Until I can accept as legitimate Chicano Texas Spanish, Tex-Mex and all the other languages I speak, I cannot accept the legitimacy of myself" (*Borderlands/La Frontera*). She yearned to connect her past, her present, her family, her job, her colleagues, her students, and her readers. One-way connections meant nothing to her.

Communicating with Anzaldúa

She gets her wish as she forges connections in my classrooms and fosters communication among students. But, at first, discussion of Anzaldúa's work always begins the same way. Armor clanks shut. "Who does she think she is? She's lucky to be living in the United States." "What's she complaining about? If you're going to live here, speak English." "Why should I learn her language? I never even heard of it." "She's not really a philosopher. I mean like Aristotle or somebody." I prepare myself for such outcries every time. The scales soon balance, however, as other students offer new insights. Shields drop. "I do assume English will be spoken everywhere and sometimes I make fun of an accent different from mine." "I know just how she feels. It's awful." "It has never once occurred to me that someone wouldn't listen to me. What if you (me!) mispronounced my name all semester?" Anzaldúa's writing inspires respectful conversation between students who disagree. Voices with differing viewpoints from diverse backgrounds dance back and forth. Stances soften and shift. More questions are asked and fewer answers given. Students tell childhood stories, admit their ignorance of other cultures, and use their imaginations to enter Anzaldúa's world as best they can. "I know how it feels to be made to stand in the corner and I really *was* sassy to the teacher!" "Did you know that 'Chicana' registers as a misspelling on computer programs but 'Chicano' is acceptable? No wonder she searches for a 'new Mestiza,' a fresh meaning for women with her cultural background." Talk of language and its power breaks out! She fires up dialogue and knocks down barriers between herself and my students. While they may disagree with specific points, they hear her. Though they may choose to resist her description of injustice, they hear her. If her look at the history of the American Southwest differs from what they were taught, they hear her.

"Loving struggle" is combat of sorts, Jaspers reminds, and students honor her passion with their own questions: "Why are you angry? Have you become a victim? Are you imagining lots of these problems? Why don't you write more about your successes? What is so important about having your own language?" Her work is done, however, and such questions continue the conversation.

Speaking One Language

Yes, Anzaldúa's writing is unsettling. Her work, inseparable from her life, is a wake-up call. What about the borderlands lurking in our minds and hiding in our hearts? What lessons can we draw from her story? How can we apply these lessons? What questions can we ask now? She wanted to be met halfway. How can I meet *you* halfway? How can I make it easier for you, for anyone, to communicate with me? She needed her voice, to find and to speak her voice authentically. When have I lost my voice and suffered as a result? Do I own my voice? Do I have the courage to speak it? Have I allowed others to speak for me? When do I ignore your voice, any voice, without having heard it? Why do I shut you out? How did *my* voice become "right"?

She loved her language and felt its living presence. Can I learn a little Chicano? Can I make a genuine effort to understand my Latina/o neighbor, my Korean or Ethiopian neighbor, despite the difficulty? What an accomplishment to learn to speak English as a *second* language!

She looked at a specific geographic area and its borderlands. Have I unknowingly embraced external blockades as well as mental borders? Inner city, gated community, public housing, North and South America . . . the "wrong side of the tracks"? "To survive the Borderlands / you must live sin fronteras / be a crossroads" (*Borderlands/ La Frontera*).

Communication? How can we relate to one another as crossroads rather than checkpoints?

DISCUSSION QUESTIONS

- What is the meaning of communication?
- What are the essential ingredients of good communication?
- Is thinking about the importance of communication new for you? Is it difficult to think and talk about it? Why? Why not?
- Describe the significance of communication in your life. What is its value?
- What sounds comfort you? Inspire you? Complete you?
- Do you know the sound of your voice?
- What are some ways to communicate your ideas and your feelings without using spoken or written language?
- Reflect on a few significant conversations that have stayed with you as time passes. Can you explain their power?
- Why is communication both desirable and at the same time difficult?

- Are you an attentive listener?
- Recall conversations through which you resolved a problem or learned something new *as you talked*. Were you surprised?
- Are there limits to communication? Are there thoughts and feelings that cannot be reached or shared in words? At all?
- Describe in detail how you imagine a life without genuine communication. Do you know anyone living in this way?
- What are some obstacles you face in expressing yourself?
- Does honest communication frighten you? Explain. When you welcome the opportunity to join someone in heartfelt conversation, can you articulate what entices you?
- How do you feel when you are listened to openly and attentively?
- Do you reject some people outright as worthy partners in conversation?
- What are five ideas from Karl Jaspers that are especially relevant to you?
- What did you learn from Gloria Anzaldúa that is useful in your everyday relationships?
- Why might we lose our taste for communication?
- If communication is a teacher, what are its lessons?

HOMEWORK

Listen and Hum

Music *is* communication. It is the connection between the artist's self-expression and the listener's attention. Divide these four categories among the members of your group, several people taking responsibility for the "letters," others for "duets/harmonies," for example. When you meet in your smaller group, listen/watch your selections together. At your regular meeting, be prepared as a group to share your songs and scenes with vocal or silent commentary.

Letters	**Trouble**
Robert Plant & Alison Krauss	Leonard Bernstein
	Peter Tchaikovsky
Peter Tchaikovsky	Charles Gounod
	Aretha Franklin &
Wolfgang Amadeus Mozart	Barbra Streisand
	Lisa Loeb

Clear Cuts	**Duets/Harmonies**
Ludwig van Beethoven	Ali Farka Touré / Ry Cooder
Lucinda Williams	Jerry Garcia / David Grisman
Dinah Washington	The Wailin' Jennys

Is a letter important to you? To write? To receive? It really matters:
- to Robert Plant & Alison Krauss, as they beg together: "Please read the letter I nailed it to your door / It's crazy how it all turned out. . . ." Their voices blend in mutual urgency, "Please!" How can a letter help when verbal communication falters? Why is it important to be understood? Even though the prospects are not good, their request burns in "Please Read the Letter."

- to Countess Almaviva and Susanna in Mozart's *The Mar-riage of Figaro*. Their "Letter Duet" is one of the opera's highlights as they compose a letter designed to untangle a humorous knot of confusion. Susanna writes as the count-ess dictates. Has a letter solved a miscommunication for you? How?
- to love-struck Tatyana in Tchaikovsky's *Eugene Onegin*. Her letter, in Act I, expresses her overwhelming love for Onegin and carries the tale until his letter to her at the play's climax. Watch/listen to the "Letter Scene." What emotions does Renée Fleming's Tatyana convey vocally that the letter, if delivered by hand, could not?

Difficulty brews at the first unraveling in the line of communication. You can feel the beginning of the break:

- in Lisa Loeb's frank admission: "You say I only hear what I want to / I don't listen hard . . ." In "Stay" she acknowl-edges talking rather than paying attention to, well, any-one. She chooses to hear only what suits her. How easy is this?! Can we train ourselves to "listen hard"? Loeb regrets her hearing problem now. . . .

Inspired by Shakespeare's *Romeo and Juliet*, miscommunication ends tragically:

- in Tchaikovsky's *Romeo & Juliet Overture*. Listen to Tchai-kovsky use viola, woodwinds, lower strings, and French horn to communicate anxiety, feuding, love, and sorrow. Describe the change in his music as it expresses hatred between the Montague and Capulet families followed by the love between Romeo and Juliet.
- in Gounod's *Roméo et Juliette*. Is hearing the opera in

French any barrier to your emotional response? Describe your experience as you watch or listen to his masterpiece.

- in the music of *West Side Story* by Leonard Bernstein. The tragic tale of Romeo and Juliet moves to New York City with the clash of Puerto Rican and Anglo gangs. Chita Rivera, as Anita, expresses the drama's underlying tension through her passionate dancing and expressive eyes as well as through her voice. The characters' remorse at the play's end at the unnecessary loss of life is painfully obvious. What happened? Can communication overcome difference, as Jaspers maintains? Tony and Maria never realize their dream.

But . . .

- in Aretha Franklin's version of "Somewhere," she makes finding "a time and a place for us" seem likely. Aretha's vocals and pensive piano, accompanied by tender saxophone, suggest a different ending. How can different voices interpret one song so differently in the numerous versions of "Somewhere"? Barbra Streisand's soaring rendition moves the listener "somewhere" new. Choose other songs performed by various artists and appreciate different interpretations.

No doubt about:

- Lucinda Williams's sincerity in "Something About What Happens When We Talk." She slowly sings, "It wasn't your face so much as it was your word," remembering the bond with her slow guitar. Describe what happens when _____ talk.
- Ludwig van Beethoven's imagination in *Symphony No. 6 in F Major*, the *Pastorale*. It invites the listener for a frolic

in the countryside. Listen to this forty-minute symphony. Let it play for a second time as you write a poem in tune with Beethoven.

- Dinah Washington's pronunciation of lyrics in "I Get a Kick Out of You." You know it's *you*! She delivers a song and communicates with her band as well as the audience. Her playful conversation with trumpeter Clark Terry showcases a voice that is hers alone, distinctive but not flashy. Her diction is impeccable, no guessing at the lyrics. Have you been frustrated at not being able to understand the words of a song? Why does good communication require clear enunciation? Do you mumble?

Is music the one language we share? Join:

- Malian roots and blues guitarist Ali Farka Touré and American slide guitarist Ry Cooder as their guitars make language/cultural/instrumental boundaries disappear. The blues connection between western Africa and the United States reverberates in "Amandrai" and "Ai Du." Are the touch and the sound of the blues scale instinctive? Listening to "Gomni," can you separate the two musicians? Could this be a four-handed guitarist playing two guitars?
- Jerry Garcia and David Grisman as they joke, strum, and chat with guitar and mandolin on the soaring "Arabia." This sixteen-minute trip, a jazzy-gypsy, swinging-bluegrass, Cuban-influenced fusion, takes you there. Describe the sights.
- Canada's Wailin' Jennys as they grow from one to two to three voices to become "One Voice." Three singers with successful independent careers met by chance, listened to one another play, and surrendered "to the mystery" of their voices in harmony. How do you feel when you hear a solo

voice become a duo and finally a trio? What is the difference between philosophizing alone and with a group?

Recite and Write

Savor *each* of these poems as they are read by *two* members of
your group. Notice what a particular voice brings to the same poem.
Listen as the two who read the same poem discuss *with each other* their
feelings about their shared poem. Gradually, one at a time, everyone
join in the conversation. Choose a poem to share outside your gathering. Write at least one poem in your journal just for you (at least
for now).

- William Shakespeare in his Sonnet 116 reminds himself:
  "Let me not to the marriage of true minds / admit impedi-
  ments." How does communication "marry minds"? Love
  that deserves the name is not altered by time or difficulty,
  Shakespeare enthuses. How can we keep such unions from
  fraying? How can we learn to be careful with love?

- Listen again, this time with Edna St. Vincent Millay, to
  Beethoven's *Pastorale*, his Sixth Symphony. In her poem "On
  Hearing a Symphony of Beethoven," Millay pleads: "Sweet
  sounds, oh, beautiful music, do not cease! / Reject me not
  into the world again." How does Beethoven transport Millay
  into the countryside to listen to the brook and the clap of
  thunder, to feel a part of merriment? How does his music
  bring her peace? What instrumental piece moves you in a
  similar way? With whom would you like to share it?

- "Before I built a wall I'd ask to know / what I was walling
  in or walling out." Robert Frost shares his disdain for borders in "Mending Wall." If apples and pinecones are no
  threat to each other, why does his neighbor insist that a
  fence will improve *their* relationship? Frost knows that his

neighbor is repeating what he was taught by his father, but he wishes he would realize that fences do not make good neighbors. "Living in a state of psychic unrest, in a Border-land, is what makes poets write and artists create. It is like a cactus needle embedded in the flesh" (Anzaldúa, *Border-lands/La Frontera*). How would Anzaldúa respond to Frost, his friend, and their fence? Why do we build walls? (Not an easy question.)

- Is it possible to know the innermost place in others that gives birth to their words? Shinkichi Takahashi hints at the possibility of moving behind words to this tender spot. "Whatever that is . . ." that makes "you" speak and "him" want to listen. What makes you talk? Who really listens? Read "Words" aloud. Silently. Aloud. "Whatever that is . . ." What is *it*?

- Maya Angelou feels the gnawing presence of a silent tele-phone for an entire week. This quiet, inanimate object "ignores" her and increases her loneliness. She bemoans the fact that "Its needle sound / does not transfix my ear—" in "The Telephone." What is it about the sound of a voice? Whose touches you every time?

- Pablo Neruda turns language into fireworks. In "Poetry," he remembers when his futile search for words caught his soul on fire and this futility exploded into poetry: "I wheeled with the stars / my heart broke loose with the wind." Discuss how he feels. In "Ode to the Dictionary," Neruda's thrill in finding his words and knowing their meaning, rolling them around on his tongue, is contagious. He helps us imagine "words exploding in the light." How does it feel to find your words? Do you agree with Neruda's proclamation in "Verb" that to express strong feelings you "want rough words / like virginal stones"?

Read and Talk

- Share (it's a big book!) Doris Kearns Goodwin's *Team of Rivals*. Goodwin's biography of Abraham Lincoln is a vivid testimonial to the value of encouraging different view-points, disagreement, and welcoming every opportunity for dialogue. Lincoln chose to surround himself with his ideological opposites as advisers and Cabinet members so that he could consider diverse perspectives and ponder new alternatives. "Yes, you're right. I have changed my position" was Lincoln's familiar refrain. "We want to ac-cept the other, to try to see things from the other's point of view; in fact, we virtually want to seek out opposing views" (Jaspers, *The Question of German Guilt*). As you share different chapters of this book with one another, cre-ate your Cabinet in Lincoln's spirit.

- Enjoy becoming a part of Japanese court life at the begin-ning of the eleventh century. The exchange of short, spon-taneous poems was a central form of communication. "He silently placed his poem before her on the end of his fan. . . . She drew it towards her with her own." In *Diaries of the Court Ladies of Old Japan*, vivid descriptions of daily life, charged by poetic exchanges, draw you into a delicate and refined world. Devote an evening to poetry. Have conversations in pairs using five-line poems passed back and forth with no verbal disclaimers. What happens to your choice of words when limited to five lines? What is the difference between poetry and prose?

- "*Be impeccable with your word.* . . . With clear communica-tion, all of your relationships will change. . . . You won't need to make assumptions because everything becomes so clear. This is what I want; this is what you want. . . . All human problems would be resolved if we could just have good, clear communication." Don Miguel Ruiz, with his roots in ancient Toltec wisdom, issues this challenge in *The Four Agreements*. What is your response? Do you think that "clear communication" can resolve "all human problems"? Do you agree with Ruiz that everyone desires such honest communication?

- David Sedaris is a master storyteller. His humor is irresistible, often laced with subtle pathos. His power of observation is a lesson in itself. How can you sharpen your awareness and sensitivity? Read Sedaris's essay "Us and Them": "Behind my mother's words were two messages. The first and most obvious was 'Yes, I am talking about boat trailers, but also I am dying.'" The foibles of family life and persistent problems with communication feed Sedaris's work: "Because they had no TV, the Tomkeys were forced to talk during dinner. They had no idea how puny their lives were." Yes, but you can sense his envy. Enjoy his storytelling on tape and appreciate the jolt of humor added to the written word by his unique voice. What happens when his tales are lifted from the page and transmitted orally? Be careful driving! You would have more time for conversation, like the Tomkeys, if _____.

- Orhan Pamuk proves his belief in the power of words in everything he writes. Accepting the Nobel Prize for Literature in 2006, Pamuk's lecture, "My Father's Suitcase," is a stunning victory for language. You hear his voice, become a part of his conversations with his father, walk the streets of Istanbul, and feel the process of a writer finding his words. What does his father communicate to Pamuk as a young man that gives him faith in pursuing a writing career? What *doesn't* his father say that also serves as inspiration? How palpable is Pamuk's longing for his father's presence as he receives the very prize predicted by his father? "As we hold words in our hands, like stones, sensing the ways in which each is connected to the others, looking at them sometimes from afar, sometimes from very close, caressing them with our fingers and the tips of our pens, weighing them, moving them around . . ." Such expressive love of language. Do you agree with Pamuk that words create new worlds?

- Daniel Pink suggests *A Whole New Mind* for better communication, emphasizing the central place of storytelling in human interaction. "We are our stories. We compress years of experience, thought, and emotion into a few compact narratives that we convey to others and tell to ourselves . . . context enriched by emotion, a deeper understanding of how we fit and why that matters. . . . We must listen to each other's stories . . . we are the authors of our own lives." What stories do you remember from your childhood? What stories do you enjoy retelling? Choose a story to tell your group that communicates something invaluable to you that you cannot express with a list of events or a fact-filled presentation. Storytelling is a universal activity. What appeals to you about narrative? Why might someone think that telling a story wastes time? In your philosophy journals, jot down ideas for a short story of no more than three pages. Tell it like it is.

Watch and Reflect

- Feel the human hunger for communication as you admire Helen Keller's courageous spirit in *The Miracle Worker*. Her frustration captured in the opening minutes of the film is almost unbearable to watch as she snatches buttons to use as eyes for her doll from a relative's dress. Annie Sullivan's determination to liberate blind and deaf Helen from her solitary darkness through the power of touch succeeds against all odds. Never has the alphabet seemed so precious or the ability to fold a napkin so extraordinary. Watching Helen's entire body register her first connection to the world is beyond words: W-A-T-E-R.

• Costello: "I said I don't give a darn!" Abbott: "Oh, that's our shortstop." Bud Abbott and Lou Costello memorialize miscommunication in their timeless exchange in *Who's on First?* The hilarity begins the moment peanut vendor Costello asks baseball manager Abbott the names of his players. No wonder they were inducted into the Baseball Hall of Fame in 1957. Providing a laugh every time is serious communication! Bud and Lou make it okay for us to forget the demands of Jaspers's "loving struggle" if only for a day and to try again tomorrow. "Tomorrow?" That's the pitcher's name!

• Among the world's most famous percussionists, Evelyn Glennie excels at "finding sound way down." Deaf since the age of eight, Glennie knows that "hearing is a form of touch." Enter her sensitive musical conversation with guitarist Fred Frith in *Touch the Sound*. Glennie caresses sound from her drum in Grand Central Terminal in New York at the film's opening and the beat "almost hits your face." Experience sound as it reverberates through her body. What do Evelyn's feet hear? What sounds might she hear that ears cannot perceive? Do you think it is possible to sharpen your sense of touch to discover sound? Before your next gathering, have each person spend time touching the strings, keys, skin, pedals . . . of a musical instrument. Talk about what your fingers and toes can hear.

Get Up and Do

- Take a mental snapshot of a vivid childhood conversation. Freeze the frame. Write a description of this remembrance, every detail keenly rendered.
- Practice listening. Birds, traffic, rain, a snore, splashing water.
- Think of someone you know whose voice is not heard. What can you do?
- Intentionally engage in conversation with someone whose lifestyle and viewpoint differ from your own. You won't have to look far for this opportunity.
- Write a letter that matters to you and that you know will make a difference to the recipient. Buy stamps.
- Draw or make with your hands an artistic representation of wordless, direct communication.
- Spend some uninterrupted time listening to yourself. In many ways, making this connection takes more effort (and courage) than any other.
- Think about what passes for conversation in your life that is often a waste of time. Technology makes instant communication commonplace. Does your use of technology sometimes interfere with communication? Make two lists with all the members in your group participating. One list is titled: "Good Communication" and the other: "Constant Rattle." Talk about it. Laugh.
- Publications of collected and selected letters abound: Martha Gellhorn, Wallace Stegner, Flannery O'Connor, and Ralph Ellison and Albert Murray, for example. Can you explain the popularity of letter collections? Have members of your group read sample letters from these or other collections of their own choosing. What do letters tell us

about the writer? Write a letter that you would be happy for the recipient to keep always.

- Arrange a time with a friend to meet on a regular basis. Together carve out time for conversation and try your best to keep the appointment even when it is inconvenient. See what happens. Use the telephone if distance is a problem.

- Have a poetry party. Enjoy the strains of Tejano legend Lydia Mendoza playing in the background. Her music is part of Anzaldúa's childhood memories and Anzaldúa mentions "Tango Negro" in *Borderlands*. Everyone bring a dish reminiscent of childhood. Anzaldúa is bringing hot-in-every-way tamales! Read aloud favorite poems and some of your own creations, as well. Go around your circle reciting an Anzaldúa poem in her language; one person read to the nearest punctuation mark and stop, then on to the next person.

- Illiteracy poses a huge obstacle for many in American society. Consider volunteering your time individually and/or as a group to teach adult learners to read and write.

- René Descartes is the model of seventeenth-century rationalist philosophy, which emphasizes the mind and its powers. In isolation the "thinking self" can discover certain truths without interference from sensory input or other people. "Thought and thought alone cannot be taken away from me. I am, I exist. That much is certain. But for how long? As long as I think" (*Meditations on First Philosophy*). How far can your mind reach? What can you know with assurance through solitary reflection? Think on your own and talk as a group.

- Invite a storyteller to your gathering. Wrap yourself into a warm evening. At some other time, talk about the intimate experience of communication that comes with a story. What is the teller revealing? What happens for the listener? Imagine one specific story that you would like to hear Jaspers tell. If you could listen to one narrative from Anzaldúa's storehouse of memories, what would you request? What period of the two philosophers' lives would you most like to enter?

Resources

Music

- *Raising Sand* by Robert Plant & Alison Krauss: "Please Read the Letter."
- *Wolfgang Amadeus Mozart: Le Nozze di Figaro (The Marriage of Figaro)* (Full Opera), The Metropolitan Opera, James Levine conducting: "Letter Duet," featuring Dawn Upshaw and Kiri Te Kanawa (CD).
- *The Marriage of Figaro* (Highlights), Berlin State Opera, Karl Böhm conducting: "Letter Duet," featuring Edith Mathis and Tatiana Troyanos (CD).
- *W. A. Mozart: Le Nozze di Figaro*, Glyndebourne Festival Opera, London Philharmonic, John Pritchard conducting: "Letter Duet" featuring Kiri Te Kanawa and Ileana Cotrubas (DVD).
- *Signatures—Great Opera Scenes*, Renée Fleming, soprano; London Symphony Orchestra, Sir Georg Solti conducting: "Letter Scene" from *Eugene Onegin*, by Peter Tchaikovsky (CD).
- *Tchaikovsky: Eugene Onegin*, Metropolitan Opera 2007, Valery Gergiev conducting: "Letter Scene," Renée Fleming, soprano (DVD).
- *Roméo et Juliette* by Charles Gounod, Royal Opera Covent Garden, Brian Large conducting (DVD).
- *Gounod: Roméo et Juliette*, Paris National Opera, Alain Lombard conducting, Original Recording Remastered (CD).
- *West Side Story* by Leonard Bernstein, Arthur Laurents & Stephen Sondheim. Original 1957 Broadway Cast Recording: "Somewhere" (CD).
- *Queen of Soul: The Atlantic Recordings* by Aretha Franklin: "Somewhere."
- *The Broadway Album* by Barbra Streisand: "Somewhere."
- *Tchaikovsky: 1812 Overture; Marche Slav; Romeo & Juliet Over-

ture, New York Philharmonic Orchestra, Leonard Bernstein conducting.

- *The Very Best of Lisa Loeb* by Lisa Loeb: "Stay."
- *Sweet Old World* by Lucinda Williams: "Something About What Happens When We Talk."
- *Beethoven: Symphonies No. 4 & No. 6 (Pastorale)*, Columbia Symphony Orchestra, Bruno Walter conducting.
- *For Those in Love* by Dinah Washington: "I Get a Kick Out of You."
- *Talking Timbuktu* by Ali Farka Touré and Ry Cooder: "Gomni," "Amandrai," "Ai Du."
- *Grateful Dawg* by Jerry Garcia and David Grisman: "Arabia."
- *40 Days* by The Wailin' Jennys: "One Voice."
- *La Gloria de Texas* by Lydia Mendoza: "Tango Negro," "Amor Bonito."

Poetry

- *Shakespeare's Sonnets and Poems*, edited by Barbara Mowat and Paul Werstine: Sonnet 116.
- *Collected Sonnets* by Edna St. Vincent Millay: "On Hearing a Symphony of Beethoven."
- *The Poetry of Robert Frost*: "Mending Wall."
- *Triumph of the Sparrow* by Shinkichi Takahashi, translated by Lucien Stryk and Takashi Ikemoto: "Words."
- *Oh Pray My Wings Are Gonna Fit Me Well* by Maya Angelou: "The Telephone."
- *I Explain a Few Things* by Pablo Neruda, translated by Bly, Merwin, Peden, Reid: "Verb," "Ode to the Dictionary," "Poetry."

Prose

- *Team of Rivals* by Doris Kearns Goodwin.
- *Meditations on First Philosophy* by René Descartes.
- *Diaries of the Court Ladies of Old Japan*, translated by Annie Shepley Omori and Kochi Doi.
- *The Four Agreements* by Don Miguel Ruiz.
- *Dress Your Family in Corduroy and Denim* by David Sedaris: "Us and Them."
- "My Father's Suitcase" by Orhan Pamuk, translated by Maureen Freely.
- *The Question of German Guilt* by Karl Jaspers, translated by E. B. Ashton Karl.

- *Basic Philosophical Writings* by Karl Jaspers, edited and translated by Ehrlich, Ehrlich, and Pepper.
- *Correspondence, 1926–1969, Hannah Arendt & Karl Jaspers,* translated by Robert and Rita Kimber.
- *Borderlands/La Frontera: The New Mestiza* by Gloria Anzaldúa.
- *Selected Letters of Martha Gellhorn,* edited by Caroline Moorehead.
- *Selected Letters of Wallace Stegner,* edited by Page Stegner.
- *The Habit of Being: Letters of Flannery O'Connor,* edited by Sally Fitzgerald.
- *Trading Twelves: The Selected Letters of Ralph Ellison & Albert Murray* by Ralph Ellison.
- *The Story of My Life* by Helen Keller.
- *A Whole New Mind* by Daniel H. Pink.

Drama
- *The Miracle Worker* by William Gibson, directed by Arthur Penn (DVD).
- *Baseball's Greatest Hits, Vol. I: Who's on First?* (Rhino Records) by Bud Abbott and Lou Costello (CD).
- *The Abbott & Costello Show Featuring "Who's on First?"* by Bud Abbott, Lou Costello, Lon Chaney, and Sid Fields (DVD).

Documentary
- *Touch the Sound* featuring Evelyn Glennie and Fred Frith, directed by Thomas Riedelsheimer (DVD).

Perspective

~~~~~

Man is a brief episode in the life of a small planet in a little corner of the universe. . . . For aught we know, other parts of the cosmos may contain beings as superior to ourselves as we are to jelly-fish.
—BERTRAND RUSSELL, An Outline of Intellectual Rubbish

THE TOPIC

Jealousy mingled with admiration as I watched my kindergarten classmates draw lifelike birds and boots. How did they do that? Why couldn't I transfer the images in my head to my drawing paper? The world I had drawn looked completely flat—a flat-footed Pied Piper fumbling his way among crushed trees. My horses lay in a jumble of tangled legs. In my heart I was a five-year-old skipping with full-bodied delight through a forest, and I longed to portray *that* world. Horses and trees and the skinny piper and me, all in proportion to one another. I was looking for perspective, and though I didn't know it at the time, it would be a lifelong quest. Perspective plays a mean game of hide-and-seek.

Most of us can relate to those moments when nothing appears as it really is, when everything feels out of place. In discussions about lost perspective with philosophers eager to reclaim it, their laments have a familiar ring: "I don't have any perspective about ____." "I've lost my perspective and my priorities are all wrong." "It's crazy at work; my supervisor blows everything out of proportion." "I can't see the forest for the trees." "I am always fired up!" Sitting on the edge of their chairs at library and cafeteria tables, many newly determined thinkers are quite animated on this topic. They want to spend their time more wisely; they want relief from misplaced priorities. Fingers drum on tabletops.

We talk and talk some more. Two general variations on the theme emerge. The first admission is easier to discuss. "Everything that happens in my life automatically assumes the same importance and, as a result, I'm constantly on full-alert." Equal intensity greets a stubbed toe and a broken relationship, a spilled cup of coffee and a friend's loss of a job, a child's incomplete homework and that child's poor nutrition—it's all the same. Proportion means nothing. Such panicky, unmeasured reaction to *every* event is usually conscious, as well; most people claim that they realize within moments that "it wasn't really *that* important." Still, frustrated philosophers marvel at their repetition of the same behavior at the very next opportunity. A wet newspaper and world events reported within its soggy pages receive identical responses.

Blinkered perspective takes another form as well, and this embarrassing recognition is often accompanied by group laughter at shared folly: I am the center of the universe. In *fact*, everything is out to get me in a world designed to make *my* life harder. A woodchuck in the garden? Infuriating. A rained-out concert? Tragic. Unprepared students? Insufferable. A train whistle that broke my concentration? That does it! I fume as victim of my concocted conspiracy rather than watch a suddenly animated woodchuck or appreciate needed rain. Trapped by and within my own mind, each of my problems seems monumental. Life is unfair . . . to me. Why would I need a thermostat to regulate my reaction to difficulty? Everything is well-regulated by its relation to me. Or is it?

Realizing the extent to which our perspective is skewed is the important first step. As we sit together the not-so-easy question remains: What *is* perspective? Thinking back on my artistic struggles in kindergarten, I now realize that perspective is the ability to see the world as it is. Refusing to be locked up and preserved, healthy perspective welcomes new information and nimbly adapts as yet another angle appears. Good perspective is consistently accurate due to its willingness to *review*. It shifts and flows, adjusting and readjusting its take on things.

A sound perspective is one that acknowledges a vast world while at the same time appreciating one's private life: it can see the forest *and* the trees, shoes and the stars. Picture a panorama opening in all directions like the circular brim of a big straw hat. Constantly circling, I can see more with every turn. My range of vision extends ever-outward, and when I look up the wild geese fly high and out of sight. New images appear—a house in a distant clearing—and my curiosity perks up. What lies beyond that road as it disappears around the bend? How far does the mountain range extend? My wide-brimmed viewfinder fills me with endless possibilities; the more I experience the more I anticipate. The world is always bigger, wider, and deeper than I guessed. I am tiny in comparison, tiny . . . yet important.

When we cultivate an ever-broadening perspective in our daily lives, events become more transparent. We can see them as they really are. What changes do I notice? A raised voice, an unintentional slight, a challenging question . . . I can sift and sort through these events, measuring their relative importance with the huge world as my yardstick. Wilted spinach and a computer malfunction receive just the right amount of *in*attention. Sliding snugly into place, the pieces of my life come together like the scattered fragments of a jig-saw puzzle.

Philosophy's very existence depends on perspective. Without the impulse to question and to know, money would matter more than mind. My culture would be the only one. Constantly reminding us that life is many-sided and that there are infinite ways of experiencing it, philosophical reflection and dialogue deepen and enrich perspective.

Bertrand Russell teams up with Mary Wollstonecraft (WOHL-ston-craft) to give us twenty-twenty vision. He points to the mystery-filled cosmos as fuel for a wise and humble perspective. Wollstonecraft rejects her tightly wound social milieu and creates an outlook all her own. Both philosophers prescribe bifocals: Wollstonecraft for up-close vision of the possible, and Russell for long-distance appreciation of an unimaginable universe.

THE PHILOSOPHERS

> *What may be happening elsewhere we do not know, but it*
> *is improbable that the universe contains nothing better*
> *than ourselves. With increase in wisdom our thoughts*
> *acquire a wider scope both in space and in time.*
> —BERTRAND RUSSELL, "If We Are to Survive This Dark Time,"
> *The New York Times Magazine*

Bertrand Russell's vigorous life spanned a century. International peace activist, pacifist, educator, philosopher, scientist, and mathematician, this Englishman was a formidable global presence until his death in 1970. Upfront and controversial, he was jailed for protesting his country's involvement in the First World War, outraged at the second major war, outspoken against the war in Vietnam, and was returned to a jail cell at eighty-nine for speaking out against nuclear arms. Russell proclaimed invigorated mental lives to be the only solution to the shortsighted stupidity of war. Only a warped, stunted perspective could endorse and feed on armed conflict. Philosophy's rewards are bigger minds with open, evolving viewpoints, and such minds sow seeds of peace. Russell's fiery philosophizing uproots our lazy complacency and thrusts us into an awe-inspiring cosmos.

A child philosopher, pondering his philosophy with me and her classmates, summed up the heart of Russell's approach perfectly: "I need to get over myself." Perspective withers with a self-centered focus. The "practical man" is Russell's off-kilter model of this withdrawn mental outlook. Everything is distorted because it is processed *through* him. A co-worker's illness inconveniences him. Thoughts of flood victims elsewhere recede when the danger to his own neighborhood passes. He cares only about those in his tightly wrapped circle who share his beliefs. Fiercely determined to fulfill his mounting material needs, this "instinctive man" sees others as means to his ends—a promotion at work or a free ticket to a concert. His unchanging interests are few. His self-revolving private world is pathetically small, and it never occurs to him that "if . . . life is to be great and free we must escape this prison and this strife" (*The Problems of Philosophy*). Russell painted an impoverished picture of a self-satisfied fellow, unaware that he is starving for "goods of the mind." Indeed, he has lost his mind in his fraught and "feverish" attention to himself, oblivious of the world's majesty, of its immensity. Stalemate.

Relief for the "Practical Man"

Russell offers the "practical man" in all of us a way out. I like to imagine a ride with Russell in a hot-air balloon. As the balloon rises slowly, objects on the ground grow smaller. I am in the treetops! A faraway river. The valley. A passing cloud. The world is big and getting bigger! I never suspected such variety; quickly more layers unfold. Suddenly I realize that I see no sign of my house or my neighborhood or any human being. No human being at all? Nothing looks familiar from this height. My outlook is profoundly altered. Apparently, my perception of the world had drawn humans, and me in particular, far out of proportion. I feel shaken and short but this brief, fanciful flight teaches Russell's lesson perfectly, that "the more we realize our minuteness and our impotence in the face of cosmic forces, the more astonishing becomes what human beings have achieved" ("If We Are to Survive These Dark Times," *The New York Times Magazine*, 1950). I must keep alive this incredible view from the treetops upon landing and take a fresh look at the world from its own perspective. Time to dress myself down.

Russell's approach accomplishes this dressing-down and therein lies its incalculable value. He makes a convincing case that philosophical wonder grants perspective. He reminds us what philosophy holds dear and why: a steady diet of "goods of the mind" that enrich our humanity. I develop my potential as I dine on curiosity, intrigue, and mystery. Philosophy asks the unanswerable questions and thrives on this very uncertainty about . . . whether or not the universe has a purpose, the nature of consciousness, how humans fit into the grand scheme, and on and on forever. As mysteries stack up through contemplation, my mind races to keep pace. Why reduce my perspective to the narrow confines of known facts and human concerns? Why rely on inherited beliefs about what to think and do? The moon, ocean, mountaintop, meteor . . . the sun unveiled by the earth's spin on its axis . . . breathtaking and life-restoring.

I grow in stature as my perspective includes more and more of all there is; contemplating all there *may* be opens my mind and heart. Contemplation of the cosmos rescues me from fear and arrogance.

All I can do is partner with the universe; I am too small to do anything else. My exhausting, fanatic clutch on my personal viewpoints is rather embarrassing. Did I really think that I was the center of the universe? Gradually, I grow into impartial reverence for the world in its entirety. As my mind roves in an infinite universe, it is brushed with a dash of this infinity. Walls tumble down and I become a citizen of the universe. Relieved of my shabby, self-centered way of looking at the world and finally at home in the universe, my now trustworthy perspective will guide me well. It points in the direction of peace. Its North Star is nondiscriminating love. We are not "destitute of wisdom . . . incapable of impartial love" (*Portraits from Memory*).

Russell will not allow the "practical man" to forget his prior folly; his former mind-set inflicted too much harm. Like a stalled truck blocking traffic, he blocked out the world. Running away from possibility, his inner life was repressed, closeted, carefully contained, and hidden. Content as the authority in his tiny realm and secure every time he locked his door, his smug conceit was deadly. He chose limits and thereby demeaned all humanity by imposing his limits on others. Dismissing mental challenge and excitement, his consequent malaise left him with a bleak outlook; he had nothing to offer, no contributions to make. His seclusion made him fearful; aggression was his outlet.

The Beautiful Not-Self

Russell gives us his vision of a better and wiser human being, one who chooses the perspective of the "not-self" with which to view the world. "We start from the 'not-Self,' and through its greatness the boundaries of the Self are enlarged" (*The Problems of Philosophy*). Then, Russell encourages, and only then, can the world's beauty take over and reality present itself as it is. The "not-self" must guard, always, against the return of the "practical man's" instincts. "Thought is great and swift and free, the light of the world" (*The Principles of*

Social Reconstruction), but the instinct to cower and lash out from fear is tempting. Watch out, Russell warns. "Neither a man nor a crowd nor a nation can be trusted to act humanely or to think sanely under the influence of a great fear" (*Unpopular Essays*). The tendency to revel in self-importance still beckons. The relentless obsession to proclaim and to defend one viewpoint remains appealing. Don't let the world slip away again. "The true philosophic contemplation . . . finds its satisfaction in every enlargement of the not-Self, in everything that magnifies the objects contemplated" (*The Problems of Philosophy*).

Is the hard work worth it? Is it so tough to find and preserve perspective? Who would want to be a "practical man" when his point of view isn't even practical? Russell's long experience in human affairs prompts his frustrated response. How smart is war? How effective is aggression? Where is the comfort in national pride? Do we educate our children about the world? Do we offer them creative expression and the freedom to shape their own viewpoints? Why all the sad faces marked by fear? Must we live in a hot-air balloon to have a sense of proportion? Endless conflict and untold misery—is our callous memory loss inevitable? Why is the "practical man" far outnumbering the philosopher? What about loving the world? What about peace?

Russell felt that dark, foreboding days haunted the twentieth century, and this dire reality drove his philosophical work. Yes, small minds shrink the world's magnificence to their insignificance. True, furious nationalism and desire for domination repeatedly reduce the world to a battleground. Sadly, unused minds are repossessed by the powerful, lured by slogans and lulled into false security. The "not-self" repudiates the senselessness of the bomb, yet the arms business is booming. Still, the world is as grand as ever, and Russell spurs us on with his optimistic outlook and his daring activism. "Our age is so painful that many of the best men have been seized with despair. But there is no rational ground for despair: the means of happiness for the human race exist, and it is only necessary that the human race should choose to use them" (*Education and the Social Order*). Get out the telescope of the "not-self." Shooting stars! The cosmos is as old as time itself and it extends into an unknowable future. Gain perspective on the past and imagine a better future. "If we are to retain calm and sanity in difficult times, it is a great help if the furniture of our minds contains past and future ages" ("If We Are to Survive This Dark Time," *The New York Times Magazine*, 1950). Look up. Think. Wonder. Try. Is there anything more important than peace?

Wearing New Glasses

Adult and child philosophers alike warm to Russell's perspective. In its vast expanse, "the universe has room for me." Feeding on "goods of the mind," I can be wisely human. The long view makes sense of my life. If Russell's "not-self" perspective takes hold . . . If philosophy's promise appeals to young and old around the globe . . . Each of us might be able to say:

I don't play favorites. Cultures and traditions other than my own are a valuable part of my mobile perspective. As I pick and choose less and less, I can pull more and more into my embrace. As my mental world stretches toward the unknown, so does my love. My heart lifts as this warmth of affection reaches past those I know intimately, outward to those I can never know, and even beyond humanity. My mind roams spontaneously. I laugh a lot, especially at myself, appreciating humor's gift of humility. Trivial complaints evaporate at the thought of untrammeled wilderness. Peace.

Just watched my first movie with subtitles! Read a book on South American history written by a Norwegian. Almost got knocked down by children running lickety-split for the school bus. Listened to a radio broadcast from another country. Borrowed from the library a book on ancient myths as well as a science fiction novel. Made friends with my new neighbors. Voted against the war. Cooked an international meal with locally grown produce. Talked so long with everybody at the dinner table that my back hurts. Walked to work. Hosted my philosophy club.

> *Those who are bold enough to advance before the age they live in, and to throw off, by the force of their own minds, the prejudices which the maturing reason of the world will in time disavow, must learn to brace censure. We ought not to be too anxious respecting the opinion of others.*
> —MARY WOLLSTONECRAFT, "To Mary Hays,"
> *Collected Letters of Mary Wollstonecraft*

"Where are the female philosophers?" I asked as an undergraduate and graduate philosophy student. "There aren't any," was the consistent reply. How remarkable! I thought it surely strange and suspected that it wasn't true. Future research confirmed my hunch. In bookstores and in basements, rookie philosophers register their surprise when I introduce them to a woman's philosophical work. "I've never heard of her," is the common refrain, and though pleased at the discovery of Beck or de Beauvoir or Addams, they look puzzled as they repeat the names . . . Manning, Spelman, Anzaldúa. . . . Is the discipline of philosophy suffering from shortsightedness? Why don't the massive tomes that feature the classic works of Western philosophy include such sterling seventeenth-century female philosophers as Mary Astell and Catherine Trotter Cockburn? And what about the self-educated star who wrote some twelve books in her short life from 1759 to 1797? Mary Wollstonecraft stands tall in spite of omission, and her *A Vindication of the Rights of Woman* is a provocative and enormously influential work. While Russell advocates the perspective of the "not-self," she shakes off bonnet and bodice almost two hundred years before his death and proclaims: not-this-society.

Wollstonecraft had a tough childhood, a cruel father who rebuffed her educational aspirations, and a distant, traumatized mother. She endured and overcame her early exposure to poverty, taking care of her siblings and always finding employment and managing to pay off debts. Job options for women were few: teacher, paid companion, governess, seamstress. Hungry for knowledge all her life, she read and researched, carving out her own education by taking advantage of every opportunity. Moody, critical, strong-willed, and independent from the start, this feisty young philosopher chafed at the stuffy propriety that choked her vision of the possible. Her confidence was staggering in the face of social lockdown, and her accomplishments came quickly. She published, under a pseudonym, *The Female Reader* in 1797, in which she encourages women to educate themselves and their daughters. The United States was born at this time; it is a revelation to see Wollstonecraft's courage in light of the prevailing perspective on women, and men, during her lifetime.

Courage in All Directions

"Woman is intended to please man . . . as masterfulness is his special attribute. . . . The male is only a male at times; the female is a female all her life and can never forget her sex. . . . They ought not to have the same education. . . . Make her a good woman, and you can be sure that she will be worth more for herself and for us. . . . The doll is the special plaything of the sex. Here the girls' liking is plainly directed towards her lifework. . . . The time will come when she will be her own doll. . . . They should be kept under control from an early age. . . . The first and most important quality of a woman is sweetness. . . . Don't make your girls theologians and dialecticians. . . . Sophie's mind is pleasing but not brilliant, solid but not deep." Jean-Jacques Rousseau perfectly embodied the accepted viewpoint on woman's innate nature as well as her future in *Émile*, a work detailing the proper education for a boy complete with instructions for training a girl whose destiny is to be his submissive wife. Rousseau penned his influential *The Social Contract*, a liberal treatise arguing for liberty from society's constraints, while blithely endorsing bondage for women. His cultural blinders outraged Wollstonecraft, who considered it audacious for men to demand "spaniel-like affection" from *their* women! "Dialectician" was Rousseau's name for a philosopher, and it is "as a philosopher, I read with indignation the plausible epithets which men use to soften their insults" (*A Vindication of the Rights of Woman*). She vetoed his prohibition against her dynamic intellectual life and vowed that "sweetness" and the "doll" will not be woman's future in her crackling masterpiece. "Had I allowed myself more time I could have written a better book," she writes to William Roscoe, and "I am dissatisfied with myself for not having done justice to the subject" (*Collected Letters*). Readers inspired by *A Vindication of the Rights of Woman* disagree. Her refusal to buckle under the status quo is proof that anyone can develop and maintain perspective independent of society.

Women can enjoy spirited, accomplished lives. Social barriers do not reflect any innate deficiency in those born female. There is nothing whatsoever "natural" about woman's preestablished subservience to man. Nowhere did Wollstonecraft suggest that women are better than men; everywhere she reiterated that they share equal intellectual capacities. Then and now her writing shouts a wake-up call to women who have been dulled into their servant's role, accepting their debased humanity as their rightful due. A monster system is in place that must be ignored, attacked, changed, bypassed. Be careful not to play the game; it need not be the only game in town. Ask more of yourself as you ask more of everyone. Win your own mind; envision a future and make it a reality. Swing open the parlor doors because "the return of the fine weather has led me to form a vague wish that we might *vagabondize* one day in the country" (*Collected Letters:* "To William Godwin"). Stomp down the carriage steps and jog to a bookstand.

Everyone in society suffers from inequality. Wollstonecraft targeted structures and systems without blaming individuals. She focused her renegade glare on issues other than female subservience as she challenged any practice that rests on inequality. Imagine *anyone* speaking up and out in her day about the evils inherent in slavery, the ownership of personal property, and the disparity between fixed socioeconomic classes that guarantees poverty. Imagine an advocate for national co-education for girls and boys despite Rousseau's renown. "I might have expressed this conviction in a lower key; but I am afraid it would have been the whine of affectation, and not the faithful expression of my feelings, of the clear result which experience and reflection have led me to draw" (*A Vindication of the Rights of Woman*).

Imagine her bravery to state without compromise that poverty shames the privilege of upper-class wealth. Listen to her! How can abject poverty coexist with pompous luxury? Money protects the affluent; the poor are not in their circle. Personal property is the institution that does much to ensure this grotesque disparity between poor and rich. "How much misery lurks in pestilential corners" (*A Vindication of the Rights of Men*). And the pride of ownership stretches to include women and children, as property, under its banner. Furthermore, the perverse mind-set that invents and condones slavery is galling. The institution of slavery epitomizes the outrageous lock on ownership of the moneyed caste. "Why is our fancy to be appalled by terrific perspectives of a hell beyond the grave?—Hell stalks abroad;—the lash resounds on the slave's naked sides" (*A Vindication of the Rights of Men*). Wollstonecraft hiked up her petticoat and walked out of her century in her condemnation of slavery and elitism. To ensure a humane future, she proposed national education for all children and co-education for girls and boys. Boys and girls playing together at recess and sitting side by side at their desks? Crinoline sales plummet! Never letting up, Wollstonecraft demanded female representation in shared governance. The perspective of one's peers counts.

Wollstonecraft looked through the lens of Russell's long-range telescope long before he built it. As we begin our study of her work in my college classes, I read selections of her work and ask students to guess when or by whom these words were written. By a platform speaker during the equal rights conventions in the 1980s? By a suffragette campaigning for women's right to vote in this country in 1848? From the mission statement of a political action committee arguing for equal pay for equal work in Congress today? Part of a speech by a woman running for political office in 2008? "I here throw down my gauntlet" (*A Vindication of the Rights of Woman*). The vagabond's voice reverberates still.

Her Humanity and Her Legacy

Wollstonecraft endured intense scrutiny of her personal life. Feeling the tug at her heels of her accepted customs and traditions, domestic life held some appeal for her and she gave herself with abandon to romantic liaisons. She despaired at her failed relationship with Gilbert Imlay, yet her unconventional viewpoint still shines through. She suggested to Imlay that she move in with him and his wife, thereby enabling them to raise their child together as well as giving her a chance to improve the other woman! Though Imlay did not agree to this inventive household, Wollstonecraft suffered ridicule for her nonconformist lifestyle and the ripping boldness of her philosophical works. She was scoffed at for her lack of scholarship, and her work was mostly forgotten for decades. Was she indignant that many male philosophers are forgiven their shortsightedness because they are "just products of their times"? Plato owned slaves, Kant thought women too weak to use his moral theory, Aristotle fabricated anatomical deficiencies that justified female servitude, but Wollstonecraft paid a price for *not* being bound by her cultural traditions. Russell shared her "unpopular" perspective: "It would seem that to judge women without bias is not easy either for men or for women" (*Unpopular Essays*).

Mary Wollstonecraft never minced words. A response to her friend Mary Hays after reviewing Hays's manuscript pre-publication serves as a good example. She reprimanded her friend for her timid view of her own abilities and prospects. "This kind of vain humility has ever disgusted me. . . ." Letter-writing was Wollstonecraft's hobby, a necessary outlet for her emotions, and a productive way for her to understand varied views. Just as she challenged Hays's perspective, she dares all readers to see past their society and to earn their own perspectives. Creating a way of looking at the world preserves your humanity. Whoever you are, it *is* possible to see with your own eyes and to use your own mind. Her work invites us to experience the joyous freedom of living life independent of conventional expectations. Choosing your friends, your clothes, your career, your causes . . . , your point of view is yours to make.

Ironically, she and her best friend from childhood, Fanny Blood, both died in childbirth. "True it is wisdom to extract as much happiness, as we can, out of the various ills of life" (*Collected Letters*: "To Mary Hays"). Wollstonecraft's daughter, Mary Godwin Shelley, wrote a book sure to have pleased her saucy and unpredictable mother: *Frankenstein*. As she was dying, Wollstonecraft summed up her life and her work in a letter to Mary Hays: "I *rest* on my own."

Her long legacy is full lives for generations of girls and women who may never know her name.

DISCUSSION QUESTIONS

- What does perspective mean to you? What are its essential ingredients?
- How can balanced perspective enhance everyday living? How can you weigh the relative importance of your interests and concerns more accurately?
- What happens when you "lose" your perspective? When does your sense of proportion disappear?
- How can you develop the ability to see things as they are? Is it possible to do this completely? Explain.
- Is it hard for you to look at things from perspectives other than your own? Why?
- Can you live more fully by expanding your point of view? Is considering other viewpoints an attractive proposition?
- Is it possible to maintain a healthy, consistent perspective in your daily life while at the same time remaining flexible and open to change? How?
- How does Bertrand Russell explain the value of philosophy? Do you agree?
- Is Russell's concept of the "not-self" hard to grasp? Explain. How can your humanity be enlarged and strengthened by viewing the world from the perspective of the "not-self"?
- In what ways are you similar to Russell's "practical man"? In what ways are you a Wollstonecraft revolutionary?
- As your perspective widens, do you have more to offer the world? Give specific examples. What is your response to

Russell's belief that through appreciating the vastness of the cosmos, our minds and hearts will expand as well?

- Do you agree with Russell that the perspective of the "not-self" leads to peace?
- How do you explain Mary Wollstonecraft's courage to break with commonly held perspectives? Can you apply her work in your life?
- Do you think that any of Rousseau's suggestions for a girl's education and her eventual social role are alive today? Give examples. Are you surprised?
- Can you identify with Wollstonecraft's frustration at the narrow perspective of female abilities so prevalent in her day? Do you have anything in common with her?
- Is it possible to be a part of your society and hold fast to a perspective that differs from the norm? Can you widen your perspective on gender expectations for both females *and* males? Why? Why not?
- How can Russell's view from the "not-self" open a wider perspective on gender assumptions?
- Has your point of view limited you? Have your viewpoints limited others?
- What three core ideas will you remember from Russell's work? What three assertions by Wollstonecraft will you recall?

HOMEWORK

Listen and Hum

Listen to many-sided, multicolored music with Russell and Wollstonecraft. It's a relaxing and festive way to delve into casual conversation about perspective. Mix and match these selections within your group. Choosing a genre or an artist unfamiliar to you is especially appropriate for our two philosophers.

Bertrand's Picks

- Travel among the stars to other *Planets* with Gustav Holst. The journey begins as the sound of his ominous, turbulent "Mars" flings the listener into the cosmos; this piece influenced John Williams's *Star Wars* score. "Mercury" assists us in our gradual transition from one world to another. This feeling of progression from planet to planet fires the imagination. Venus is the "Bringer of Peace" while Jupiter is the "Bringer of Jollity." Why? The contrast in moods between the final calm, induced by a female choir in "Neptune," and the early jolt from Mars, is striking. How does contemplation of life on other planets affect your perspective?
- Yo-Yo Ma steers with his cello as we caravan along ancient trade routes that connected Western Europe with the Far East. Accompanied by the Silk Road Ensemble, Ma plucks his strings and transports us into another world. Feel the heat, hear the clamor of the marketplace, taste the dust of such places as Mongolia, Iran, Azerbaijan, Turkey, Armenia, and Afghanistan. His two albums titled *Silk Road Journeys* are appropriately named *When Strangers Meet* and *Beyond the Horizon*. Ma designed the Silk Road Project to make cultural connections around the globe despite time's passage. Why would Russell suggest that we listen?
- Flooded with bluebirds, "nothing but blue skies / do I see." Willie Nelson's version of Irving Berlin's 1926 classic, "Blue Skies," serves as a lovely example of this "outlaw" musician's versatility. Nelson's ability to mesh his unique

sound and styling with so many other genres, and his joy in singing in tune with such a long list of diverse artists, are both in keeping with his instinct for charitable work. Big, open, fluid perspective opens the heart, Russell reminds, and Nelson's heart beats for family farmers in his annual Farm Aid concert and on behalf of animals and the 2004 tsunami victims. The Willie Nelson Biodiesel Company, distributing this "alternative" fuel to an ever-widening clientele, gives "blue skies" a chance.

Mary's Medley

- "Freedom's just another word for nothing left to lose. . . ." Janis Joplin belts the blues and twists freedom's meaning round and round in her throaty twang in Kris Kristoffer-son's "Me and Bobby McGee." Her sound blasted into the turmoil of a decade grappling for perspective—on civil rights, the war in Vietnam, the policing of freedom, the length of a boy's hair as well as a girl's skirt. Joplin stirred the pot to a boil. Her sound defied categorization; "la da la la la, la da la la la da la . . ." and crowds cheered. "Hey hey hey Bobby McGee, lord." That was the sixties. What is your perspective on freedom now?

- Musical "Soirées" for piano, composed by a girl of sixteen or seventeen around 1835, applauded by audiences and greatly admired by the famous composer Robert Schu-mann? Her name is Clara Wieck. Who? How can a young girl in this or any day reach for the powerful emotion she taps in "Nocturne"? Young Miss Wieck is perhaps better known as Clara Schumann, Robert's wife, the volume and variety of her compositions shrouded behind her husband's fame. She is a grand example of Wollstonecraft's dream of woman's excellence thriving even within cultural binds.

Both women, controversial philosopher and celebrated pianist, raised children, cared for family members, and invented their lives as best they could.

- "Don't Fence Me In." Ella Fitzgerald's voice with its three-octave range roamed in unheard reaches from Harlem in the 1930s, into countless American homes in the 1950s, and eventually onto turntables worldwide. She defeated her severe stage fright with quiet spunk, and this shy, somewhat reclusive performer became one of the most irresistible improvisers ever. In "Scat Medley" she uses her trilling vocal cords as different instruments, interacting with band members as she matches their virtuosity note for note with her voice. When Ella goes "Stomping at the Savoy" with Louis Armstrong, her scatting whisks the listener onto the dance floor. Grit and grace.

Tunes for Two: Four for Mary and Bertrand

- A prodigious talent born into poverty in 1910, Mary Lou Williams's life embodies Wollstonecraft's leap over barriers and Russell's ever-expanding vision of life's possibilities. This eight-year-old sang and played piano at parties (before women had the right to vote) and became a traveling musician at thirteen. In the thirties, when vocals were women's place in the music industry and long before civil rights was a familiar term, Williams was a successful arranger/composer and instrumentalist. Duke Ellington and Benny Goodman were among those conducting her arrangements. In 1945 she composed the Zodiac Suite, twelve instrumental jazz pieces written to commemorate the astrological signs of her beloved musical contemporaries. "Aquarius," a solo piano piece she first improvised live on radio, is dedicated to President Franklin Roosevelt. Commissioned by the Vatican, *Mary Lou's Mass* was celebrated in St. Patrick's Cathedral in New York City in 1975. It included a children's choir and was the first jazz played during Mass in that cathedral. Applause erupted as the *Mass* ended to the strains of "I Have a Dream." Williams's legacy is at the heart of her *Mass*: "Peace I Leave with You / Alleluia."

- Mary Lou Williams shared her birth sign with Duke Ellington and dedicated "Taurus" to her world-renowned friend and colleague. From the perspective of composer, conductor, arranger, producer, and pianist, Ellington elicited an unmistakable sound from his unique mix of the sax, trumpet, trombone, and rhythm sections of his orchestra. The Duke absorbed the diverse notes of Harlem music in the late twenties and thirties and whipped them together to create "American" music. His elegant, innovative piano-playing came from a secret place. Then and now, tapping feet scamper to "Take the A Train," which makes stops for any "Sophisticated Lady."

- "So I take a few steps back / and put on a wider lens," and the world changes for backpedaling, electric guitar–playing Ani DiFranco. Skin color, gender, social class . . . all disappear at the bottom of the Pacific and on the top of "Everest." At a distance, we become silhouettes of one another. DiFranco refuses to bite at the "corporate carrot" of big-label marketing, founding her own record company in Buffalo and helping to produce and release her music. Righteous Babe Records is home to one hip folksinger.

- Do Russell and Wollstonecraft recommend "Waiting on the World to Change"? John Mayer looks at today's cowardly apathy in the face of social problems, mocking the common tendency to give in to the "system" and buy into media spin. Life isn't fair, you know, so "we just feel like we don't have the means / to rise above and beat it. . . ." Russell's "practical man" waits. What if Mary Wollstonecraft had waited? If our perspective of the possible shrinks . . .

Recite and Write

Read each of the following poems silently. In your philosophy journals, jot down your response to the *one* that really grabbed you, and describe an appropriate setting in which to recite the poet's work. What special place would evoke the poem's feeling? Take turns reading the poems aloud and picture your ideal setting for all to envision. Choose a spot at your meeting place to recite your chosen poem that also suits its meaning. Stand or sit or walk. . . .

- A dog in a previous life finds disappointment in "The Promotion" to human being the next go-round. Oh, for the dog's life guarding sheep with a farmer who loved him. Kids to play with and all the love in the world brought such pleasure to this good dog. Living now in a high-rise, eyes full of tears gazing from the window, the trip from canine to human seems a painful demotion. "At my job I work in a cubicle and barely speak / to anyone all day." Why does James Tate write this poem from the dog's perspective? Can we nab a glimpse of the world from a nonhuman perspective? How?

- "I Am a Black Woman." Mari Evans offers her cultural perspective in this poem that hums with shared black-skinned history. Tears shed from slave ship to cane fields, from world war to Vietnam, and the black woman survives it all. She thrives and remains untouched. Her strength, "defying place / and time," is uniquely hers. How might her perspective on the loss of a son in wartime differ from that of another parent? How can a person's history affect perspective? Give specific examples. Do we unwittingly assume that others share our perspective?

- There are "Thirteen Ways of Looking at a Blackbird" for Wallace Stevens. Do you prefer "the blackbird whistling / or just after"? As soon as he notices the slight movement of a blackbird's eye against the backdrop of snowy mountains, Stevens looks at the world from shifting perspectives. He would not trade this vision from his window for the sight of golden birds. Fly with the blackbird and admiring poet to sit in the cedar limbs. Feel the icicles and catch your breath as the blackbird flies from sight. Let your topic come to you as the blackbird did to Stevens, and write a poem titled "Thirteen Ways of Looking at _____."

- Kenneth Koch stares at the motionless top of a snow-covered "Mountain," captivated by its solitary and imperturbable remove from human access. He loves the complete silence that grows within mountain stillness, taking comfort that neither subdivisions nor heartbreak will mar its existence. This peak does not have a history, or "do you, mountain top?" he inquires. The places left bare by the melting snow can never be Koch's home. "But I'm moved," he tells the mountain. How does perspective change when the world is viewed from above? From below? Does the natural world lend proportion to your perspective? When?

- "We Alone" can change our perspective. Whoever, wherever, whenever, the option to shift our vantage point is ours. "We alone can devalue gold," Alice Walker encourages. It is possible to opt out of the race for expensive things. A stone shaped by the sea is a treasure. Rejecting the gold standard "could be our revolution." Do you agree with Walker that anyone can depart from society's consumer mind-set? Can we choose to love the commonplace? A feather?

- Russell challenges us to expand our horizons. Wollstonecraft insists that we push back imposed constraints. Both philosophers envision change, growth, and ceaseless questioning. This can seem daunting, but in his *Four Quartets*, T. S. Eliot welcomes all traveling philosophers home. Our explorations will bring us full circle, back to the same world but with new eyes, and we will "know the place for the first time." Renewed by our journey, the life taken for granted sparkles upon our return. "And all manner of thing shall be well. . . ." Eliot's fourth quartet, "Little Gidding," is breathtaking in its promise of the rewards of heightened perspective. Catch its fire.

Read and Talk

- Billie Jean King's defeat of Bobby Riggs in their 1973 tennis match, billed "The Battle of the Sexes," symbolizes this woman's victory over societal barriers at every turn. One of the greatest tennis players of all time, King uses her stature to carve new roads for women in sports—prize money equal to their male counterparts and the same access to opportunity, for example. Among other causes, she is an agent of change for AIDS research as well as environmental advances in the sports world. In *Pressure Is a Privilege*, King enthusiastically offers insights drawn from pivotal events in her life. The Billie Jean King National Tennis Center, home to the U.S. Open, celebrates more than a tennis champion. King is a tireless advocate for fair play on all fields. Though it is tricky to see one's own time in historical perspective, how far have we come in the two centuries that separate her and Wollstonecraft? How can we do better?

- "It is inconceivable to me that an ethical relation to the land can exist without love, respect, and admiration for land, and a high regard for its value. By value, I of course mean something far broader than mere economic value; I mean value in the philosophical sense." Aldo Leopold's *A Sand County Almanac*, written in 1949, extols the merits of a philosophical perspective that extends beyond humanity. Economic motivation for conservation always falls short; we must move beyond valuing things, songbirds and creeks, only as they relate to human beings. The land, the "fountain of energy," has intrinsic value in and of itself. List some of the current environmental dilemmas. Use his belief in the innate, inherent value of all things as a way to address each issue.

- Jane Austen created many of her memorable characters during Wollstonecraft's lifetime. Until her fame was secure, Austen's books were published mysteriously "By a Lady." This British "lady" illuminates the trap and trappings of social class and gender restriction in *Emma*. Though she is smart, high-spirited, and financially independent, Emma spins in her squeezed, hand-me-down orbit. When her governess marries, Emma laments that she is "now in great danger of suffering from intellectual solitude. She dearly loved her father, but . . . he could not meet her in conversation, rational or playful." She frustrates herself with an often-haughty attitude and in her delight at interfering in others' affairs. "Warmth and tenderness of heart . . . I have it not—but I know how to prize and respect it." How does Austen's *Emma* showcase Wollstonecraft's period? Are there parallels to our own age in this 1816 work?

• "Messages from the Past" and "Journey into a Lost World: The Beginnings of Civilization" are two of the enticing chapter titles in Riane Eisler's *The Chalice & the Blade*. Eisler takes Russell's long view and retraces human development from prehistoric times to the present. She offers a startling new perspective on the past in the hope that modern society can move from power to partnership as its enduring foundation. "Cultural bias has led to mistakes" in anthropological and archaeological research, so that our view of the past is distorted. Eisler's look at the culture of ancient Crete is especially revealing. For approximately four thousand years, beginning in 6000 BCE, this society knew equal partnership between the sexes. Wealth was shared and poverty nonexistent. In a city built without military fortifications, gardens and artistic activity flourished. Eisler does not portray a perfect society; that it knew peace for millennia, however, is her proof that we can enjoy a "cultural transformation." Discuss Eisler's research and conclusions. Take one chapter at a time, as each is rich and ripe for dialogue.

• The opening of new vistas through a very long trip into the past continues with Gregory Curtis's *The Cave Painters: Probing the Mysteries of the World's First Artists*. To think that the artwork reproduced on the book jacket is thirty thousand years old! The paintings and engravings discovered on cave rocks in Altamira, Spain, in 1879 and Lascaux, France, in 1940 spark continuous wonder and debate about our silent ancestors from the Stone and Ice Ages. Why so few people in the drawings? What do the animals symbolize? Pablo Picasso marveled at the creativity of the Neanderthals upon his visit to Lascaux, admiring lifelike horses sketched in full-bodied perspective. What philosophical musings occur as you look at the cave paintings? What perspective on our day could be garnered from *our* artwork in thirty thousand years?

- "A great tall cloud moved elegantly across an invisible walkway in the upper air, sliding its flat foot like an enormous proud snail. I smelled silt on the wind, turkey, laundry, leaves . . . my God what a world. There is no accounting for one second of it." Annie Dillard's joyous romp as a *Pilgrim at Tinker Creek* unveils an intimate way of seeing the world. When she forgets herself and experiences the cicada or the muskrat as it is, Dillard and her readers are awash in wonder. What a world, indeed, from every "not-self" angle. "We are making hay when we should be making whoopee. . . ."

Watch and Reflect

- The vast silence of Antarctica, a sandstorm in the desert, the eruption of a volcano, an avalanche picking up speed, forests of rhododendron, flapping wings scaling Mount Everest, a waterfall and swirling rapids . . . "What a world we live in!" conclude those playing their part in filming, producing, and narrating the BBC series *Planet Earth*. This documentary is more marvelous, more unimaginable than any cinematic simulation. The heart softens as you enter the habitat of the ibex, the macaw, the snow leopard, and as you search with elephants and buffalo for water. Though there are six billion people on the planet, there remain places untouched by humans. Penguins, pandas, and caribous are on the move; grizzlies, pumas, and eagles stand guard. Huge scale and minute detail, the wilderness and the frog, every moment captured in this documentary sings of the world's majesty. The "not-self" appears unasked, and this humble perspective makes human domination seem neither possible nor desirable. How did you feel watching the film? Is it possible, as Russell maintains, that by stepping out of ourselves and into a mysterious world we can inch toward peace?

- Norwegian playwright Henrik Ibsen features the inner lives of women in many of his works, perhaps most famously in *A Doll's House*. Imagine Mary Wollstonecraft at a performance in 1879 as you watch Nora evolve from her husband's "flittering lark twittering" to a woman awakened to and horrified by her stunted development. Nora's only perspective is the constricted one given to her by society. Slowly, slowly she develops fresh determination to become a full-bodied person. "I must try to educate myself. You could never help me do that; I must do it quite alone." Her husband, Helmer, greets her pronouncement with scorn and disbelief: "You are ill, Nora; you have a touch of fever. . . ." Nora persists in leaving Helmer and their three children. How can she rear children if she is a child herself? She ignores her husband's pleas to stay, just as Ibsen resisted requests to change the ending of his play. "I want to find out which one of us is right—society or I."

Enjoy experiencing the diverse perspectives offered in *A Doll's House* in two ways. First, have a "play reading." Read Ibsen's dialogue aloud. There are three acts, so everyone in the group can read a part; switch parts after each act to experience new angles. Another possibility is to imagine the director's perspective. While a novel actually tells a story, a play consists almost entirely of dialogue, with minimal stage directions from the playwright. "A comfortable room furnished with taste, but not expensively" is the first instruction in Ibsen's play. Have fun as a group as you imagine bringing the play to life in *this* age. Describe the setting as your play opens. What set changes will you make as the storyline progresses? What about costumes, lighting, and sound effects?

Get Up and Do

- Spin a globe. Rotate it slowly. Notice the space taken by the oceans and the deserts. Look carefully at the relative size of different countries. Discuss unfamiliar regions. Perhaps some of you have studied or traveled to such places and can share your experiences.

- Use a telescope to explore the sky. Perhaps a neighbor has a good one, or you can check with a local university, science museum, or your Parks and Recreation Department can direct you to a public observation spot. What do you make of the difference between your vision with and without the telescope?

- Visit a natural history museum. If there is not one nearby, use the local library to track the dinosaur and trace the flight of migrating birds.

- Select a piece of sheet music. A fine first choice could be the musical score for "Ac-Cent-Tchu-Ate the Positive." Many are familiar with the tune and the upbeat lyrics: "You've got to spread joy up to the maximum / bring gloom down to the minimum. . . ." Already knowing the melody, you can watch it come alive on paper from the composer's perspective. Forget the words for now. Look at the notes and watch the melody take shape, maybe as a mountain or a city skyline. . . . Where is the high point, the composer's

climax? Draw or trace this melody as you listen to Bing
Crosby sing the lyrics. Discuss this musical experience
from an insider's perspective. If your group repeats this exercise, be sure to choose a familiar tune and you can hum
along as the notes spring to life.

- Think of people in your community who have shown
  Wollstonecraft-like courage by choosing a "different"
  frame of reference to guide their lives. Invite one or more
  to join your circle and describe their insights and lifestyles.
  Discuss the benefits and difficulties of breaking with social
  expectations. What is it like to be in your given world
  and at the same time moving beyond it? A former banker
  now an organic farmer, or an old engineer now a young
  teacher . . .

- Turn a world map upside down. Point to a random spot
  from this altered perspective. Step into this heretofore unknown place through music. Everyone should bring to the
  next meeting a musical selection from your newly discovered place on the planet. Research a bit. For example,
  travel to Uganda and listen to xylophone and yodeling
  while picturing the playing of thumb piano and horizontal
  harp. You can introduce the group to this traditional music
  through "Warumbirigwe" or "Kawairanga." Perhaps your
  spot on the map is Venezuela. The legend of a passionate
  singing contest between a cowboy and the devil has a special place in Venezuelan culture. Florentino wins this poetic duel in Antonio Estévez's third movement in *The One
  Who Sang with the Devil*. Discuss the ways in which music
  effortlessly enlarges your perception of the world.

- Listen to a news broadcast or read a translation of a political commentary from a country other than your own.
  Take a specific event in history and read about it from a

variety of cultural perspectives. The Industrial Revolution, famine, sports, economic developments, *any* war . . .

- To fine-tune your perspective, use Russell's wide-angle lens and Wollstonecraft's barrier-breaking ability to rank ten concerns in your life from lesser to greater importance. Share as a group. Talk about the ways in which these two philosophers can help you rearrange priorities and make changes.

- Individually, make a point of seeking and hearing the perspectives of those whose viewpoints are often unsought. Learn as you listen to varied outlooks on the same or different topics from the following people: an elderly person, a child, a newcomer to this country, a worker at a minimum wage job, a deaf or blind acquaintance. . . . Share your conversations and new vantage points with the group.

Resources

Music
- *The Planets* by Gustav Holst, Chicago Symphony Orchestra & Chorus, James Levine conducting.
- *Silk Road Journey: When Strangers Meet; Silk Road Journey: Beyond the Horizon* by Yo-Yo Ma & The Silk Road Ensemble.
- *Stardust* by Willie Nelson: "Blue Skies."
- *Pearl* by Janis Joplin: "Me and Bobby McGee."
- *Clara Schumann: Piano Works: "Soirées Musicales"* for piano, Op. 6, Konstanze Eickhorst, piano.
- *Ella Fitzgerald Sings the Cole Porter Songbook* by Ella Fitzgerald: "Don't Fence Me In" (CD); *Live at Montreaux:* "Scat Medley" (DVD).
- *Ella Fitzgerald/Louis Armstrong* by Louis Armstrong and Ella Fitzgerald: "Stompin' at the Savoy."
- *Zodiac Suite: Revisited* by Mary Lou Williams, performed by The Mary Lou Williams Collective, Geri Allen conducting.
- *Mary Lou's Mass* by Mary Lou Williams (Smithsonian Folkway Recordings).

- *Ellington at Newport 1956* by Duke Ellington: "Take the A Train," and "Sophisticated Lady."
- *Up Up Up* by Ani DiFranco: "Everest."
- *Continuum* by John Mayer: "Waiting on the World to Change."
- *Secular Music from Uganda, 1950 & 1952*: "Warumbirigwe," and "Kawairanga."
- *The One Who Sang with the Devil* by Antonio Estévez, performed by Simón Bolivar Symphony Orchestra of Venezuela, Eduardo Mata conducting.
- *Golden Greats* by Bing Crosby: "Ac-Cent-Tchu-Ate the Positive," music by Harold Arlen, lyrics by Johnny Mercer.

Poetry

- *Return to the City of White Donkeys: Poems* by James Tate: "The Promotion."
- *Continuum: New and Selected Poems* by Mari Evans: "I Am a Black Woman."
- *The Collected Poems of Wallace Stevens*: "Thirteen Ways of Looking at a Blackbird."
- *A Possible World* by Kenneth Koch: "Mountain."
- *Her Blue Body Everything We Know: Earthling Poems (1965–1990)* by Alice Walker: "We Alone."
- *Four Quartets* by T. S. Eliot: "Little Gidding."

Prose

- *Pressure Is a Privilege* by Billie Jean King.
- *A Sand County Almanac* by Aldo Leopold.
- *Emma* by Jane Austen.
- *The Chalice & the Blade* by Riane Eisler.
- *The Cave Painters: Probing the Mysteries of the World's First Artists* by Gregory Curtis.
- *Pilgrim at Tinker Creek* by Annie Dillard.
- *The Problems of Philosophy* by Bertrand Russell: "The Value of Philosophy."
- *The Basic Writings of Bertrand Russell*, edited by Robert E. Egner and Lester E. Denonn, preface by Bertrand Russell with writings from various works and publications, neatly arranged by topic.
- *Émile* by Jean-Jacques Rousseau.
- *A Vindication of the Rights of Woman* by Mary Wollstonecraft, edited by Miriam Kramnick.
- *A Vindication of the Rights of Men* by Mary Wollstonecraft.

- *Collected Letters of Mary Wollstonecraft* by Mary Wollstonecraft, edited by Ralph M. Wardle.
- *Thoughts on the Education of Daughters* by Mary Wollstonecraft.

Drama
- *A Doll's House* by Henrik Ibsen, directed by Patrick Garland (DVD).

Documentary
- *Planet Earth*, produced by the BBC (DVD).

Flexibility

~~~~~

Walk on!
—ALAN WATTS, *The Spirit of Zen*

THE TOPIC

His kind and sad face lingers in my memory. For the first few
weeks of class, he sat with bowed head in my introductory philosophy
course, at times appearing to restrain himself from making a comment or asking a question. He bolted from the room at the end of
each class. Absences piled up, writing assignments were carelessly
dashed off and then nonexistent, and any interaction with other
students was carefully avoided. My unsettled student stopped coming
to class altogether toward the end of the semester. Months later I
received a two-page, impeccably written letter from him. He insisted
that he had tried to force himself to come to class and to do the readings, but everything we discussed contradicted what he had been
taught and believed all his life. He confessed that he felt miserable
and that the misery escalated with every class; furthermore, he
couldn't write about ideas that he refused to consider. His letter
concluded with an admission that though he hated feeling "wrong,"

he liked talking with me *outside* the classroom. I liked talking with him, as well, and his "misery" stays with me as the understandable yet unfortunate and unnecessary consequence of inflexibility.

A child philosopher once asked me if I thought "upside-down thinking" was a good definition of philosophy. Absolutely, and I wish I had thought of it! She shook her head as she elaborated, "It makes you think brand-new and not like you used to and simple things seem hard and hard things seem easy." Philosophical discussion does unzip certainty by calling our ideas and actions into question. Philosophy exercises the brain. Its practice thrives on open-ended dialogue un-restricted by a predetermined destination. Robust conversation, ex-posing us to ideas that compete and conflict with our own, gives us a way to think about our convictions as if for the first time. What does it mean to be a good person? Where did I get that idea? How do I know the things that I think I know? Why am I so sure that my opinions are right and adamant that others agree with me? Do I think for myself? Philosophizing works our minds into supple shape.

Whenever I engage in a conversation about flexibility with my sidekicks in "upside-down thinking," comments quickly spill out about a topic that many claim is long overdue: "I'm totally set in my ways." "Just a detour on the way to work throws me for a loop." "I make lists constantly." "Retirement scares me." "It's too late to change now." Is flexibility desirable? Oh, yes, they agree wholeheartedly. Will it take some work to lubricate our lives? Eyes roll in acknowledgment that flexibility comes with a price; otherwise we would be less resis-tant to change. Entertaining new ideas can transform lifestyles; facing changing circumstances shakes up comfy routines. Will becoming more flexible prove valuable? What *is* flexibility?

Flexibility is the ongoing practice of moving *with* life. Just as the sails of a sailboat catch the wind as the vessel glides smoothly through the water, accepting change as an inevitable aspect of being alive allows us to flow more easily with life's movement. If I know deep down that the world renews itself in every moment, I learn to expect change as a natural part of life. My agility increases as I respond to this and then to that and move here and then there. Serendipity keeps me on my toes. I bend, swivel, rotate, and pivot with little friction. Job transfer, fluctuating finances, flooded basement, un-house-trained puppy . . . no problem. When I get stuck in a rut, I limber up once again . . . and I follow life's lead and live my life as it happens, as best I can.

In contrast to smooth sailing even in rough waters, inflexibility saps energy. Resistance is exhausting, and this chafing at change often leads to missed chances. We stagnate when we refuse to consider changing an opinion, altering a practice, adjusting a priority, or simply listening to those with whom we disagree. We miss openings and opportunities . . . and regrets begin to stack up. Stories of clashes with inflexibility abound among newly stretching groups of philosophers. For example, parents often bemoan the extravagance surrounding children's birthday parties, yet they stubbornly stick with the rituals in vogue on their child's big day. On one occasion, listening to repeated parental laments in our circle, a tired grandmother of eight asked her daughter, "Why not celebrate the way you want?" "Because *we* can't be the ones to disappoint everybody," her daughter explained assuredly. "I think that as adults we ought to model for our children how to withstand peer pressure," a determined father respectfully proposed. A club member's response to him ended our meeting in a frenzy, all talking at once, both to themselves and to one another, amazed and dismayed. A single mother on a tight budget smilingly recounted the agreement she made with her teenage daughter to forgo new shoes and clothes for the start of the school year. The girl already had everything she needed; her classmates nosily disagreed among themselves, however, and some of them went home telling tales after the first day of school. That evening, this happy and hardworking mother received several calls from parents "worried" that she might be sick because her daughter had not been "school shopping." Birthday parties and shopping rituals set in stone.

Change and innovation will come despite our attempts at stalling and standing firm. Change occurs due to time's passing, and flexible lives move in step with time. If time were to stand still, everything would freeze and stop. Time and its companion, change, hold endless fascination for philosophers. Is time real? Does it apply only to humans? Must we heed its demands? Can we live without it? What does "timeless" mean? Is change really necessary? "Why can't I get my life just right and cement it in place?" "What if I'm happier dwelling on the past and counting on the future, especially when life is hard?" "I try to set my mind in fixed ways so that I can feel secure."

Approximately 2,600 years ago, Heraclitus dipped his toes into a river in Greece and instantly understood that change itself is the one unchanging reality. Everything is in flux; change is the source of life, the one thing you can trust. He realized that he could never—as hard as he might try or as much as he might like—step into the same river again. Change is here to stay. The moment when you read this word . . . is *now* gone. The case for flexibility is made; if life is moving, I'd better get going if I want to live.

Where to go for workouts in limber living? Socrates (SAH-kruh-teez) and Plato (PLAY-toh) suggest a fitness program that frees thinking by tossing out mental baggage. Conversation is hot. Alan Watts offers a Buddhist training regimen that frees movement by welcoming impermanence. Insecurity is cool.

> *I am better off . . . I neither know nor think that I know . . .*
> *I seem to have an advantage.*
> —Socrates, in Plato's *Apology*

In 399 BCE an Athenian jury convicted a philosopher of corrupting the local youth and sentenced him to death. At his trial, Socrates

maintained that he was far from the wisest man in Athens as an ora-
cle had prophesied; in fact, it was merely his awareness of how little
he knew that gave him a better chance to acquire knowledge than
those who were set in their opinions. One of the very first to refer to
his vocation as "philosopher," Socrates strolled the streets of Athens
for generations, asking questions and persisting in his inquiries with
those who professed expertise in any field. Barefoot and toga-clad, he
trolled for know-it-alls and begged them to share their wisdom, embarrassing the pompous and the privileged much to the youths' delight.
He testified before the jury that he had neither invited nor in any way
coerced young males to follow him; rather, they had enjoyed wit-
nessing his cross-examination of "authorities" and were emboldened
by their own mental stimulation. Silent grudges against him festered
nonetheless and rumors surrounded Socrates' straightforward life; his
legend outstripped his simple daily regimen dedicated to enlivening
Athenian minds. Despite his fervent entreaty that his accusers speak
so that he could defend himself, no youth came forward to accuse him
at his trial, nor any offended family member or aggrieved citizen.

Socrates' method of inquiry proved an unbearable aggravation to
those in power, his attempts to invigorate the intellectual life of Athens too threatening to the comfortable status quo. Plato, Socrates'
pupil, witnessed his mentor's trial and his defense, and while Socrates
never wrote about his theories, as the central character and star of
many of Plato's early dialogues, he is forever immortalized. Though
more than two millennia have passed since he was sentenced to sip
hemlock, these dialogues continue to push philosophers to nourish
an active, flexible mental life.

Meet the Wise Man Who Knew Nothing

With his admission that he was keenly aware of how little he
knew, Socrates shouts a rallying cry from ancient Greece to philosophers in every age. How can we learn *anything* if we think we know

everything? His admission of ignorance frees my philosophizing friends to challenge customary thinking, both personal and societal. While some backs initially bristle at a perceived threat to their long-held beliefs, ears soon perk up and the pace of conversation accelerates. His realization serves as profound incentive for each of us to embrace what we don't know. When I assume I know it all, questions disappear. My mind locks shut with a satisfied click. If wonder and curiosity peak because I am humbled by my ignorance about so many, many things, then the search for knowledge can begin at last. One question gives birth to another, and Socratic dialogue guarantees a flexible mind that is perpetually on the go.

Why are we so afraid of our ignorance? Perhaps because from an early age it is impressed upon us that there is so much we do not know that we *should* know—how to dress, how to talk, how to interact with others. We learn our first lessons in expected thinking and behavior quite early. As we mature, the sheer volume of hand-me-down ideas clutters our minds to the neglect of those essential gems of wisdom that we must discover on our own. Socrates reminds us that these inherited ideas are often merely unexamined assumptions that warrant our close-up scrutiny. He readily acknowledged that his ideas weren't his own *until* he asked his first question. What's going on? What am I thinking? What is the source of the ideas that are guiding my decisions? Do my senses convey everything to me, or is there a world hidden from my perception? Where exactly have the "experts" found their special knowledge? Parroting tried yet potentially untrue opinions has nothing to do with acquiring real knowledge. Among Socrates' favorite targets were those who professed certainty that death was the greatest evil. Facing his own imminent demise, he further aggravated his accusers at his trial: "This fear of death is indeed the imitation of wisdom, and not real wisdom, being the appearance of knowing the unknown" (*Apology*). Plato and Socrates plead with each of us to think for ourselves. Why not? How else can we know what we really think? Ideas, whether fuzzy or bright, motivate all our actions. Use your mind. No longer rattled by fear of the unknown, we begin to question everything with Athenian fire.

The Lifelong Quest for Eternal Truths

Plato and Socrates benefited from a fertile intellectual climate stoked by the musings of earlier thinkers. Pre-Socratic philosophers such as Thales and Empedocles joined a band of contemplative Athenians searching for truths unaltered by change. Socrates agreed with his predecessors that change rules the physical world. Buildings crumble, people age, seasons come and go. He and Plato offer us a mental refuge from physical change, however: a permanent sanctuary in an unchanging world of ideas. Stability can come from the practice of philosophy, as we talk together and unveil razor-sharp ideas that will stand the test of time. Walk with me, Socrates waves invitingly; never "hate reasonable discourse" (*Phaedo*). We quicken to keep pace with a troublemaker who wants the very best for our intellects. Imagine mixing with the crowd that listens to his animated celebration of eternal truths:

Perfect, eternal ideas *do* exist untouched by time. These pure concepts are true for all time and in all places, concepts such as Love, Truth, and . . . Flexibility. Take for example the one essential meaning of Shape: "this which applies to the round and the straight and the other things which you call shapes and which is the same in them all" (*Meno*). This never-changing definition of Shape itself, one that requires constant probing and rethinking, withstands changing circumstances. While the physical world shifts to and fro, nontangible ideas remain the same—Joy, Friendship, Equality—and as philosophers we must reevaluate our understanding of them through reflection and dynamic conversations. What is the *all-time* meaning of flexibility? Magnificent revelations await us if we are willing to utilize our innate intelligence to grapple with these concepts and reach for their eternal meaning. We are born with pure knowledge that soon grows cloudy from exposure to society's mixed messages. My inquiry and my faith in dialogue, Socrates explains, stem from my conviction that "searching and learning are, as a whole, recollection" (*Meno*). For example, originally we understood pure Freedom and the basics of Devotion, and just as we must wipe the dust from an old lightbulb so that it can gleam anew, we must dust our minds with the practice of philosophy to get closer and closer to reclaiming our knowledge and claiming it as our own. In the struggle to retrieve and receive pure understanding, be flexible in following your mind wherever it leads. Distrust certainty. Throw away whatever your hearty questioning invalidates if you are "to act intelligently in public or in private" (*Republic*). Clear thinking equips us for good living.

It comes as no surprise that Socrates walks away without providing a complete definition of any idea, content with planting the seeds for our self-awakening.

Plato's Dark Cave

One of Plato's enduring gifts to future philosophers is his "Myth of the Cave." In this "strange picture" with its "strange prisoners" (*Republic*), Plato symbolizes a world of people locked in the darkness of their own minds. His goal is that we recognize ourselves as these prisoners. Let's enter the Cave, confident in an exit plan!

Imagine the members of our philosophy club jailed from birth, shackled by the neck and the ankles, unable to move and seeing only what passes directly in front of us. Wedged in fixed positions, we watch as firelight casts flickering shadows on the cave's wall. This puppet show is all we know, and with no reason to doubt its authenticity, we accept its reality. We sit, inflexible in virtual darkness, staring straight ahead with no inkling of the glimmer of light at the mouth of the cave. Eventually, one of us shakes loose, spurred perhaps by natural curiosity and the stirrings of memory, and he begins the arduous journey toward the light, a painful journey for a stiff, newly mobile body. Up, up, up until at last . . . bright sunlight! A dazzling sun shines on the real world of ideas. Ahh. Courage itself. Peace in its pure form. Happiness is real, the former prisoner rubs his hands, and as he continues to gaze, he can see its meaning more and more clearly. Real learning is "this turning around" (*Republic*) from slumbering minds to supple intelligence. Compassion Itself. The undaunted escapee, Socrates hurries back to tell us about a world we knew before, a world in which we fed our souls and steered our lives with clear thinking. The rest of us barely noticed he was gone. . . . Plato suggests that as cave dwellers we would reject immediately the notion of another, truer world and be furious with the messenger pointing toward the sunlight. Get out of here! Socrates shouts at us, to no avail unless . . .

Plato admits that exercising the mind to its new potential is hard work and that a retreat to the Cave is often alluring. "I believe you may feel irritated at being suddenly awakened when you are caught napping" (*Apology*). It takes time to get used to the sunlight and to admit that we mistook the shadows for reality. Awareness of new ideas shocks complacency. Rediscovering our mental mobility is the work of a lifetime, and we never quite regain perfect understanding; we can never know the pure concepts with absolute certainty so we must keep seeking. But it's the process, the struggle, the small and larger visions of true meaning that matter. "It is then our task . . . to follow that upward journey" (*Republic*). Cave-bound living epitomizes inflexibility, and "the life which is unexamined is not worth living" (*Apology*). Never again such willful ignorance.

Dinner with Socrates

Well versed in the rewards of hearty conversation, Athenian thinkers gathered regularly for philosophical dinner parties. Good food and drink, a little flute music, and girls to clear the tables . . . let the party begin! In the *Symposium*, Plato writes about an evening devoted to discussion of the topic of Love, with dinner guests, including "Socrates fresh from the bath and with shoes on his feet, two circumstances most unusual with him." Round and round it goes, one description trumped by another, back and forth, and then the Socratic reminder that their goal is to move from specific examples of Love toward understanding Love's core meaning. He cautions us not to isolate "a particular kind of love and appropriate for it the name of love, which really belongs to a wider whole" (*Symposium*). More talk until Socrates tosses out his idea that Love is the search for Beauty and Wisdom. Conversation dwindles and only Socrates remains alert and eager for another round, "using pure thought alone" as he "tries to track down each reality pure and by itself" (*Phaedo*). Are we willing to stay up with him all night chasing ideas, trying to gain ground on wisdom? "What if their prison had an echo" (*Republic*) that reverberates from Plato's Cave to ours?

In the *Symposium*, Socrates never tires of wrangling with the assembled guests over the slippery concept of Love. Almost all budding philosophers long for a round in the ring with their antagonist, and he always spoils for a joust. Socrates enticed one philosophy club in particular with his tease to ask *him* questions. All right, they answered in chorus! Eavesdrop as they cheer one another on and one by one give Socrates a philosophical roughing-up: Phooey on those unchanging ideas, Socrates; everything is culturally relative. Just look at Athenian folkways such as slavery and female repression, and in the United States slavery has been deemed both right *and* wrong. Bet you can't think of any idea that is universally valid. And just as the effort to recollect perfect forms confounded your followers, "we cannot find the one which covers all the others" (*Meno*). One size does not fit all; courageous acts vary, the definition of justice depends on circumstance, and no two of us in our group can agree on love's meaning. Quit your badgering interrogations, Socrates. What about all the wondrous pleasures of the body and savoring being part of this world here and now? The Cave surely has its perks or so many wouldn't choose its faint light and security. Given our local and global differences and animosities, how can you cling to the notion that all people have the same perfect ideas stored in their minds at birth? How can you possibly suggest that *you* and *I* possess the same stash of wisdom? Flexibility an *unchanging* concept? Hilarious.

Socrates stifles a pleased guffaw. "You will please me and mine and yourselves by taking good care of your own selves in whatever you do, even if you do not agree with me now" (*Phaedo*). He stands and excuses himself from the table, grateful for new ideas to consider as he, and we, move closer to the sunlight. Nothing like a good chat with folks so attuned to their ignorance, and how cleverly they turned on me my very own Socratic method of asking one question after another. "Would he not reckon himself happy for the change?" (*Republic*) A real comeuppance at last! Thrilled with his new companions in thought, imagining all the daily upgrades opening for him and for each of us, Socrates departs in search of dessert and late-night companions.

> *Be as spontaneous and unfettered as life itself.*
> —ALAN WATTS, *The Spirit of Zen*

Anglican priest and author Alan Watts brought the philosophies of the Far East to Western cultures in the twentieth century through lectures, books, radio and television series, and tape recordings. He hooked audiences with his knack for simple presentation coupled with his subtle display of similarities among varied religious traditions. By the time of his death in 1973, Eastern philosophies had taken firm root in the West. His life was testimony to the joy to be found in spontaneous living; he included cooking and singing, calligraphy and dancing among his many passions. Zen Buddhism, centered in flexibility, served as the foundation of his personal philosophy.

From the perspective of Zen Buddhism, our desire for permanence in a swirling world that never stands still promises anxiety. Continuous striving to fix things firmly in place and thereby halt the passage of time belies an eternal truth: the process of change never lets up. Time passes. When we attempt to drop anchor in an effort to hold fast against the shifting tides of our lives, we struggle against the flow of life's energy. The moment will not wait; the anchor will not hold. Like a river, life keeps flowing. Watts reminds us that "nothing in the universe . . . is completely perfect or completely still" (*The Spirit of Zen*), and as part of this world we, as well, are always on the move. Hiding from change is impossible because "everything is perpetually becoming new" (*The Spirit of Zen*).

Accepting impermanence, on the other hand, frees us to ride life's current. Members of philosophy clubs today ask the age-old questions: How can we bend flexibly with life's fluctuating tides and variable winds? If we expect change as a natural part of living and adapt to it, can this flexibility lift life's burdens and quash its worries? And if so, why do we race against time and resist change so determinedly?

Time Nibbles at Our Heels

What is it about human nature that makes us resist fluid movement with life? Understanding this puzzle a bit better marks a good place to begin loosening up. As we leave early childhood, time sneaks up on us; at first unnoticed, it increasingly makes its presence known.

Longing for days gone by or the ones to come kicks in more often. Human capacity for "memory and foresight" can have the unpleasant side effect of making the past and the future seem *so* real that we often award them undue significance. Lingering in the past or anticipating the future, mistakenly feeling immune to time's passing, we miss life's ever-changing colors.

Watts helps me recognize that I am caught in time's trap, that "when you hold your breath you lose it" (*The Wisdom of Insecurity*). Ah. I begin to see how much *real* time I spend rushing backward or forward, seldom, if ever, present in my life as it is happening. Unfortunately my spotty attendance record tends to worsen when difficulty arrives; straying from living *now* poses an attractive alternative to facing my life. I forget, stall, ignore, and wait, safely ensconced in the past and future. Afraid of time's march, my tactic is to be tardy, absent from my life, unmoving . . . stiff as an iron rod. Unwilling to cope with change, I give up on life. It is at these times that Watts's challenge surfaces: "To be afraid of life is to be afraid of yourself" (*Cloud-hidden, Whereabouts Unknown*).

We all experience it. Racing here and there, we are merely running in place. We grant the clock ever-increasing control over our lives. Newspaper and coffee at seven, lunch at noon, job finished by five, bed by eleven. Repeat. Dinner at eight, never be late. "A less brainy culture would learn to synchronize its body rhythms rather than its clocks" (*The Wisdom of Insecurity*), but time "management" builds. Fun only on the weekend. One-a-day vitamin. Eventually a predictable routine will make all my decisions for me. No picnics in winter. Brunch once a month. Avoid serious conversation. Deviation from this pattern now strikes me as foolhardy. Why take any chances when I'm getting this life business down? Watts whispers his warning that "we can only understand life by keeping pace with it, by a complete affirmation and acceptance of its magic-like transformations and unending changes" (*The Spirit of Zen*). Ignoring him, my rut solidifies. Fretfully, I overthink everything. "If . . . then . . ." scenarios spin me around. "Maybe . . . but . . ." possibilities dizzy me. I make lists and longer lists to plot a certain future. If I have definite plans, maybe I can pull out of this shaky tailspin. "By Monday," "at the end of the month," "when it snows," "after the holiday": all these exact calculations protect against any unforeseen events. I grab a stranglehold on security. I've got my job, my exercise group, an intimate love and friends I call on specific days, a reliable car and a faithful dog. All set!

And all this time, life passes me by. How could I think that investing my time in recalling past pleasures and pretending future successes would absolve me from living? Sad, frustrated, and on edge, I'm going nowhere at top speed. Obviously, it is absolutely necessary that I make friends with change. But how can I get time on my side?

Letting Life Live You

Watts is adamant that the time to start living is NOW. Where to begin? Stretch with him as he launches a training program that will strengthen your concentration. Do you notice your focus flitting from this to that, here and there, fidgety and unnerved? Stop it. Settle yourself on whatever is immediately present. Focus. When your attention first wanders, hustle back to the moment. "This is the real secret of life—to be completely engaged with what you are doing in the here and now" (*The Essential Alan Watts*). Drop everything outside the instant and wrap your attention around . . . the timbre of a voice, the boiling kettle, the taste of a melon, a song on the radio, a clap of thunder, the touch of a hand. Developing such a "one-pointed" attitude will take willpower; as with any skill, fine-tuning comes with practice and paying attention gets easier. Fleeing from change was hard work and self-defeating "but, as soon as you let life live you, you discover that you are living life with an altogether new fullness and zest" (*The Meaning of Happiness*).

As you hone your powers of concentration, the more flexibly you "take each thing as it comes, finish with it and pass on to the next" (*The Spirit of Zen*). Oddly but happily, you discover that living in the present yields that long-sought sense of permanence. Getting *with* the flow of time *in* your life, cartwheeling and back flipping, though changes brew, you remain limber *and* centered. There is more magic still to come: the division between work and play softens and fades. "There was a man who was making shoe-shining a real art. He used his cloth to beat out a rhythm. He had just the same fascination in shining shoes as one has in spinning a prayer wheel" (*The Essential Alan Watts*).

A sink full of dishes: no problem. Washing them one at a time, I complete my rhythmic scrub-and-rinse task painlessly. No time is awarded to thoughts of being finished or to prospects of another sink full of dirty dishes after the next meal. Ironically, rolling with my life without resistance allows me to meet responsibilities more quickly and efficiently. I forget to worry. The breeze of spontaneity blows through me. No chores this Saturday. Going to call that friend. Off on a walk, bye. Think I'll read that interesting article now. No longer immersed in manipulating my life's course, I have more time to live. I wave a nimble wrist and motion one surprise after another my way, no longer trying to predict the future, to return to the past, to control the present, to plot my life on a grid.

"Life, change, movement, and insecurity are so many names for the same thing" (*The Wisdom of Insecurity*). Joy and pleasure garner their intensity *because* they are fleeting. Living with this insight instills calm and cool reserve, come what may; on the move, happiness can pass this way again. Sorrow and pain gather their power from our attachment to them. Though we may cling to them, they, also, are momentary. Such a basic truth frequently appears a revelation. "Does this simply mean I should just live life?" a wide-eyed, slack-jawed student asked as our study of Watts came to a close. Yes, that's what it means. "All this mental effort to realize *that*? Just live? How would you sum up his philosophy?" she asked me.

"Perfect timing."

Walking On

Watts leaves us with the clear lesson that hardship and heartache are inevitable. Both will present themselves in our lives without fail. He contends that much of the nagging pain revolves around our dogged attempts to dodge difficulties rather than to deal with them head-on. As a surfer waits for the wave, catches it and rides its natural unfolding, we paddle out from shore and learn to ride with our lives. "Freedom comes through complete acceptance of reality. Those who wish to keep their illusions do not move at all; those who fear them run backwards into greater illusions, while those who conquer them 'Walk on'" (*The Spirit of Zen*).

Talking with newly flowing philosophers about the possibility and the practicality of accepting change, most feel encouraged to share their qualms: "Walk on" sounds attractive, but "having no direction at all feels sort of derelict!" "Does this mean I should make no plans at all?" is usually the first reservation voiced after students warm to Watts. He maintains that future plans need not diminish our focus on and enjoyment of the present. A note of caution, however: preparing for the future requires a flexible lifestyle that allows switching course, backpedaling to go forward, and perhaps choosing another direction altogether. To encourage dialogue, I provide examples from my life of the rewards of trusting chance; with new proofs surfacing for me all the time, there are countless possibilities. . . . Here's but one: during my first two years in college, I reveled in the feast of academic offerings, scrolling in order down the alphabetical listing of courses from art, to chemistry, to economics. Drawing closer to the time to choose one subject as my specialization, I had difficulty making the commitment. By chance, at that time I had arrived at the letter P. I took my seat in an introductory philosophy class, and here we are!

Testimony to the happy consequences of trusting chance and embracing happenstance has inspired philosophizing groups over the years. A sampler: tutoring co-workers in French for lunchtime fun led to a more interesting job with the State Department; my allergy to grass kept me from playing field sports but now rowing crew is my passion; loving Monopoly as a kid was my inspiration for pursuing a career in banking. Around the circles we go, sharing examples of living with focus but without a fixed plan and arriving at just the right spot. Our conclusions: "When I listen, life lets me know." "Life is the teacher." "When work is play, it all works." "I think that if you take care of the present, the future will take care of itself."

"For the animal, happiness consists in enjoying life in the immediate present" (*The Wisdom of Insecurity*). Think of dolphins bobbing and gliding . . . birds dipping and soaring . . . dogs chasing and napping. Life moves . . . not along a fixed, linear line with predetermined stops along the way, but with irresistible energy. Now.

DISCUSSION QUESTIONS

- What is flexibility?
- Is increased flexibility appealing? Why?
- What does it mean to be inflexible? Physically? Mentally? Emotionally? Are they connected?
- How do you respond to change? Do you resist it?
- Is change inevitable? Avoidable?
- Are you trapped by time's constraints? In what ways are time's restrictions real?
- How do you impose deadlines and demands on your life unnecessarily?

- Is there security in inflexibility? Safety in refusing to change?
- Do you take pleasure in being right? What is satisfying about proving your point?
- In what ways are you a prisoner in Plato's Cave? What ideas would you like to understand more clearly? How would improved vision make for better living in each case?
- How would you describe a flexible mental life?
- Do you enjoy good conversation? What are its ingredients?
- Do you like to ask questions? Do you like to be asked questions?
- What is a firmly held belief that you discarded upon further reflection? What are some assumptions that you regret?
- Do you spend much time thinking about the past and imagining the future? Too much?
- How does it feel to be fully attentive in the moment? Is time an issue when you are completely engaged *now*?
- Do you use time to your advantage or do you waste it worrying about unimportant things? How can you spend time more wisely?
- Is there freedom in accepting that everything, including you, is changing constantly? What new freedoms appear when you befriend change?
- If you were more focused on the task at hand, could you be more flexible come what may? Can you give an example?
- What does "forever" mean? Are there things that time cannot change? What?
- What tips for flexing will stay with you from our philosophers? How can you become more limber on your daily climb out of the Cave? How can you glide with life's current?

HOMEWORK

Listen and Hum

Music is the artistic arrangement of continuous sounds in time; tempo is the speed, the pace at which the composition moves. Music depends on time for its creation. Musicians showcase fluid movement. Enjoy further exploration of aspects of flexibility through free-flowing discussion of the following musicians and their works. Choose one from each of the three categories, making sure that every selection is taken by a member of your group. As you listen, contemplate the nature of Music, Time, and Change. In your journals write a sharp description of the essence of these three concepts in as few words as possible. Share the findings of your Platonic investigation.

What Is Music?

- Jazz becomes art as Charlie Parker curls his fingers around his saxophone and gives birth to bebop. Yardbird's heyday marks the postwar years of the forties and fifties and his innovative compositions elicit attentive listening. Though he lived for thirty-four short, tumultuous years, his revolutionary take on music is alive in countless recordings and many recorded tributes from other musicians. A sculpture of his likeness in Kansas City proclaims: "Bird Lives." Listen to his riffs of Watts's belief that "Now's the Time." These familiar notes inspired the Hucklebuck, a dance requiring great flexibility! With Charlie Parker as background, the question remains: What is Music?

- A mezzo-soprano performs the music of the Beatles and Monteverdi, George Gershwin and John Cage, Stravinsky and Debussy? Music is not confined by genre nor limited by Cathy Berberian's range of talents. While her version

of "Ticket to Ride" is twisty fun and Gershwin's "Summertime" unusually warm, it is her own composition,
"Stripsody," that defies any possible expectation. One
voice sings chicken and cat, classical and contemporary,
silent and soaring. Listening to her rooster's cackle, one
wonders how Berberian would describe music's essence.

- John Cage's total absorption in the process of composing
  music results in curious sounds blended with periods of
  striking silence. At times the strings are struck from inside
  the piano! The score for his *Music of Changes* is inspired
  by the ancient Chinese classic the *I Ching, The Book of
  Changes*, a work setting forth techniques based on chance,
  used for predicting the future. As if with the roll of the
  dice, Cage uses chance operations that find their way into
  a complete composition. Buddhist concepts of chance
  and change likewise influence his *Seven Haiku*, short
  pieces mirroring the Japanese poetic form of three lines of
  five-seven-five syllables. Compare Cage's musical haiku
  with Basho's poetry when you meet him later in this chapter. Are music and poetry alike? How? Can you discern
  qualities of musical composition shared by Parker, Berberian, and Cage?

- Is music yours to define? Elizabeth Cotten and Jimi Hendrix use their left hands to turn music inside out. These
  natural lefties whirl right-handed guitars upside down and
  have at it! "Cotten Picking" is her unique style that reverses the usual roles of thumb and finger as she alternates
  between bass and treble. A girl eleven years old, listening
  to the familiar rumble of the number 9 speeding by, she
  writes and strums about that "Freight Train" that keeps
  "comin' round the bend" . . . and then it's "gone again."
  Hendrix's huge hands nimbly rove over his guitar as he

plays it behind his head and with his teeth. His mastery of
the "whammy bar" turns "The Star-Spangled Banner" into
his signature song. No rules govern the talent of Cotten
and Hendrix. Does music conform to *any* rules?

What Is Time?

- Enya's Irish lilt conveys future uncertainty with assured
serenity. "Only Time" will answer the questions it poses.
Does anyone, ever, really know "where the road goes /
where the day flows"? Do love's ties promise a certain future? Explain and share examples.

- Is memory the thread that binds together the moments of
a life? What connects your youth with your later years? Iris
DeMent poignantly reflects on her "Childhood Memories"
of time spent with her father, Patrick. Collecting lightning
bugs in a canning jar, playing grown-up in the driver's seat
of Daddy's car, gathering around the piano . . . Do such
reminiscences hold our lives together? "Time, it moved so
fast, those days are over now . . . but no matter where I
roam I've got you here with me." Can you relate to De-
Ment's astonishment at time's quick passage? Is your childhood present in your life now?

- Kicking dirt, shuffling around, wasting "Time" in the old
hometown, and all of a sudden ten years pass by. Taking life
for granted, Pink Floyd sings the sinking feeling of knowing
you "missed the starting gun" for your life. Now, desperate
to catch up, but "every year is getting shorter, never seem
to find the time." Can you find "more" time? Where? Do
you waste time? How? Strange questions . . .

- Time's steady movement passes through much of Judy Collins's music. "Who Knows Where the Time Goes?" and
how do birds know it's time to fly and why does love grow

even though time goes? If you "Turn, Turn, Turn" in the spirit of Ecclesiastes, you realize that "to everything there is a season." Planting and reaping, laughing and weeping, dancing and mourning, embracing and withholding . . . there is a time for each in its turn. It's a good thing that "Nothing Lasts Forever." Magic cooks even in shadow and "you'll get through this trouble." Time passes and soon "you'll be fine," Collins assures. What about time?

What Is Change?

- Change churns in the flowing waters of the Mississippi and the Moldau. William Warfield calls his Mississippi "Ol' Man River," and despite the suffering of those who "tote dat barge / and lif' dat bale" on its waters, that "long ol' river forever keeps rollin' on." Joe, the enslaved bargeman in Jerome Kern's *Show Boat*, longs to be like the river that moves no matter what. If humans could live with the river's fluidity, would change lose its sting? How does the river change? What qualities do the Mississippi and the River Moldau in Czechoslovakia share? Bedřich Smetana paints a musical portrait in his *Moldau*, using program notes to describe the river's path as two small streams join for a trip through the countryside. Nymphs dance, peasants feast, and castles appear; finally, the Moldau spins through rapids on its way to Prague . . . not to linger, but gracefully to merge into the Elbe. Can change be as seamless for us as the shift from Moldau to Elbe?
- "Live, love, and let live, / love, live, and let go," Sam Bush sings, picks, and dances. Accompanied first by the slow pluck of his mandolin, which then quickens into rhythmic strumming, Bush repeats his advice simply to "Go with the Flow." His animated voice makes flexible living quite ap-

pealing. In what ways does living and letting go come naturally? Why is it also very, very hard?

- Fancy clothes and cool shoes, bling and crowds, and Jack Johnson worries that "there are things that concern you more than your time." How are you spending the days of your life? Do you take care of your mind or "is it straight from the mold and ready to be sold"? His ardent voice issues the ancient Socratic warning to flee the Cave, to change before it's too late. Can we change our careless expenditure of time? Are our minds too far "Gone"?

Recite and Write

Two people share one of the following poems. Talk together about your reactions and share your responses with the group. What insights into flexibility appear?

- Is everything snatched by time's flow? William Shakespeare offers his concluding lines from "Shall I Compare Thee to a Summer's Day?" as testimony to the power of art and love to defeat time's passage. "So long as men can breathe, or eyes can see, / so long lives this, and this gives life to thee." His love's beauty glows with every reading of the poem, no longer touched by changing seasons or circumstances. Shakespeare's words make youthful loveliness eternal. Does art outlast time? Is Mozart's music alive? Can love defeat time? Will Shakespeare's love be lovelier than a summer's day forever?

- Even though all around you are satisfied with society's pat responses to every question, "Do Not Be Afraid of No." Say "no" to fast and easy answers that stifle curiosity. Saying "yes" too quickly is wonder's dead-end street. Gwendolyn Brooks smiles at the prospects: "It is brave to be involved, / to be not fearful to be unresolved." Are you sometimes afraid of learning new ideas? Is it inviting, when faced with making changes in light of these new ideas, to skip back down to the Cave? Can you become accustomed to saying: "No, I don't know"?

- "Eternity" is home to those who can embrace fleeting bliss without begging it to stay. William Blake promises constant sunrise for those who live joyfully in the present. Craving permanence ruins the immediate, fleeting experience of pleasure. Do you think that Blake is speaking truthfully in this four-line poem? Have you missed the face you love in repeated glances at the clock?

- In the hallway of an old town hall, an "ancient timepiece" remains unchanged through all the swiftly changing lives that pass before it. Do the hands of "The Old Clock on the Stairs" point, perhaps, to eternity with its repeated refrain: "Forever—Never! / Never—Forever!"? Henry Longfellow thinks of all who have passed through this building never to return and wonders when there will be an end to suffering, to separation, to death. What does the refrain mean? Is there a reality outside time and beyond death? Not here, but always there? Outside the Cave, Plato answers. Inside the moment, Watts claps. And you?

- Who better than the author of some two thousand poems to pronounce: "The Brain—is wider than the Sky." Do you share Emily Dickinson's faith in the mind? Not only does the brain's breadth stretch out of sight, but its depth reaches far deeper than the bottom of the sea. Align the brain beside the sky and . . . they are the same size! And, just think, the mind's weight matches God's heft. Socrates teaches us how little we know. Dickinson presents us with unlimited mental possibilities. How do these two approaches complement each other? Are you pushing your mind toward its potential?

• The splash of a frog in a pond. Basho, seventeenth-century Zen Buddhist poet, captures that very instant in one of Japan's most famous poems. Basho uses just a few syllables to take a snapshot of one moment—wild geese in clouds, scent of plum blossoms, cat's yelp, temple bell's toll, sea slug's shadow—and preserve it in delicate detail. He yanks the nightingale, the violet, and the firefly from time's clutch. Basho is master of haiku, three lines of verse arranged with five syllables in the first line tumbling into seven syllables in the second and finishing in five syllables in the third line. Penetrating to the essence of an instant, spring moon and monkey's mask . . . and snap! . . . his pen records the image. Basho practices Zen concentration and flowing movement as a wandering monk in nature's temple. Nature is his teacher; despite its infinite variety and transformations, Nature itself is unchanging. Wander, quietly. Focus and click in seventeen syllables. Moment. Moment. Moment. Time evaporates. Share.

Read and Talk

• "Suppose time is a circle, bending back on itself" and people repeat their lives over and over forever. Suppose you found yourself living in the past, fully aware that your decisions could alter a future that had already come to pass. Physicist Alan Lightman sneaks the reader into *Einstein's Dreams* in thirty short, poetic fables investigating the nature of time. Lightman imagines the year 1905 in Bern, Switzerland, where an unknown patent clerk moves ever-closer to divulging the "Theory of Relativity." Time is real but depends on the observer's viewpoint, Einstein discovers, so our individual relationships with time vary. Thirty nights and thirty dreams, simply and clearly rendered, whirl the reader into Einstein's subconscious musings. Could time exist as frozen moments? Each fable gives a taste of time's mystery. What do you suppose?

• Is there a word used as often with more misunderstanding than "love"? bell hooks instigates personal discussion of this elusive concept in *all about love,* recognizing that for her "it was love's absence that let me know how much love mattered." Platonic in her approach, hooks proposes a fresh search for meaning that depends on our willingness to discard society's mixed and distorted messages. Advertising, "romance" novels, magazines, music—we are bombarded by false impressions that leave us silently obsessed and cynical about love. We can experience love once more if we uncover its essential ingredients. Along with Plato and Socrates, hooks seeks love's definition because "the principles of love are always the same in any meaningful bond." Losing love's meaning results in loneliness, disappointment, and abuse. What is love? Talk about it, says hooks, often and everywhere.

• Published in 1850, Nathaniel Hawthorne's *The Scarlet Letter* portrays a puritanical society whose members are sure of their moral beliefs beyond any doubt. Established norms rule and prove deadly. Hester Prynne's pregnancy grievously offends tender sensibilities and she wears the scarlet letter A to brand her an adulteress and to separate her from the good citizens. "This woman has brought shame upon us all, and ought to die." But Hester emerges from prison and stands before the crowd and "she took the baby on her arm . . . with a burning blush, and yet a haughty smile, and a glance that would not be abashed." What about Hester's personal qualities such as loyalty, strength, perseverance, responsibility, devotion? At book's end she has retired to her "home" town where she hopes "at some brighter period, when the world should have grown ripe for it . . . a new truth would be revealed" and love would rest "on a surer ground of mutual happiness." What prevailing moral standards could use scrutiny from your group? What new truths could herald a brighter age?

- "The river laughed" because it contains the secret that "there is no such thing as time." In his novel *Siddhartha*, Hermann Hesse takes the reader on one man's lifelong quest for abiding satisfaction. Siddhartha's restless seeking begins as he leaves his youth and his parents behind. The disciplined monk Siddhartha trades fasting and a chat with the Buddha for years of indulgent sensuality; he becomes a merchant who gambles all on the roll of the dice, and eventually collapses in despair at a river's bank. The river's wrinkles answer his search for truth. "This discovery had made him very happy. Was then not all sorrow in time, all self-torment and fear in time?" Siddhartha sought what he and we always possess, the "eternity of every moment." What can you learn from his wanderings and his fulfillment? What is it about the river? Go and sit if you can. Talk about the experience together, later.

- Time-out takes on new meaning in Rae Grant's *Crafting Fun*. Grant's beautifully illustrated book offers children and adults old-time crafts to enjoy together. "In the days before ink pens were invented, people used feathers dipped in ink to write their letters or to keep family journals." After discovering a large feather on a walk, then clipping it to a sharp point with grown-up assistance, children can make entries in their "feather journal" with a quill pen. Lives spanning generations join while creating tin can lanterns, daisy chain necklaces, and rubber stamp hearts. Wooden clothespins snap; waxed paper crinkles. Such simple fun makes time stand still for younger and older participants. Swap tales; forget time.

- Vivian Stringer, women's basketball coach at Rutgers University, invites both Plato and Watts to play ball in her memoir, *Standing Tall*. Now in her fourth decade of coaching, Stringer is tough-minded and clear-sighted in her approach to the game and in coaching and mentoring her players. She challenges her team's practice ethic with the warning that "mental weakness can make you a prisoner of your body." Strengthen your mind, and the body follows. Her unwavering ability to ride the rough flow of her life's current is a model of flexibility. Just as she takes her players through the rhythm of a game, she moves through poverty, racial and gender barriers, her three children's serious health problems, her much-loved husband's death, her own bout with cancer, every obstacle met head-on with grace. What do you see of Platonic mental vigor and a Buddhist stroll with impermanence in Stringer's brand of ball and life?

Watch and Reflect

- There is "nothing magical about change. . . . Get up and take the first step. Do the work." Nobel Peace Prize laureate Jody Williams does exactly that in her tireless work aimed at the removal and banning of land mines. Join Turk Pipkin in *Nobelity* as he travels the globe for a year of asking questions and engaging in conversation with winners of the Nobel Prize. Though the pressing magnitude of global issues overwhelms the mind and weakens energy, Pipkin learns from these big minds that we should welcome change because "it doesn't have to be this way." Laureates in physics, chemistry, medicine, economics, and several Peace Prize winners offer new ways of thinking about war, famine, disease, ecology, and technology. They lend a hand up and out of the Cave. Indian economist Amartya Sen is optimistic that humans can "think through" our problems and that we "can reason our way out." Does *Nobelity* offer you new ways of thinking? Are you changing your mind? How?

• Willy Loman is a traveling salesman who never moves an inch. Scrambling "in a race against the junkyard" to pay the bills and to keep his head up, his solace lies only in memory and dreams. Arthur Miller brings inflexibility alive in *Death of a Salesman* as Willy tries to "remember those days" cruising in a 1928 Chevy and assures his wife that "I'll knock 'em dead next week." The misery of a life stuck on hold replays itself with wrenching regularity. Though he has lost his job, he proclaims that "some day I'll have my own business." Infuriated that his wife purchased American whipped cheese knowing full well that he only eats Swiss, he vehemently reminds her, "I don't want to change." His grown son bears painful witness to his collapse, and Biff begs his father to "bury that phony dream, Dad." Watching Willy's inflexible nature harden serves as warning and reminder of the need to move with life. His bags are so heavy. What mental baggage weighs you down? What realities in your life tug at you to deal with them directly? Do you have anything in common with Willy?

Get Up and Do

- Have great fun at a dinner party sure to pique the interest of Socrates and Plato. Everyone bring a dish, and perhaps choose a specialty to prepare as you gather. Franz Joseph Haydn's *Symphony No. 22*, "The Philosopher," is appropriate background music. Pick one appetizer for a philosophical taste test . . . a dip, sauce, cheese, olive. Take turns describing the taste in one (just one) word. Discuss varying sensory experiences. Does everyone interpret the world differently? Is there one right descriptor? Relax and enjoy a festive meal and good conversation. In keeping with Greek tradition, devote the time during and after dessert to one philosophical topic. I guarantee one concept sure to stimulate, confound, and make merry: *Time*. What is it? Musings from the turn of the fifth century come alive as Augustine sits perplexed in his monastery, contemplating the meaning of time and its stark contrast to eternity. Eternity? Maybe time is an illusion, "but there is a present act of attention, by which what was the future passes on its way to becoming past" (*Confessions*, Book XI). That moment right here that just this second passed . . . What is the nature of time? Is it real? Is it time to go?!

- Sip tea. Pay attention to the taste on your tongue and the texture in your throat. Slowly. No gulps. Relish the aroma.

- Try a steady hand at sumiye, the ancient Chinese art of black ink drawing on thin white paper. Art supply stores have inexpensive brushes as well as ink and rice paper, or you can use any white paper and a thin brush. Because the paper absorbs the ink immediately, the brushstroke must be continuous. Enjoy an endeavor that requires and teaches complete concentration. David Bowie's awareness of "Changes" haunts him, as the "warm impermanence" of ripples in a stream reminds him of passing days. Time chases Bowie, "but I can't trace time." "Trace time" in black ink. Is your unbroken tracing linear? Circular?

- Spend quiet time sitting in a breeze or walking in the wind. Think of the breeze and the wind as teachers. What specific lessons about flexibility can you learn? Think of ways to apply your insights.

- Discuss your educational experiences. What were/are your best teachers? Is learning best described as receiving and storing information or, as Plato insists, an uncovering of innate ideas and abilities through reflection and dialogue? How are you learning in your philosophy club? What are you learning? Be specific. What are your hopes for your ongoing, lifelong education?

- Become absorbed in the open spaces that fill the canvases of Chinese and Japanese landscape paintings. If a visit to a museum is not possible, look through art books at your local library or perhaps view slides in a college collection. Illustrations of Chinese and Japanese artwork appear throughout Watts's *The Spirit of Zen*. Space invites the viewer into the painting; it pulls you into the scene. And, just as physical exercise requires room for stretching and extending, mental and emotional flexibility relies on space as well—to flow and to adapt with change. What impinges on your mind's movement? Discuss practical ways to improve mental agility.

- Greek art flourished in the days of Plato and Socrates. Flip through art books and see through their eyes the extra-

ordinary drawings on drinking cups (kylixes) put to very
good use at their dinner parties, or the artistic tales painted
on large ceremonial vases (amphoras) reserved for special
occasions. The sculpture of Kritios and the architectural
triumphs spreading across the Acropolis, the hilltop with
a view of Athens below, transport us into an accomplished
world. Even in ruins, the Parthenon stands in beautiful
tribute to the goddess Athena.

- Abrupt change presents a challenge in any life. Are you
aware of people coping with a sudden shift in circumstances? Where are they? Near or far? Is there something
you can do to increase their flexibility? Rest for the tired
caregiver? Time with the painfully lonely?

Resources

Music
- *Now's the Time: The Revolutionary Charlie Parker*: "Now's the
Time."
- *Magnificathy: The Many Voices of Cathy Berberian*, with Bruno
Canino, piano: "Stripsody," by Cathy Berberian; "Ticket to Ride,"
by John Lennon and Paul McCartney; "Summertime," by George
and Ira Gershwin.
- *The Complete John Cage Edition, Volume 29*, Martine Joste, piano:
Music of Changes and *Seven Haiku*.
- *Elizabeth Cotten Live!* (1984) by Elizabeth Cotten: "Freight
Train."
- *The Jimi Hendrix Experience Live at Berkeley* by Jimi Hendrix: "The
Star Spangled Banner."
- *A Day Without Rain* by Enya: "Only Time."
- *My Life* by Iris DeMent: "Childhood Memories."
- *Dark Side of the Moon* by Pink Floyd: "Time."
- *Forever: An Anthology* by Judy Collins: "Who Knows Where the
Time Goes," "Turn, Turn, Turn," "Nothing Lasts Forever."
- *Greatest Hits: Broadway [Cast Recording]*: "Ol' Man River," from
Show Boat, by Jerome Kern and Oscar Hammerstein II, featuring
William Warfield, baritone.

- *Howlin' at the Moon* by Sam Bush: "Go with the Flow."
- *On and On* by Jack Johnson: "Gone."
- *Smetana: Má Vlast: Moldau*, Česká Filharmonie, Rafael Kubelik conducting.
- *Best of Bowie* by David Bowie: "Changes."
- *The Best of Chubby Checker 1959–1963*: "Hucklebuck."
- *Haydn: Symphonies Vol. 9*: Symphony No. 22, "The Philosopher," Northern Chamber Orchestra, Nicholas Ward conducting.

Poetry
- *Shakespeare's Sonnets and Poems*, edited by Barbara Mowat and Paul Werstine: "Shall I Compare Thee to a Summer's Day?"
- *Selected Poems* by Gwendolyn Brooks: "Do Not Be Afraid of No."
- *Complete Poetry and Prose of William Blake*, edited by David Erdman: "Eternity."
- *Longfellow: Selected Poems* by Henry Wadsworth Longfellow: "The Old Clock on the Stairs."
- *The Poems of Emily Dickinson*, edited by R. W. Franklin: "The Brain—is wider than the Sky."
- *On Love & Barley* by Basho, translated by Lucien Stryk.

Prose
- *Einstein's Dreams* by Alan Lightman.
- *all about love* by bell hooks.
- *The Scarlet Letter* by Nathaniel Hawthorne.
- *Siddhartha* by Hermann Hesse.
- *Crafting Fun* by Rae Grant.
- *Standing Tall* by Vivian Stringer.
- *Apology, Symposium, Republic, Meno, Phaedo* by Plato.
- *Confessions* by Augustine: Book XI.
- *Herakleitos & Diogenes*, translated by Guy Davenport.
- *The Spirit of Zen; The Wisdom of Insecurity; The Essential Alan Watts; The Essence of Alan Watts; The Meaning of Happiness; Cloud-hidden; Whereabouts Unknown.*

Drama
- *Death of a Salesman* by Arthur Miller, directed by Volker Schlöndorff (DVD).

Documentary
- *Nobelity*, directed by Turk Pipkin (DVD).

Empathy

~~~~~

Is your heart right? If your heart isn't right, fix it up today.

— MARTIN LUTHER KING, JR.,
The Autobiography of Martin Luther King, Jr.

THE TOPIC

It looks something like this. A victorious athlete tastes the loser's disappointment and tones down an instinctive victory celebration. Students satisfied with their well-earned grades, sensing a room full of deflated spirits, discreetly slide their papers into their notebooks. Standing alone on the outskirts of a party, a first-year teacher gladly shakes hands at a veteran's welcoming tap on the shoulder. Aware of the chronic fatigue that marks a neighbor's life, an excited traveler refrains from talk of holiday plans. It looks nothing like this: making fun of someone's fear of heights; gloating over a promotion in the presence of underpaid colleagues; brandishing endless pictures of the new baby unmindful of a companion's lost child.

Sensitivity to another's feelings requires no grand gesture. Seemingly intuitively, people such as the subdued athlete, the modest students, and the experienced teacher easily add "kind" to their list of things to be. Perhaps the frustrated opponent and the complaining classmates did not notice the thoughtful gestures, but empathy expects nothing in return. It springs unsought from a wide heart. While stores devote entire sections to "sympathy" cards, most expressions of empathy are subtle, often wordless.

Why is empathy such a powerful force? Recall occasions when someone has crept through the gossamer-thin fabric of separation and fallen in step with your life. Partnering on a silent walk with you and your frantic worry. Calling to chat about nothing in particular to diffuse the pressure of your increasing responsibilities. Experiencing afresh your memory of old heartache. How to explain the immeasurable comfort provided by these simple acts?

What *is* empathy?

Empathy is the direct experience of another person's feelings, often to the extent that the very concept of an *other* no longer exists. It is the use of one's imagination to project another's life into our own. Such pure feeling moves rapidly, barely discernibly . . . from feeling *for* you, to feeling *with* you, to feeling *as* you feel. This intimate identification that blurs the distinctions between us gives birth to compassion, kindness, and love. Acts of empathy lift our burdens, shining new light on lusterless days. Though we parade about in different bodies, we all know salty tears, anxious hearts, drained spirits, and weary footsteps. Empathy acknowledges this sameness; while it requires a leap out of my life and exposes me to your pain, empathy fine-tunes my heartstrings. My heart expands to make room for your feelings. Bigger is better. Empathy elicits my best instincts, polishing my jagged edges to soften your entry into my life. Boldly, an empathetic person continually gives the benefit of the doubt, putting a kind first foot forward.

Talking about empathy causes some initial awkwardness in most groups of philosophers. Defensive poses strike first. Feet shuffle, legs cross and uncross, eyes look down and straight ahead. Opening remarks usually conform to an expected pattern. Assurances that "I'm always full of empathy" and "I'm a naturally empathetic person" imply that this particular philosophical discussion may very well be unnecessary. I can count on familiar choruses of "casseroles (tuna) for the sick neighbor," "volunteering (three days every week) at a soup kitchen," and "setting aside money for charity (a lot) at the end of the year." Throats clear as more voices chime in with comparable proofs of kindness; rarely is tribute paid to the empathy of others. Given time, the talk drifts of its own accord into first one and then many admissions that . . . "I've learned how it is to get dragged into somebody's life," and "I try not to be open as much to protect myself," and "It is hard enough trying to live my own life." Early assertions of natural empathy give way to reluctant confessions of selfishness; frequently the softly spoken and painful insight dawns that "I didn't know I don't have it."

Group posture relaxes and our circle comes alive once these preliminaries are behind us. We remember together that our exploration into the meaning of empathy is no different from our look at any other topic. We seek clearer understanding of empathy in order to foster its growth in our lives. If I know better *what* it is, I can know better *how* to live it. Of course! Any relationship calls for keen awareness of another's life. Suddenly our task appears less daunting. Comments are tinged with hope. "If I were not so hard on myself, I could stop blaming others and start forgiving them *and* me." "When I discount someone else's heart, I shortchange mine." Though we at present may lack a trusting, empathetic heart, we now know for sure that we need one.

Ancient philosophers from Augustine in the West to Sun Tzu in the East debated the ethics of war, and modern philosophy continues this conversation in depth. But thoughtful philosophers sit with me and consistently question the time devoted to discussions of war. Fresh to the practice of philosophy, their comments cut straight to the point. Doesn't the outbreak of violence announce the failure of reasoned discourse? It is not naive to counter cruelty with a clear comprehension of empathy, they hope. Can't we combat violence peacefully if each of us stokes the fires of empathy? Jesus thought so. Confucius recommended self-cultivation as the cure for war in ancient China. Yes, there is a way to revive our hearts in spite of and in response to the widespread violence that plagues our planet. How? One person at a time.

Two tough guys, far from naive and plenty smart, have won legions of fans and Nobel Prizes for Peace. They welcome us to join them in waging love and kindness against war and bigotry. Saturate a world thirsty for your natural empathy, the Dalai Lama (DAH-lie LAH-mah) beseeches. Fight injustice and change society with the gale force of empathy at your back; Martin Luther King, Jr., marches on.

THE PHILOSOPHERS

*Each of us can inspire others simply by working to develop
our own altruistic motivations—and engaging the world
with a compassion-tempered heart and mind.*
—The Dalai Lama, *The Washington Post*, October 21, 2007

In 1998 I attended a talk given by a merry man of many faces. The Dalai Lama, spiritual and political guru to millions of ethnic Tibetans, was the featured speaker at a conference of Nobel Peace Prize laureates. Solemn, laughing, inquisitive, pensive, his pace was at once unhurried and on the go. He was dressed in inner peace. The former Tenzin Gyatso was intensely aware of his surroundings, whether a dropped pen, a child's giggle, an outstretched hand in the distance, or movement in the balcony. He did not miss a thing, yet he never lost his concentration on the present moment. His de-meanor was at the same time self-effacing and self-assured. Laugh lines crossed a brow furrowed with concern; his eyebrows lifted en-gagingly when he spoke or entertained a question.

Exiled since 1960 in Dharamsala, India, witness to the murder of millions of his people and the destruction of Tibet's cultural heritage by the Chinese government, the Dalai Lama travels the globe in love with life. His mission is peace. His strategy is to unite countless indi-vidual lives, as many as he can, in the warmth of empathy's power.

Let's settle in for an audience with His Holiness at your group's favorite meeting place. Though he travels the world pleading for political reconciliation, the Dalai Lama will now focus our attention inward. He includes everyone in his insistent call that "we need a fundamental shift in our attitudes and our consciousness" (*The Wash-ington Post*). Empathetic identification with others, neither syrupy nor superficial, requires rigorous, persistent self-improvement. Kind-ness and compassion call for steely, unshakable good intentions. For all our technological advances and scientific discoveries, we fail at educating our hearts. The Dalai Lama tells us: "In the end . . . what matters is that one be a good, kind and warmhearted person" (*The Washington Post*).

According to the Dalai Lama, goodness lies at the core of human nature. This conviction, that humans are basically good at heart and united in spirit, informs his "policy of kindness." Feeling empathy comes naturally; we need only work on our inner lives to release it. And empathy, "the ability to appreciate another's suffering" (*The Art of Happiness*), is contagious. One life guided by altruism encourages others to tap into their reservoirs of goodwill. His concept is clear and bone simple. Everyone wants to be happy; most despise conflict. "True peace with ourselves and with the world around us can only be achieved through the development of mental peace" (*A Policy of Kindness*). Peace comes one calm and contented person at a time. At war with ourselves—intolerant, negative, greedy, suspicious, agitated—why talk of nuclear disarmament? *Internal* disarmament is the Dalai Lama's blueprint for world peace. "Let us talk of what is human. Love is human. Kindness is human" (*Essential Teachings*). Private arsenals of selfishness, anger, and resentment eventually pull triggers. If we educate our hearts, we can lay down these three weapons. The Dalai Lama targets them, slowly, one at a time.

Selfishness

First, the Dalai Lama examines the crucial distinction between actions motivated by inner peace and those driven by selfishness. Inner peace generates empathy from a deep heart that bestows and welcomes kind offerings. I'm okay and therefore ready for you. In contrast, self-absorption severs ties; looking out for number one leaves no room for two. Eye-pleasing kindness often rots at its self-centered core. Private motives hide behind public applause: "Working with refugees looks fabulous on my résumé." As I turn my gaze inward, self-serving motivation looms large: "Offering you temporary lodging guarantees me a free babysitter." Although I advertise my kindness and *act* compassionately, I may not *be* that way. The Dalai Lama warns us that such consuming selfishness—always restless, never satiated—splinters humanity. Further, selfishness is self-defeating in an undeniably interdependent world; it is futile to expect happiness in isolation.

Because empathy is tucked into our beings, our happiness depends on the happiness of others. Our capacity for bearing sorrow depends on a boost from another's show of empathy. We are all children of the earth; my motivation for actions large and small should be my intimate grasp of this truth. Cleansing my heart of insistent self-regard opens new channels for empathy's flow. When a colleague suffers, workplace demeanor changes. Sorrow in one house mutes laughter in the neighborhood.

Anger

Anger is the second weapon we must confiscate in our quest for inner peace. Jealousy, rage, vengeance, regret . . . anger wears many masks but in any form, if left unchecked, it muddies the waters of mind and heart. Agitated about this and that, mixing old grievances with new grumblings, I revel in my fury about anything and everything. Opposing opinions, alternative musical tastes, unfamiliar dialects—all have the power to infuriate. Latching onto anger eliminates any possibility of identifying with anything other than my anger. I stay mad, on guard, and untrusting. Aggressive posturing confirms my sense of well-being; swagger and strut pave my way. When I lash out I feel safe; fear of being confronted keeps you at a distance. Blowing up gets people's attention; just watch! Bullying boosts my pride; rudeness puts people down and off. Phew. I'm all worked up! Can this be right? Don't you see, the Dalai Lama warns, that living well with anger is impossible? Anger consumes; even without physical manifestations, it breeds disaster. Anger always spoils for a fight—hitting others with neglect, with words, with shoves, with missiles.

Happiness begs for anger's release. Can't we grasp its destructive potential? One angry person at a meeting disperses the group. One angry voice at the table silences the rest. One angry group shatters the community. Think, the Dalai Lama gently chides, of the consequences of anger in your life. Its folly is quickly apparent. Did screaming end the disagreement? "Anger cannot be overcome by anger" (A Policy of Kindness). Did gossip inflict sufficient hurt? Did taunting prove gratifying? "But even if your enemy is made unhappy through your actions, what is there for you to be so joyful about? If you think about it carefully, how can there be anything more wretched than that? Carrying around the burden of such feelings of hostility and ill will" (The Art of Happiness). Think. Will that slap in the face lay the groundwork for future violence? Will the slamming door close without retaliation?

Our Tibetan guide invites us to analyze our anger, to understand its selfish roots and heavy costs. Anger eats at our humanity and jeopardizes everyone; it is an unwelcome visitor that can call at any time. Practice replacing its tumult with the ease brought by inner calm, and the world opens wide with rich possibility.

Resentment

The last weapon is particularly fierce. Uncovering long-harbored resentments for all sorts of insults, slights, and harms stirs this emotion afresh. Memory bitterly stores and catalogs grudges as we wallow in self-pity while plotting our revenge. Holding tight to our ever-growing stack of bitter complaints oddly instills a sense of self-righteousness. "You did not invite my child to your child's birthday party." "You gave me a failing grade and I lost my scholarship." "You wrecked my car." "You fired me." "You stole my credit card." Our hearts fall into foreclosure; we could not pay the price of inner peace. Forgive, the Dalai Lama exhales, and put an end to this wretchedness. We pound our collective fists in immediate response. Forgive? Are you kidding? "Your country attacked mine." "You stole this land from my ancestors." "Your way of life threatens good people everywhere." He waits until we fold our hands. His straightforward testimony to the human capacity for forgiveness amazes: "So I think we, as Tibetans, contributed to this tragic situation. It's not fair to blame everything on China" (*The Art of Happiness*). Yes, forgive.

Forgiveness liberates both the forgiving and the forgiven. The heavy lifting of grudge-bearing exhausts personal resources. Though the memory of hurt remains, cutting the cord of attachment deprives the wrong of its stinging power. And, once cut free, true problems can be met with the welcome infusion of new energy.

"We need to embrace a more realistic approach to dealing with human conflicts, an approach that is in tune with a new reality of heavy interdependence in which the old concepts of 'we' and 'they' are no longer relevant" (*The Washington Post*). How can such a simple philosophy of interwoven kindness rouse hope worldwide? Is His Holiness dreaming? Does he read the newspapers? Isn't he telling us what we were taught as children, that "love and kindness are the very basis of society" (*A Policy of Kindness*), only to learn as adults that war and hate are inevitable? What kind of man delivers a message brimming with optimism, insisting that the world gets better every day? A man who is a scholar of Buddhist theology and Western philosophy; a world traveler whose daily regimen of prayer and meditation begins around 3:30 A.M. regardless of time zone; a sage to his beloved Tibetan people, rejecting the desire of many for a fight with the Chinese; a lecturer at the annual meeting of the Society for Neuroscience in 2005 who is willing to put aside any Buddhist theory contradicted by scientific evidence; an exiled radio repairman who says he is never lonely; a world leader who stoops to chat with one child as if she were the whole world.

This simple monk never strays from his basic teaching. Inner qualities determine our outlooks. When grounded in steady contentment, we know with certainty "how petty our squabbles are" (*The Washington Post*). Hearts stripped of selfishness, anger, and resentment regain their vigor. Restored hearts can pump kindness and rest in happiness.

> *I was a drum major for peace.*
> —MARTIN LUTHER KING, JR.,
> *The Autobiography of Martin Luther King, Jr.*

In the summer of 2005, while I was awaiting my luggage in a Barcelona hotel lobby, the rhythmic cadences of a well-known voice filled the room. "Isn't that Martin Luther King?" I asked my friend, who smiled in confirmation. As we reached the check-in desk, the clerk turned from the computer on which King's "I Have a Dream" speech played. "It is so beautiful, yes, so hopeful," he said with emotion. Later that afternoon we walked through streets crowded with protesters marching in peaceful opposition to the war in Iraq. They chanted the name of a Baptist preacher; though dead at age thirty-nine in 1968, Martin Luther King, Jr., is still at work. "World peace through nonviolent means is neither absurd nor unattainable. All other methods have failed" (*Autobiography*).

From the time he left Boston University with his doctorate in theology in 1955, until his final proclamation "I've Been to the Mountaintop" in Memphis in 1968, this warrior waged love on humanity's behalf. Through sit-ins, boycotts, marches, speeches, sermons, and meetings, his tireless defiance of injustice lit fires of change that glow today.

King's nonviolent strategy was rooted in two things: Jesus' command to love coupled with Mohandas Gandhi's successful tactic of peaceful active resistance in India. King showed us that love fueled by empathy has immense power in effecting social change. Never forget, however, that his brand of Christian love is not for the faint-hearted; his plan of action counts on dogged determination and courage. He gathered with his ever-growing number of comrades in motel and living rooms, holding cells, and hospital lobbies, to plot their course. Just as Socrates was a gadfly on the hide of Athenian citizens, King whipped up creative tension in American cities comfortable with blind segregation and its killing consequence. Let's join him in Birmingham in 1963.

Walking with Dr. King in Birmingham

"I am in Birmingham because injustice is here," and it is undeniable that "injustice anywhere is a threat to justice everywhere" ("Letter from Birmingham Jail"). According to King, everyone is endangered by unbridled hate; no society can endure its pervasive presence for long. Hate corrodes clear thinking and concludes that

Negro humanity is second-rate. We forget that we are brothers and sisters; love and justice are obscured by complacent condemnation of the once and still enslaved Negro. Hate makes our identification with others impossible; "other" lives are *not like mine*. Oppressors refuse to thaw their frozen hearts, and even with nagging consciousness of wrongdoing, they hold fast to their power. King invites both those working *with* him in protest as well as those fighting *against* the specter of shared humanity to purge their hearts and to fill them with a special kind of love.

Faced with overwhelming racial injustice in Birmingham and elsewhere, King takes his troops through four stages in their program of active resistance. First, a fact-finding mission to determine whether or not injustice truly exists, discarding rumor and conjecture; second, good-faith efforts at dialogue and negotiation to avoid confrontation; third, self-purification of hate and anger and cultivation of empathy and love; and, finally, direct action. Nonviolent resistance to injustice is not to be entered into lightly; it demands much of the protester's humanity. Only diligent self-analysis, on guard against revenge and bitterness, ensures that love motivates the movement. "There's a tension at the heart of human nature. And whenever we set out to dream our dreams and to build our temples, we must be honest enough to recognize it" (*Autobiography*).

In Birmingham, as in cities from Montgomery to Selma to Memphis, determining the facts is tragically easy—beatings, drownings, lynchings, disappearances, barred schools and playgrounds, all with no accountability. Repeated entreaties for negotiation with "city fathers" are rebuffed outright or soon dishonored. Merchants break their promises to remove "whites only" signs from their storefronts; motel owners hang up and cling to their "no vacancy" signals of segregation. No alternative remains but to prepare hearts and bodies for direct action through a process of self-purification. Jesus' commandment to love, even your enemies, serves as the rallying cry of

King's nonviolent campaign. King's invitation is "for a worldwide fellowship . . . an all-embracing and unconditional love for all . . . not . . . that force which is just emotional bosh" (A *Call to Conscience*: "Beyond Vietnam").

Unconditional Love

King sponsored and hosted workshops on nonviolence for his army. He and his soldiers had to be willing to lay down their bodies without retaliation. As an archer trains his gaze on the target, each member of the campaign must train her eye to see God in every face. While despising hate-fueled acts and the broken systems that promote and allow them, activists must perceive godliness within each individual. As Jesus' love is unconditional, human love must be non-discriminating, as well. No more grueling regimen can be imagined than this practiced preparation to throw love at every challenge. By identifying God's face in all faces, the distinction between friend and enemy vanishes. So many events and actions to condemn; every person without exception to love. "Now, I'm not talking about a sentimental, shallow kind of love . . . I'm talking about *agape* . . . the love of God in the hearts of men" (A *Call to Conscience*: "Give Us the Ballot"). What do we learn at the workshop in 1963? We know now that when moved by bitterness to even the score, we must retrain our gaze away from violence and toward across-the-board, godlike love. Agape (ah-GAH-pay) training in this selfless, other-centered love empowers the fight against injustice.

Unless my mind and heart are right, I am not a worthy opponent for hate and injustice; in fact, I join forces with the opposition. Practicing empathy, I realize that my aggressors were born into the trap of a hate-filled environment not of their own making. Continuing my practice, empathy comes more quickly as I recognize my own blind spots and find solace in keeping my seat at the human family's table. "Willingness to use nonviolence as a technique is a step forward. For he who goes this far is more likely to adopt nonviolence later as a way of life" (*Autobiography*). Direct action now begins, deliberately, carefully, forcefully.

The purpose of direct action is to force the negotiation that pleading failed to win. Rather than blow up the bus, I refuse to ride it. When I ride, I ignore the order to sit in the back and ride for free to jail. "I" grows in numbers and businesses suffer economic jolts. Protesters en masse incite others to join in boycotting stores and transit systems. Sit-ins at lunch counters ruin everyone's meal, with "love correcting that which revolts against love" (*A Call to Conscience*: "First MIA Meeting"). Eventually the larger community, the nation, and the world take notice of a different kind of battle. In this nonviolent fight, the means of attaining justice are just as important as the goal. Taking aim at aggression with petitions and peaceful demonstrations is a novel approach to war. "It is no longer a choice between violence and nonviolence in this world; it's nonviolence or nonexistence" (*Autobiography*). Loving, active resistance topples hate and its by-products. The Civil Rights Act of 1964 sent the Negro to the voting booth and to college. Peace wears violence down and out. Though many revile love as weak and passive, it has the power to stop the crazed spin of the cycle of violence. "I was much more afraid in Montgomery when I had a gun in my house" (*Autobiography*), King confessed after his house was bombed. Unarmed bodyguards provided him and his family with the surest safety. King did not pride himself on his goodness and admitted his shortcomings; he did *live* his philosophy of nonviolence.

King Speaks Today

Can empathy wrap itself around our everyday lives? Can King's workshops also guide our direct actions as we work, love, and face difficulty? "The way to be integrated with yourself is be sure that you meet every situation of life with an abounding love" ("Loving Your

Enemies"). Students from all backgrounds enjoy testing and applying King's four steps to a nonviolent campaign in their daily lives. Together we propose new and better questions and "cop an attitude of love." His warning to be sure to collect the facts reminds us to slow down and collect ourselves, as well. "What actually happened?" "What did you say, exactly?" His appeal for negotiation encourages conversation and averts standoffs. "Can we find a compromise?" "What goals do we share?" "Is it possible that we are not so far apart, you and I?" The process of self-purification fosters introspection. "What am I thinking?" "Why am I so quick to attack?" "Can I train my vision to look for and to expect love?" "If I humbly admit my shortcomings, will I be quicker to forgive?"

Steadfast empathy surely demands the best of human beings, and the lofty aspiration for agape creates tension within us. Jesus "realized that it was painfully hard, pressingly hard" ("Loving Your Enemies"). Our nature is speckled with selfish tendencies; we foolishly and intentionally harm ourselves and one another. Many times we know better and we act worse. But self-purification removes some stains and my behavior benefits. My tendency to answer with curt retorts decreases, I seldom raise my voice, my ability to separate individuals from their harmful actions improves. Can I take Jesus' insistence on love to heart even when disappointed? If so, at last, my direct relationships with my neighbors near and far thrive as I keep my eye on the prize. "Jesus ended up saying this was the . . . great man, because he had the capacity to project the 'I' into the 'thou,' and to be concerned about his brother" (*Autobiography*). The prize is a wellspring of empathy that "makes a career of humanity" (*Autobiography*), yours and mine.

I like to imagine Martin Luther King, Jr., resting with the Dalai Lama on a Himalayan mountaintop overlooking a Free Tibet. Two hardworking contemporaries, practical fellows seeking peaceful change by the path of least resistance, the Buddhist host shares his Christian guest's problems and his solution. Loving kindness for all, generated in recognition of our human sameness and our godly likeness. As empathy ties the knots between us, intelligent, unconditional love unleashes a torrent of peace.

DISCUSSION QUESTIONS

- What is empathy? What are its essential ingredients?
- Do you experience empathy naturally? Can you express empathetic feelings?
- What does empathy ask of you? Is it too much?
- Can you distinguish between superficial words and actions in contrast to true expressions of shared feeling? Can you give examples of each?
- How do you respond to the Dalai Lama's insistence on pure motivation? What are some good motives for compassionate action? Can kindness spring from selfish intentions?
- What can identification with others bring to your life as well as to theirs?
- How do larger communities benefit from any bond forged by empathy?
- In what specific ways have you suffered due to your anger? At the expense of another's unmanaged anger?
- What is the connection between anger and violence? Is anger itself a form of violence?
- If you work on disarming yourself as the Dalai Lama recommends, what thoughts and emotions will you try to reduce and/or eliminate?
- Is forgiveness a natural response for you? Who gains from an act of forgiveness? If you could find it in your heart to forgive inexcusable hurt, would you?

- Do you agree with Martin Luther King, Jr., that love is the most powerful force, that it can "move mountains" in human relations?
- How do you respond to King's concept of agape? Is unconditional love an ideal worth striving for? Is it possible to increase your capacity for this kind of love? In little steps? Completely?
- What does Jesus' command to "love your enemies" mean to you? Can you apply it in your life?
- Do you agree with King that hate destroys the hater? In what ways is hate corrosive?
- Do you agree with Gandhi and King that humble, loving noncooperation is the most effective and longest-lasting solution to conflict? Can you name a war that has brought lasting peace?
- What three ideas from the philosophies of the Dalai Lama and Martin Luther King, Jr., can you put to good use? What is one lesson from both lives that you will carry with you?

HOMEWORK

Listen and Hum

Assign each of the musical selections randomly among the members of your group. Enjoy exploring both these particular recommendations as well as other works by the artists; perhaps learning about their backgrounds and careers can make for good conversation. Listen to the many notes of empathy.

Protest

- Miriam Makeba, "Mama Africa," raised her unmistakable voice against vicious apartheid in South Africa. In 1963 at the United Nations, she detailed the persecution of blacks in her homeland, and her protest of segregation in the United States in the 1960s proved equally controversial. For a time Makeba was unwelcome in either country and spent her exile as a delegate to the UN from Guinea. "To Those We Love" is her 1965 tribute to jailed South African leaders, including Nelson Mandela, who in 1990 persuaded her to come back to the home they shared. Makeba joins Jamaican humanitarian and social activist Harry Belafonte, the "King of Calypso," in "Malaika," and their poignant longing for peace strikes a universal note. Is music an effective agent for social change?

- The sound of Sam Cooke's conviction that "A Change Is Gonna Come" echoes King's weary, frustrated, yet hopeful voice in the 1960s. Cooke knew segregation firsthand; he was once arrested with his band when trying to register in a "whites only" motel. Eerily, his song, conveying his belief that though "there been times that I thought that I couldn't last for long / but now I think I'm able to carry on," was released after his shooting death in 1964. Cooke's promise, an anthem of hope during the civil rights era, gives us pause to ask how much change *has* come? How far must we travel?

- If you viewed our planet from above, "you might think it was paradise," but it's not; "How Long" will it be "before you ask yourself why?" Jackson Browne challenges. How long will we accept missiles masquerading as weapons of peace? "Why?" do we wait to use our talents and get busy with the business of peace? When will we say "enough" and mean it? Browne means it, using his voice in support of children, the Tibetan people, and environmental innovation.

- "Somebody please stop that war now!" Jimmy Cliff chants in "Vietnam." His reggae beat and insistent voice sound more urgent with every intonation of "Vietnam." Happily he receives a letter from his buddy promising he'll be home soon, but a telegram beats his soldier friend back from Vietnam: "Mistress Brown, your son is dead." What are the lessons of the war in Vietnam? Cliff's clip, playful Jamaican versions of "Wonderful World, Beautiful People," and "I Can See Clearly Now" provide welcome alternatives to war. How do the timbre and resonance of his voice differ in these two songs from his tone in "Vietnam"?

Identification

- "Lord, Help the Poor and Needy." Cat Power repeats this slow, heartrending request in the name of the human race. We live and we die together, "and we face the morning sun." This desperate plea was written and first sung by Jessie Mae Hemphill in the unmistakable blues of the Mississippi Delta. Religious traditions in all times and places mandate compassion for those in need, and this tune recalls the spirit of the Old Testament's Forty-first Psalm. Find similar, specific requests on behalf of the "poor and needy" running throughout various religions.

- "I Believe the South Is Gonna Rise Again," and King pulls for "outlaw" country musician Tanya Tucker's vision of brotherhood when she quickly adds, "But not the way we thought it would be back then." Tucker was just a teen in 1974 when she belted Bobby Braddock's lyrics of "a brand-new breeze blowing cross the southland." Poverty taints every skin color; we can rise against it hand in hand. Human kindness has the power to heal the wounds of the past, Tucker sings. How did/have we become distracted by color of skin rather than paying attention to killing poverty? Will we remain distracted?

- At the end of your stamina and hope, when you are as low as can be, Paul Simon and Art Garfunkel pledge to be your "Bridge over Troubled Water." Slow, soulful piano complements Garfunkel's intimate rendering of Simon's lyrics, and the lilting violin trills at song's end extend comfort. "I will lay me down . . . take your part" and you can rest assured that I am "on your side." How does it feel when someone "takes your part"? What difference does it make?

- "Peace Comes Stealing Slow" for a young man and an abandoned woman who never expected their fates, and Kate Campbell lines up "on their side." Barely twenty-one and a hometown boy, he signs military papers never imagining that he will recite the Twenty-third Psalm for the last time in a foxhole. Homeless and aimlessly walking the streets, she dreams of being a little girl when this destiny was unthinkable. Campbell asks that we bow our heads with her in "petition" and in "prayer" that peace soon "falls like silent snow . . . swings down sweet and low."

Action

- Lucy Kaplansky offers each of us a job. At least "For Once in Your Life," walk empathetically in the worn shoes of a loved one's hard life. Appreciate your easier lot in comparison; understand why it might be hard for someone to express feelings or to move past deep hurt. Though Kaplansky laments that she did not find this empathy soon enough, she knows that she has been forgiven. "I don't think I deserve it," she sings, and then stumbles into the heart of forgiveness: "Maybe a person forgives so they . . .

don't have to be alone." Is she right? Borrow a shoe from someone who struggles to make a comfortable home on the planet. Can forgiveness spread all around?

- Jean-Paul Samputu sings and dances in his homeland's traditional 5/8 beat, bearing tidings of peace in his *Testimony from Rwanda*. He spends "Ten Years Remembering" on two tracks, closing with an a cappella version; as a survivor of the genocide, Samputu invites Rwandans to come home again. His music is joyous, snappy, and earthy, supplanting a nightmare with musical celebration of a beloved culture. Look to the future and "Karame Mwana," cherish the children—he claps and dances. How can we cherish *all* children?

- Martin Luther King, Jr., shares the stage with his role model, Mohandas Gandhi, in the Philip Glass opera *Satyagraha*. In his meditative, minimalist style, Glass showcases human heartedness as he gives musical expression to Gandhi's work in South Africa from 1893 to 1914. It is as if Gandhi passes the torch of nonviolent activism to King in Act III. Gandhi sings contemplatively downstage; upstage, and with his back to the audience, King mimics the familiar gestures of his "I Have a Dream" speech to a distant throng. The Hindu classic the *Bhagavad Gita* exerted great influence on Gandhi and it serves as Glass's inspiration for the libretto. "A man finds peace in the work of the spirit," Krishna tells Arjuna in the *Bhagavad Gita*, which closes with an invocation of "Peace. Peace. Peace."

- A children's advocate sings her signature tune to close a benefit concert for victims of the 2004 tsunami. "Reach Out and Touch (Somebody's Hand)," the familiar voice invites. Take the time to share another's problem and to give encouragement "to someone who's lost the way." Diana

Ross sings convincingly that kindness "comes very naturally" and that "we can change things if we start giving." Philosophers, poets, musicians repeat this message. Well?

• Richard Gere's humanitarian organization, Healing the Divide, sponsors a Concert for Peace and Reconciliation to support the Tibetan Health Initiative. The Dalai Lama speaks. Tom Waits mixes his gravelly voice with the strings of the Kronos Quartet, huskily advising that "wherever you may wander / wherever you may roam," always keep a "Diamond in Your Mind." R. Carlos Nakai's Native American flute lends backing to Tibetan composer Nawang Khechoq in "Peace Chants." Philip Glass's ensemble combines with the Gambian harp of Foday Musa Suso. Sit quietly and picture a "diamond in your mind."

Recite and Write

Read each of the following poems on your own prior to your group's next meeting. Write a spontaneous response to each poem in your philosophy journal. Recite the poems, share your notes, and chat about any new glimpses into empathy's essence.

• Mary Oliver carries in her heart the disfigured, perspiring face of a boy begging on the streets of Jakarta. Though their paths most likely will never cross again, his memory finds a home in her imagination and it serves as a token of empathy's stirring. Slipping under the wire of separation, "you can creep out of your own life / and become someone else—." Oliver fills her life with the boy's. This "becoming someone else" defines empathy. What one experience similar to Oliver's comes immediately to mind? Why do you carry it with you? Can you relate to her "Acid" feeling of futile indignation?

- "The Wellfleet Whale," foundering and leaking life on the shores of Cape Cod, makes eye contact with Stanley Kunitz; their close kinship secures a lock on Kunitz's heart. The poet sees himself in the whale's huge, glistening eye, and identifies with the finback as humans carve their initials in his gull-pecked flank. The "unearthly outcry" of this once majestic, powerful, and graceful whale draws his human family to a bonfire at his side. "You made a bond between us," wrapping us in a circle around you in "your hour of desolation." Can such an experience expand our empathy in a lasting way? Have you identified, gut-level, with nonhuman life? Did this intimate bond bolster compassion for humans?

- Martin Luther King, Jr., nominated this exiled Vietnamese Zen Master for the Nobel Peace Prize in 1967. Why does Thich Nhat Hanh implore "Call Me by My True Names"? When we identify with humanity, we share sameness with All. Our "true names" are not only sufferer, refugee, and pacifist, but also dictator, abuser, and arms dealer. Every name is my "true name." Humility demands that we see ourselves everywhere; empathy must not be reserved for a select few. Why call me marauding pirate *and* starving child? "So I can wake up and the door of my heart / could be left open, the door of compassion." What are some names to add to our own? Sneak as well as volunteer? User as well as friend?

- How can we cultivate "Kindness"? Endure loss and sink into loneliness. Naomi Shihab Nye counsels that "before you know kindness as the deepest thing inside, / you must know sorrow as the other deepest thing." Intimate knowl-edge of sorrow makes sense of kindness; deep-down kind-

ness makes sense of our lives. Kindness flavors even our
smallest acts once we are aware that *any* life could be ours.
Shoes can be tied and letters mailed with kindness. Do you
agree with Nye that kindness can become a way of life? Is
it necessary to know sorrow?

- Polish poet Wislawa Szymborska ensures that we never
  lose sight of the disaster wrought by hate and war. When
  the media leaves the scene to track yet another war, "someone has to tidy up"; debris, dead bodies, broken glass, and
  "bloody rags" do not remove themselves. In "The End and
  the Beginning," are we mindful of the never-ending after-
  shock of every war? What about the land, the survivors,
  the haunting residue that brews future conflict? "Hatred"
  never sleeps, fueled by misguided patriotism and religious
  fanaticism, and Szymborska dares us to realize "all the
  human carpets it has spread / over countless city squares
  and football fields." Why do we forget? Why do we lapse
  so casually into conflict? When will sharpened memory of
  war move us toward peace?

- Rumi, thirteenth-century Persian poet, paints a stunning
  image. Tired of words, icons, and causes, desperate for respite
  from madness, he pictures "No Flag" flying, "only the holder
  the flag fits into, / and wind . . . only love." As he whirls and
  dances, this Sufi mystic envisions the human community
  without territorial distinction. Can national flags wave as
  symbols of peace? How? In "Cry Out in Your Weakness,"
  Rumi celebrates the great good fortune of having your need
  met by mercy. "Let the milk / of loving flow into you." If you
  allow yourself to express your sorrow, empathy has a welcome outlet. Do we expect too little of one another? Are we
  sometimes too hardened to feel compassion's solace?

Read and Talk

- Empathy wins the match with Mr. Pneumonia in O. Henry's short story "The Last Leaf." Johnsy resignedly waits for death in old Greenwich Village, watching the leaves fall from an old ivy vine outside her window. "When the last one falls I must go, too," she confides to her friend Sue. Behrman, a failed artist, lives on the floor below them, "a fierce little old man, who scoffed terribly at softness in anyone, and who regarded himself as especial mastiff-in-waiting to protect the two young artists in the studio above." Enough said. Enjoy the surprise ending, an understated celebration of pure empathy.

- Kath Weston puts the reader in the seat next to hers for a five-year, cross-country bus trip. "I looked where I knew I would find poverty in motion." She straightforwardly and tenderly shares the lives of those broke and trying to get to a funeral, others sickened by junk food and the ensuing public humiliation, and travelers proud and searching anywhere for work. In *Traveling Light: On the Road with America's Poor*, Weston introduces us to individuals whose lives teach lessons as no statistics can. "But what will it take to see it?" she asks, to really *see* the unacceptable economic disparity between people living almost shoulder to shoulder. How did the human family grow so far apart? What to do?

- Martin Luther King, Jr., discovered lasting inspiration in Mohandas Gandhi's "Practice of Satyagraha," the revolutionary Indian leader's powerful weapon of nonviolent active resistance. "The beauty and efficacy of *satyagraha* are so great and the doctrine so simple that it can be preached even to children," its potential demonstrated by

Gandhi's rebellion against British rule. "Non-violence is . . . in its active form good will towards all life. It is pure Love." Gandhi looks to Hindu, Islamic, and Jain religious traditions for guidance while King's foundation for social protest lies in Jesus' ministry and the teachings of the New Testament. Gandhi makes "bold to say that violence is the creed of no religion." Are violence and spirituality incompatible? So . . .

- Maura "Soshin" O'Halloran never intended to be published, and it is her mother who keeps her daughter's *Pure Heart, Enlightened Mind* alive through Maura's journal entries and letters home. American-born and Irish-educated, Maura enters monastic life in Japan to satisfy her curiosity about Zen Buddhism. Unexpectedly, she completes an uncommonly arduous thousand-day training regimen, and a statue of this Catholic girl's likeness stands in tribute to her divine compassion. Always "there was much love, deep warm womb love" emanating from her life. Even when tempers flare in the monastery, "it's impossible to bear a grudge. It's true that if you love your enemy you have killed him for he ceases to exist." Zen training or a King sermon? What is "deep warm womb love"?

- The Dalai Lama writes the foreword to Charles Halpern's positive memoir of lessons learned in a life of *Making Waves and Riding the Currents*. By creating and sustaining soft, nonadversarial relationships, we can move more easily and comfortably toward lasting social changes. Halpern realizes that successful activism must be infused by compassion, and he works incessantly to foster his own inner peace. His deepened introspection earned through a five-day meditation retreat with Zen Master Thich Nhat Hanh resembles the rewards of self-purification promised by

King. If we listen calmly to wise people of all persuasions, "clarity of vision emerges." Do you agree that empathy is smart business practice? How can compassion enhance job performance?

- "No matter what anybody says to you, don't let 'em get your goat. Try fighting with your head for a change," Atticus tells Scout in Harper Lee's *To Kill a Mockingbird*. Empathy's presence in Maycomb County looms larger and lives longer than Tom Robinson's lynch mob. Scout's father agrees to defend a black man even though "in the secret courts of men's hearts Atticus had no case." When Atticus walks defeated and dejected from the courthouse, blacks relegated to the balcony stand in tribute to his courageous display of empathy. Boo Radley, Maycomb's mysterious outcast, exhibits unconditional love for Atticus's children. Scout now knows the truth about Boo: "Atticus was right. One time he said you never really know a man until you stand in his shoes and walk around in them . . . he was real nice . . . most people are . . . when you finally see them." What do you think? In your experience, are most people good at heart?

Watch and Reflect

- Emmanuel Ofosu Yeboah's life serves as compelling testimony to the power of unconditional love and the vast potential of nonviolent protest. *Emmanuel's Gift* changes the "inescapable destiny of the disabled" in Ghana, West Africa, with his determination to "turn compassion into action." Ten percent of Ghana's population, born disabled and doomed to beggars' short lives, find their best advocate in one of their own. Empathy flows through Emmanuel's veins from those of his beloved mother, whose unqualified love for her boy born with one leg spreads into two million lives marred by physical deformity. Walking proudly with her son to school and encouraging him to play sports, she counseled him at her death to "stay close with family." Emmanuel's concept of family knows no bounds, as he seeks and receives first a bicycle and then much more from Jim MacLaren and the Challenged Athletes Foundation. His one-legged, pedaling protest across Ghana earns him growing fanfare as it uplifts the disabled. Emmanuel comes to the United States for a fund-raising bike ride and goes home with a prosthesis to "explore all avenues" as a champion of the outcast. "I will share the benefits . . . stop begging in the streets . . . build a sports academy." Emmanuel grins when identifying with "what goes on in the hearts" of those riding for the first time in new wheelchairs. This gentle man forgives the father who abandoned his "deformed" child only to surface when Emmanuel returns to a hero's welcome and a King's embrace. Can he explain the unthinkable cultural change embodied in the Emmanuel Education Fund? How is he winning this selfless campaign against injustice? His empathy and motivation come naturally, "so I thank my mother a lot." What gifts do Emmanuel and his mother leave in your hearts?

- Empathy builds nests in the hearts of hardboiled characters assembled by Tennessee Williams during *The Night of the Iguana.* Reverend Shannon, inhibited schoolmarms, irrepressible Maxine, financially destitute Hannah and her grandfather all share the same thin-skinned humanity. After chastising his congregation for sitting with closed hearts in judgment of him, a drunk, dispirited, defrocked Shannon slinks from yet another town and escapes to

Puerto Vallarta, Mexico. Though he "gets the spooks" when confronting his tortured life, he instinctively protects others' feelings. He finds refuge in Maxine's rundown hotel and its unlikely cluster of guests, especially in Hannah's direct, unsolicited compassion for all. She identifies with his troubles, having endured her "blue devil," and tenderly assures others that Shannon's weakness is "not the man himself." This portrait painter feels neither shame nor guilt for leading a gypsy life with her elderly grandfather in tow because "it just happens to be what happened to us." Knowing that we all "need to believe in someone, something," Hannah wishes for "broken barriers between people," and calls home any place where two people nest and rest emotionally because "what is important is that one is never alone." How does kindness win the night? What if we could all say, along with Hannah, that "nothing human disgusts me unless it's unkind or violent"?

Get Up and Do

- Make plans for an activist group project in King's spirit. Take a look at your community, however large or small you choose to define it, and locate injustice and its specific consequences. Poverty and poor nutrition, violence and women's and animal shelters . . . pick your spot. Work through any anger about the situation. Develop a plan of action in keeping with King's rugged determination. See your active noncooperation through, and spend an evening together chatting about the process, the results, and things you might do differently. How much difference does it make to tackle a problem with empathy for *all* concerned?

- Be attentive to the spark of empathy in your own life. When it strikes, act compassionately in one particular case, however seemingly small, that you may have overlooked on similar occasions. Reflect on this private experience. Is purity of motive an essential feature of compassion for you as it is for the Dalai Lama? Is the action just as important as motivation?

- Learn about the climate, the geography, and the natural resources of Tibet. Peruse books portraying Tibetan culture—traditions, cuisine, music, dress, art, and architecture—and take a long look at its ancient heritage.

- Meet lesser known champions of the civil rights movement. Head to school at Central High with the Little Rock Nine. Vote for Fannie Lou Hamer for Congress. Attend a meeting of the National Council of Negro Women and meet its leader, Dorothy Height. Join Jo Ann Robinson in Montgomery and follow her long trail of activism. Go behind the scenes with Ella Baker and experience the power of quiet, nonstop dedication. Her mighty force rippling through the second half of the twentieth century, get to know Coretta Scott King who also gave her life to love-driven social change.

- Spend a night, or two, at the movies walking in too-tight shoes. Gain insight into the Dalai Lama's world by viewing *Windhorse*, a movie filmed on the sly that unveils the hidden plight of Tibetan people starved for freedom. Can you identify with the fears of cast and crew in making this film? Compare Tibetan oppression to that faced by King as you meet him on his last protest march in *At the River I Stand*. "I AM A MAN!" the striking sanitation workers proclaim with proud dignity, a claim denied by a deaf Memphis community whose ears open only when King loses his life to violence. What does Tibet in 1998 have in common with Memphis in 1968? Why is the truth of shared humanity such a hard reality to accept? What ideas gleaned from these films can you use in your daily life?

- On a quiet day, choose one thing for which to forgive yourself. Really do it. That same day, not much going on, forgive another's offense. Really do it.
- Paint empathy.
- Discuss together the connection between anger and violence. How do "harmless" demonstrations of anger contribute to a climate of violence? Fury at a referee's bad call, aggravation at an incompetent cashier, pleasure in a slammed phone . . .
- Think of five recent expressions of empathy that have come your way. Describe the act itself and its effect on you in your philosophy journal. Do we underestimate the empathy that surrounds and buoys us every day? Are we kinder than we think?

Resources

Music
- *An Evening with Belafonte and Makeba* by Miriam Makeba and Harry Belafonte: "To Those We Love," "Malaika."
- *Portrait of a Legend, 1951–1964* by Sam Cooke: "A Change Is Gonna Come."
- *World in Motion* by Jackson Browne: "How Long."
- *Ultimate Collection* by Jimmy Cliff: "Vietnam," "Wonderful World, Beautiful People," "I Can See Clearly Now."
- *Jukebox* by Cat Power: "Lord Help the Poor and Needy."
- *Get Right Blues* by Jessie Mae Hemphill: "Lord Help the Poor and Needy."
- *Would You Lay with Me in a Field of Stone* by Tanya Tucker: "I Believe the South Is Gonna Rise Again."

- *Bridge over Troubled Water* by Paul Simon and Art Garfunkel: "Bridge over Troubled Water."
- *Blues and Lamentations* by Kate Campbell: "Peace Comes Stealing Slow."
- *Ten Year Night* by Lucy Kaplansky: "For Once in Your Life."
- *Testimony from Rwanda* by Jean-Paul Samputu: "Ten Years Remembering," "Karame Mwana."
- *Philip Glass: Satyagraha*, New York City Opera and Orchestra, Christopher Keene conducting (CD).
- *Greatest Hits Live* by Diana Ross: "Reach Out and Touch (Somebody's Hand)."
- *Healing the Divide: A Concert for Peace and Reconciliation* with the Dalai Lama and Richard Gere, featuring Tom Waits, Kronos Quartet, Philip Glass, Foday Musa Suso, Anoushka Shankar, Nawang Khechoq, R. Carlos Nakai, Gyuto Tantric Choir.

Poetry
- *Dreamwork* by Mary Oliver: "Acid."
- *Next-to-Last Things* by Stanley Kunitz: "The Wellfleet Whale."
- *Thich Nhat Hanh: Essential Writings*, edited by Robert Ellsberg: "Call Me by My True Names."
- *Words Under the Words: Selected Poems* by Naomi Shihab Nye: "Kindness."
- *View with a Grain of Sand: Selected Poems* by Wislawa Szymborska: "Hatred," "The End and the Beginning."
- *Essential Rumi* translated by Coleman Barks and John Moyne: "Cry Out in Your Weakness," "No Flag."

Prose
- *Best Short Stories of O. Henry*, edited by Bennett Cerf and Van H. Cartmell: "The Last Leaf."
- *Traveling Light: On the Road with America's Poor* by Kath Weston.
- *Gandhi: Selected Writings*, edited by Ronald Duncan: "The Practice of Satyagraha."
- *Pure Heart, Enlightened Mind: The Life and Letters of an Irish Zen Saint* by Maura "Soshin" O'Halloran.
- *Making Waves and Riding the Currents* by Charles Halpern.
- *To Kill a Mockingbird* by Harper Lee.
- *Bhagavad-Gita*, translated by Christopher Isherwood and Swami Prabhavananda.
- *A Call to Conscience: The Landmark Speeches of Dr. Martin Luther King, Jr.*, edited by Clayborne Carson and Kris Shepard.

- *The Autobiography of Martin Luther King, Jr.*, edited by Clayborne Carson.
- *Why We Can't Wait* by Martin Luther King, Jr.: "Letter from Birmingham Jail."
- *Strength to Love* by Martin Luther King, Jr.: "Loving Your Enemies."
- "Commentary" by the Dalai Lama, *Washington Post*, October 21, 2007.
- *The Art of Happiness: A Handbook for Living* by the Dalai Lama and Howard C. Cutler, M.D.
- *A Policy of Kindness* by the Dalai Lama, edited by Sydney Piburn.
- *Essential Teachings* by the Dalai Lama, translated by Zélie Pollon, edited by Marianne Dresser.

Drama

- *The Night of the Iguana* by Tennessee Williams, directed by John Huston (DVD).
- *Windhorse*, directed by Paul Wagner (DVD).

Documentary

- *Emmanuel's Gift*, directed by Lisa Lax and Nancy Stern (DVD).
- *At the River I Stand*, directed by David Appleby (DVD).

Individuality

Man first of all exists, encounters himself,
surges up in the world—and defines himself afterwards.
—JEAN-PAUL SARTRE, *Existentialism Is a Humanism*

THE TOPIC

An enthusiastic invitation to chat with two radio hosts about the rewards of philosophizing with children fired up a cold January day. Halfway into the hour-long show, they asked if, after a break for the news, I would engage them and their listeners in a philosophical conversation similar to those I share with my fourth-grade child philosophers. Call-ins were solicited and the announcers promised great fun at the bottom of the hour. I explained why I chose humanity as the topic for our discussion: it always delights children with its surprising and laughable difficulty and incites lively, often boisterous discussion. Greeting my new on-air pupils, I eased into the topic with a question: "What does it mean to be human?" All jovial banter ceased; I beheld two expressionless faces, mouths drooping at the corners. "Who are you?" I pressed on encouragingly. They shuffled papers and exchanged puzzled looks. "What makes you who you are?"

With "live broadcast" now a misnomer and philosophers in the listening area as muted as my uncomfortable companions, I waited in what I hoped was secret enjoyment. My hosts finally assured each other that children surely can't discuss such matters. "Don't you ever wonder about yourself?" I persisted, sweeping us, laughing at last, into an unplanned break.

This good-natured almost-exchange mirrors the general consternation of most aspiring philosophers (adult!) as we begin our investigation into personal identity. Quite often they share their amazement that the question "Who am I?" is a new one. The inability to articulate "what makes me who I am and no one else" bedevils. How can I not know who I am? Is this a trick question? Am I somehow different from everyone else? Another unsettling question. Me? What makes *me* an individual? I *was* taught to look out for number one, to take care of my self. Do I prize individuality?

What is individuality? My best answer (at this moment) is that individuality is self-possession. I am the only person who can pull all the disparate pieces of *me* together as *my* self, assemble the parts into one stable, sturdy, whole being. Even though my identity is ever-changing, I will it to retain its core and shape it into my life. As I probe more deeply into the meaning of individuality, I realize that its essence involves self-*awareness* rather than self-*importance*. My mind and heart know certain things to be true for me and even though I may betray these innermost truths at times, they remain my North Star. Indeed, I can win self-respect only from myself, earning it every day.

No one descriptor can capture an individual; each of us is so much more than just an athlete, a parent, a pilot, an activist, a teacher, or an architect. Rather, we are unique mixes of many subtle components, both external and internal. We are combinations of well-worn facial expressions and frequent hand gestures; we are defined by the spirit in which we carry out tasks both large and small, and by whom and what we love.

The study of human nature has occupied philosophers forever. What does it mean to be human? Is there one answer or are there infinite answers to that question? What (where?) is our place in the universe? How can each of us carve out a separate life and also live together peacefully? How can we as individuals hold fast to our integrity regardless of society's impingements? Can we let one another be and also help one another out? If I choose to surrender my individuality, do I lose anything important?

Discussing individuality with suddenly fascinated philosophers, I usually hear quick agreement, in principle, on the central importance of individuality. "It would be awful to think my life is exactly like yours or anyone's—that there is nothing original about my experience." "I hate to think I may be copying someone's life and calling it my own." Conversation soon turns happily to some of the things that make us who we are. Shortcomings and talents receive equal attention. "I love to cook and add to my collection of secret recipes." "I use my oven as a storage area." "Snorkeling went from fantasy to my middle-aged hobby." "I feel most at home when I travel." Animated claims to an irresistible sense of humor or local fame as an all-knowing Grateful Dead aficionado combine with talk of pride in a relationship or fervent belief in a cause, all special ingredients that mark different personalities. Settling in with outstretched legs, we get to know ourselves as we get to know one another. Individually.

On the heels of such self-assured statements, however, nagging suspicions are voiced by first one and then another honest philosopher. Deep potholes have threatened the project of creating a distinct, self-aware life already. "It's like I gave up on me." "I feel like an actor watching my life from the outside, playing a role." "Integrity can be really expensive! Never free or easy to be true to yourself."

Around we whirl, individuals wondering who we are and whether or not we truly want to know. How can we be certain that our choices are our own and are not subtly (or overtly) dictated by society? Wait. Who or what is society? A chuckling chorus of "Them!" concludes that "We are."

What now? Will I have what it takes to grow my own self up? Can I be loyal to my values even with a hard life? Can a clear understanding of what it means to be an individual make it less difficult and more desirable to become one? If so, let's go.

Jean-Paul Sartre (zhanh-pohl SAHR-tr) and Elizabeth Spelman ante up with the necessary supplies. Sartre stretches a fresh canvas on a frame for each of us, placing new brushes and unopened cans of paint beside the easel: everything at our fingertips for the creation of highly individualized self-portraits. Spelman leaves a master key with the paintbrushes, there for us to use when we choose to unlock the doors that shut out the individual.

THE PHILOSOPHERS

Life is nothing until it is lived. . . .

—JEAN-PAUL SARTRE, *Existentialism Is a Humanism*

Playwright, literary critic, professor, political activist, and novelist Jean-Paul Sartre placed the human condition under intense scrutiny. Inquisitive philosophers find his works written during and immediately after the German occupation of France especially relevant in their quest for personal identity.

Sartre challenges everyone to become an authentic individual, to get to know that person, and to be true to the creation. Each person paints a self-portrait that is the action story of that one individual life. "Man makes himself; he is not found ready-made" (*Existentialism Is a Humanism*). The task of becoming myself, independent of society's norms and expectations, beckons. Though saddled with responsibility for all my past choices (as well as those decisions that I failed to make), the prospects of honing an honest life that is mine alone present a wondrous opportunity. Can I paint an accurate portrait that makes me proud? Will I prove faithful to my true self, or will I fake my life?

Because human beings are subject to constant change, this search for self-knowledge lasts a lifetime. Human nature is puzzling, fickle, exasperating, wonderful . . . so many layers, so much going on . . . moods, intellectual curiosity and frustrating limitations, whims, guilt, fear, anxiety, passion. "That being understood, does anyone reproach an artist, when he paints a picture, for not following rules? Does one ever ask what is the picture that he ought to paint?" (*Existentialism Is a Humanism*) Nothing matches the lofty achievement of personal integrity; every other goal pales in comparison.

Lunching at the Balzar

Should we accept Sartre's challenge? Let's join him at his favorite café on a bustling Parisian street and allow him to make his case for the significance of personal integrity. But before indulging in philosophical debate, he prefers that we linger over our first course. He has ordered us a round of onion soup—flavorful, rich, and delicate. He licks his lips and subtly begins his lesson by asking us to imagine such a treat coming from a prepackaged mix. Add a cup of water, wait one minute, and voilà! Just as the chef at this bistro makes every bowl of soup from fresh ingredients, continually experimenting here and there with her original recipe, so, too, Sartre assures us, can we create our lives from scratch. "*Existence* comes before *essence*" (*Existentialism Is a Humanism*). We show up in the world a blank canvas, and determine who we are through our actions alone. We make the rules as we go along, with no pre-set formula to follow or convenient one-size-fits-all definition of human nature.

At their first brush with the heart of Sartre's theory, I watch my students wrestle with a jumble of excited responses. "It takes my breath away to think that there is actually no ideal for me to imitate. Searching for a 'role model' means nothing to me now." "I've been trying to measure up to a standard not my own." So, we all show up on the playing field of life, not having asked to be here and not knowing how to play the game. Alone, we make the rules courageously, living with gusto until the game is over. "I didn't want to lose two hours of life" ("The Wall").

Wait. What's the catch? A bit of uncertainty always creeps into the buzz. As our lovely meal at the café ends, our enthusiasm wanes, as well. What kind of game constantly changes without warning? Freedom might be too expensive. I choose my life and you choose yours, with no alibis, ever, and with no outside validation. Too hard. Plenty strange . . . I am responsible without excuse for everything I do, but I had no say in the crucial fact of my existence. Not fair. Painting by numbers would be easier; this uncertainty fills me with anguish—*never* to know if I'm living as I should. Taxi!

Sartre expects our discomfort. Yes, he acknowledges, individuality asks the utmost of humans, and many prefer to flee its incessant demands. Two escape hatches open wide, inviting any and all to seek cover through self-deception and prejudice. Hmm. Might I avoid freedom and responsibility by tricking myself and/or despising a group of people? Am I already in flight? Grumbles surface quickly as our exploration takes us into sensitive territory. Happily recovered from his study of Sartre, one of my college students confided, "It was like poison dripping in my ears from the first word out of your mouth." A far cry from the delicious soup and the prospects of cooking our own lives! But the damage done by self-deception is so grave, the cycle of prejudice so deadly, that Sartre forces us to taste the poison straight-on in order to preserve our *self*-portraits.

Self-Deception

Let's pry open the lid of self-deception first. It's noteworthy that self-deception lures only human beings into its trap; only we are gullible enough to fall into its snare. Turtles and zebras never stray from their true natures, their lives self-fulfilling, all turtle, all zebra. We, tragically, can lose our human nature, self-negating, hidden from ourselves and others. "If self-deception is possible, it is because it is an immediate, permanent threat to every project of the human being" (*Being and Nothingness*). When I propose to fidgeting philosophers that humans have a regrettable knack for pretending reality away, I am rarely met with opposition. Does the following daydream have a familiar ring? I tell myself a lie. "I can't find a good job no matter what I do." I know it's a lie, of course, and it is most bizarre that the person to whom I'm lying is myself. I'm not looking for a job, thoroughly enjoying a free ride, spending my time complaining with feet propped up. Ah, but I choose to blame every would- and should-be future employer. And no, I'm not kidding; it's not a lie if I believe it. "Self-deception flees being by taking refuge in 'not-believing-what-one-believes'" (*Being and Nothingness*). I intentionally reject the truth that I am manipulative and self-indulgent, insisting instead on the *fact* that no one will give me a job commensurate with my abilities. Not only can I explain away my situation, but I can concoct a future that substitutes nicely for reality. Watch this! I am unemployed, not looking for a job, refusing to switch "careers," *and* this summer I'm living at the beach, building a boat, and looking for oceanfront property to buy (I can afford it). I barely realize that my relationship with myself is saturated by Sartre's frightening description of "bad faith." I am "living" at the beach, yes, but I'm absent from my own skin.

Laying bare such deception often elicits group laughter, soon silenced by Sartre's caution that this pattern of lying is habit-forming. Once we begin deflecting *one* responsibility, it can swiftly become automatic to shield ourselves from *any* responsibility. "I'm late because people are always cutting in front of me." "You didn't remind me to pay the bill." "A person can *live* in self-deception, which does not mean that he does not have abrupt awakenings to cynicism or to good faith, but which implies a constant and particular style of life" (*Being and Nothingness*). While at first I know I'm lying, after a while lying is what I do for a "living." I rob myself of my humanity, and this make-believe person forfeits any chance of a relationship with anyone. Sartre never lets up. Be wary of this addiction. Homespun lying may preen as a seductive alternative to being in charge of your life, but "once this mode of being has been realized, it is as difficult to get out of it as to wake oneself up; self-deception is a type of being in the world, like waking or dreaming, which by itself tends to perpetuate itself" (*Being and Nothingness*). Scary.

Prejudice

And Sartre's not done with us. Prejudice provides the second poisonous escape route from the challenge of making your life your own. "Nothing but a strong emotional bias can give instant certitude . . . and last an entire lifetime" ("Portrait of an Anti-Semite"). Pre-judging individuals because they are members of a group boosts my feeling of security and superiority. My contempt never changes, this anchor dug by hate holding me fast to a fictional notion of who I am. And when things go wrong, I know where to point the accusatory finger. Nothing is my fault; nothing is my responsibility. Don't try to reason with me and don't make me angry. "He is a man who is afraid. He is a coward" ("Portrait of the Anti-Semite"). I hitch up my pants, safely sequestered in my cocksure worldview; at least I am not a ___. I focus on *their* inferiority (and I add to the list at will) rather than my integrity; still, I'm a pretty decent chap. "But . . . what if he were only that way in regard to Jews? If he conducted himself sensibly in regard to all other matters? I answer that this is impossible" ("Portrait of the Anti-Semite"). Solid as a rock yet blinded by a prejudice that soils every encounter and relationship.

In devaluing humanity, we diminish ourselves most of all. "I am obliged to will the liberty of others at the same time as my own" (*Existentialism Is a Humanism*). Discounting your individuality, I lose mine.

Exploring self-deception is not easy. I have not encountered any group of shaken philosophers who did not temporarily fumble in bags or look out windows in an attempt to keep their distance from Sartre's portrayal of the bigot. Often I pave the way into the discussion, however far this essentially private investigation may or may not proceed, with an opening look at current events. "What are 'hate crimes'?" "Why was there so little media coverage of the mosque destroyed by arson?" So many news items to choose from that showcase prejudice, unfortunately: "Which areas received almost immediate assistance after the devastation wrought by Hurricane Katrina? Who were/are the ignored residents?" "What happens to the Native Americans living by the river when the dam is built?" The imperative to take on prejudice is clear.

On this topic especially, adults engage in dialogue more readily through the back door of their youths, recalling childhood lessons in prejudice. "I learned to feel this way about ___ at the dinner table or in the school cafeteria" symbolizes the recurring theme of inherited bias. "What were you taught in word and through example?" evokes unwanted memories. Certain groups were mocked; particular individuals were belittled. Mumbled asides were made; no questions were asked. A perfect case comes to mind. A third-grader's confident illustration of prejudice, that "all French people hate Jews," surely was not the product of his own research. When I asked, "Are you suggesting that the French are prejudiced or that you are?" he was adamant that the French were guilty as charged. His head bowed dejectedly when I posed Sartre's (a Frenchman's!) warning to the class that bigotry can change a person into an untrustworthy student, or daughter, or teacher, or parent, or friend. "A man who finds it natural to denounce men cannot have our concept of the humane. . . . One cannot localize passion" ("Portrait of the Anti-Semite"). If you can sweep aside one group, tomorrow you can despise *any* group. With five minutes left in our forty-five-minute, one-time slugfest, my new child philosopher spoke slowly for the second time. "I have an uncle who sews. People are surprised because they think that's a girl's job. That's prejudice, I think . . . and . . . if I have a best friend for six months and find out she is in a group I hate, I would either have to give up my friend or my prejudice . . . and I would keep my friend." Well! Now we newly fortified grown-up philosophers open up, stew a bit, as we rediscover some old teachings to unlearn at last. While my prejudice hurts others, it also crushes my humanity.

Sartre leaves us alone to ponder his electric philosophy. Perhaps individuality *is* well worth the effort, a better choice in the long run than either self-deception or prejudice. Death completes my self-portrait and seals the deal I made with myself. "No one can tell what the painting of tomorrow will be like; one cannot judge a painting until it is done" (*Existentialism Is a Humanism*). Did I live my life? Am I comfortable leaving my masterpiece for all to see, without excuse? "I want to die cleanly" ("The Wall").

> *The identities of persons are much more complicated than*
> *what might be suggested by the simple and straightforward*
> *use of terms like "Black," "white," "woman," "man."*
> —ELIZABETH SPELMAN, *Inessential Woman*

"How many of you have checked a box on an application or a form that identifies you as 'Caucasian,' then asked yourself what that word means?" I asked students in my Honors Ethics class during our discussion of societal roles. Hands went up and came down fast. Their incredulity grew when I gave them the most literal definition of the term: people native to the region between Europe and Asia along the border formed by the Caucasus Mountains. They stared at me. "What does that have to do with *me*?" A smiling student shook his head and ventured: "Maybe everyone born in North or South America should check the box marked 'Native American.'" "I'm from Zambia but there is no square that I can mark 'African.'" "Who should identify themselves as 'alien'?"

At what age do we learn which box to check? What purpose do the boxes serve? What happens if you leave the squares unchecked? What if there is no box for you?

Elizabeth Spelman, philosophy professor at Smith College and author of books and articles centered in feminist theory, worries about the serious threat to individuality posed by such arbitrary classification of human beings. Her eye-opening work shines a harsh light on the shrunken individuality of people trapped by stereotypes. "What is it I know if I know that I am a woman or a man, Black or Hispana or white, Jewish or Christian, straight or gay or lesbian? Could I be wrong? If others disagree with me, is there a way of deciding which of us is right?" (*Inessential Woman*). Spelman's vehement reply to her own question: You know absolutely nothing about the person; it was a mistake to assume anything; there is no "right" stereotype.

Generally Speaking

We must be vigilant in fighting the human tendency to generalize about groups of people. "All Cubans love baseball." "No tobacco farmer has a heart." "Students at community colleges couldn't get into a four-year university." "People on welfare feel no shame when they get a handout." How easily unexamined conjecture passes for actual knowledge of real people. Assume nothing. Spelman challenges Plato after all these years for forgetting his own allegiance to the carefully examined life: "Plato didn't consult with women around him to find out if they thought they were like men in the significant ways he thought they were" (*Inessential Woman*). Her rigorous inspection of the "doors" designed to channel individuals into their waiting niches reveals that these doors will disappear quickly if we look closely and see how they work and why they are constructed. Unfortunately, our relentless compartmentalizing of others, and even to a surprising extent the boxing in we do to ourselves, are both so ingrained that most often the doors remain locked.

Children Check the Boxes

Spelman laments the insidious trap of essentialism, the unspoken yet pervasively adopted doctrine that all members of a group share certain qualities *simply because they belong to that group*. And the fix sets in early. Most of us learn society's labels at such a young age that, over time, they appear natural and correct. We forget to question them. As kids, picture books showed us that girls dress *this* way and delight in ballet and sewing; boys dress *that* way and relish in rolling down hills and digging for worms. *Those* kids play street hockey and *these* children play lacrosse. Janitors look like *this;* doctors look like *that.* Says Spelman, "If we have learned the ways of our society, we have learned which doors we will be expected to pass through" (*Inessential Woman*). Humans are sorters and classifiers by nature—apples in this bin and oranges in that one, pencils in this drawer and socks in the other. But neither all apples nor all socks are the same. The classification process may seem innocent enough but the doors seep ever-deeper into our consciousness. Children get their marching orders and hasten to their assigned place: in the family dynamic, in the seating arrangement in kindergarten, in separate playground activities, in the division of household chores. Only Mexicans eat *that* food. Only Muslims celebrate *that* holiday. Father knows best.

Doors Clang Shut

The complexity of this human sorting escalates, as does the damage it causes. I identify you by your dress and accent. Labels instruct me whom to trust and to avoid. Soon, strangely, I feel lost without these descriptors to guide me even in regard to my own identity; I *am* an Italian chef. I become anxious without doors safely bolted behind me and in front of you. In conversations with would-be individuals about Spelman's doors, there is no end to the testimony of the doors' damage. Not only do we pre-judge others but we box ourselves in, as well. "I thought of myself only as a mother and fell apart when my children started school." "I was humiliated when I lost my 'white collar' job and had to become a 'blue collar' worker in order to pay my bills." "I felt like a complete failure when I reached a certain age and wasn't married." "I've been with my partner for thirty years and my parents still refer to him as my 'roommate.' I feel too guilty to tell them or my brothers that we are a couple." "I should be wary of describing my actions as 'willing' if I would have been punished for not acting in that way" (*Inessential Woman*). Shut-ins.

So much self-inflicted harm described by so many earnest philosophers over the years. "We need to ask why people are being processed through these doors, whether social and political positions and privileges are at stake in this processing" (*Inessential Woman*). Who ordered these horrible doors? Who built them? Must we allow them to win?

Understanding why we catalog one another and ourselves so strictly presents a challenge. Spelman sees nothing accidental in the distinctions we draw, stating that the doors "reflect the particular purposes of powerful members of human communities" (*Inessential Woman*). What similarities and differences are of interest and how much they are weighed mirrors a status quo that is working well in the interests of a select few. When you peruse the boxes meant to define you, what matters in your society becomes apparent—income level, skin color, gender, age, birthplace, marital status. Options for necessities such as housing, medical care, and disaster relief open and close depending on your answers. Alternatives for education and employment appear and disappear based on your check marks. The boxes justify unequal pay for equal work. Is everyone's life circumscribed by these doors? Spelman notes that it is quite possible that "those with the most power of all don't have doors" (*Inessential Woman*). The sequenced opening and closing of the doors reinforces the upper hand of the powerful. People are kept in their proper place. Must we give in to unwarranted disadvantage, or unearned advantage, and give up our individuality? What to do?

Vigilance and Impassioned Tolerance

Growing awareness of the doors undermines their power; they work best when they go unnoticed. Spelman recommends two remedies to cure their chokehold: vigilance and tolerance. Heightened vigilance sharpens our ability to detect the slightest whiff of group stereotype. Incorporating empathy into the meaning and practice of tolerance can knock the doors off their hinges.

True vigilantes stand watch over themselves on full alert. "Why did I assume that she spoke no English?" After watching a movie I now question why I identified with one character and forecast villainy for another. Recalling seemingly casual conversations at day's end, I begin to realize how certain remarks serve to rebuff others' individuality. "Did I really ask you how you could stand being a plumber?" "Did I just roll my eyes when you told me you were a regular churchgoer?" If I pay rapt attention, no door is secure.

And we must be more vigilant still. We need to do more than merely tolerate others, letting them have their say without really listening to their very personal stories. Humanity consists of a big, messy mix of individuals all with unique lives. I must seek knowledge of other experiences and invigorate and enrich my definition of tolerance; lazy tolerance is no more than a luxury bought by privilege. "In tolerating you I have done nothing to change the fact that I have more power and authority than you do" (*Inessential Woman*). Active tolerance welcomes individual self-expression; it engages and responds, person to person.

Blithe brush-offs come all too easily. The story of a walk taken by my dog, Mel, and my college student John teaches Spelman's lessons well. As I waited for their overdue return at the close of my office hours, John suddenly filled the door frame, red-faced, panting, distraught, and attached to a happy dog. "You won't believe what happened! We were walking up the hill and two people came up and asked to pet him. They carried on about how beautiful, et cetera, and then asked what kind of dog he was. I said he was my teacher's dog. They asked again. I said he's not any one thing. They backed off and said, 'You mean he's just a mutt?' and walked away as if he weren't even there." I asked Mel and his defender to sit and dispensed well-deserved treats.

Oh, John. We're all mutts. Isn't it grand?

DISCUSSION QUESTIONS

- What is individuality? What is its essence?
- Who are you? What are you?
- What qualities define you as you? Are you true to these defining characteristics? Have you given others the privilege of determining who you are?
- Do you live well with yourself? Do you know you? How can you stay in closer touch with the real you?
- What is the meaning of personal integrity? When have you held fast to integrity? When has it slipped away?

- What threatens your individuality? Are these real or imagined threats? Do you value individuality?
- To what extent are you a nonconformist? Can you be your own person under any circumstances?
- Do you agree with Sartre that the fight against self-deception is a hard one that lasts a lifetime? In what harmful ways do you succumb to self-deception?
- Have you latched on to an abiding prejudice that robs others of their individuality as it restricts your own? Are there individuals you dismiss outright due to their membership in a group?
- Do you agree with Sartre that there are no alibis for what we make of our lives? Do you accept responsibility for your life?
- Do you generalize about people? Why are humans so quick to judge?
- Do you encourage others' individuality? How? All people? Your children? Your parents?
- Have you defined yourself as well as others by using Spelman's doors? Does sorting individuals into categories pose problems? Be specific.
- Do you agree with Spelman that genuine tolerance is inviting, welcoming?
- How would you describe yourself to someone you were about to meet? What can you learn from your description?
- Is the story of your life unique? Why? How?
- Do you live with zest? Are you passionate about the project of your life?
- As our two philosophers leave you with your life to live, what three mementos from Sartre and Spelman will you safeguard?

HOMEWORK

Listen and Hum

Everyone gets three tokens for the jukebox. Spend them freely, using one token to make a choice in each of the following groups. Make sure all the musicians/composers get a spin on the turntable. Sport your dancing shoes just in case.

Renegades

- The British rock band The Who, led by Roger Daltrey and Pete Townshend, powers the individual past social conventions, singing Sartre's warning against hiding behind an "Eminence Front." They dress for parties, ride in big cars, and order tall drinks, but people "forget they're hiding" and that "it's a put-on." Self-deception powders the soul like packed snow until only the disguise remains. Are you hiding? Are you kidding yourself? Do you make excuses for your life? Townshend composed the first full-length rock opera, *Tommy*, and The Who performed it at the Metropolitan Opera House in New York. They shook the chandeliers, the first rock band to appear on this venerable stage, and audience members boogied in the red-carpeted aisles. Can you break the mold?
- You know Eleanora Fagan's voice but you might not know her name. She grew up in emotional and economic chaos in the twenties and thirties in Baltimore, catching an unlikely break while working for tips in a Harlem club when she was eighteen. Young Eleanora coined her own identity by naming herself Billie Holiday, and by performing jazz vocals with an intensity and personalized phrasing that

won her an international audience. Head thrown back with "Them There Eyes," a white gardenia in her hair, Billie Holiday speaks to her audience one-to-one with her trumpetlike voice. "Lady Day" had neither a formal education nor musical training and never outran her personal blues, but she sings an ode to longed-for independence in her "God Bless the Child," any child "that's got its own." Have you "got your own" self-sufficient means and resolve?

- Eric Dolphy carved his own controversial niche in the jazz world. His shocking improvisations drew furious criticism as well as hearty admiration from his peers; ringing applause mixed with loud jeers in concerts worldwide. Dolphy persevered, coaxing his alto saxophone into new territory and pioneering bass clarinet and flute solos. Imagine Billie Holiday experiencing his "avant-garde" interpretation of her "God Bless the Child" in 1961 in Copenhagen. On the title track of his best-known recording, *Out to Lunch*, he showcases his mesmerizing unpredictability. Can you relate to Dolphy's desire for self-expression? What are your outlets?

- Russian composer Igor Stravinsky's *The Rite of Spring* provoked quite a brouhaha at its 1913 premiere in Paris. Composers were among the clientele rushing for the doors at the screech of the opening bassoon; ballet dancers struggled to hear their cues as shouts and fights broke out among those brave enough to stay. Newly modern music was ushered in by a colorful personality with an insatiable intellect. Stravinsky, composer and conductor, resident of Switzerland and Los Angeles, France and New York, made music his lifelong experiment. That wildly dissonant celebration of a pagan spring ritual served as early symbol of his fearless innovation. Why not try something new?

Songs for Spelman

- Stereotypes abound in the *South Pacific* as Navy Seabees prepare to do battle with the Japanese. Ensign Nellie Forbush, typecasting herself as a "hick" from Little Rock and whose shipmates think of her as a "dame," must confront her unquestioned racism when she rejects the mixed-race children of her suitor. Polynesian Bloody Mary hurls furious prejudices at the sailors because her daughter, Liat, has no future with Lieutenant Cable; he knows that they would never be welcome in the high society he left behind. This gentle military man was trained from an early age that "You've Got to Be Carefully Taught" to fear "people whose eyes are oddly made, / and people whose skin is a different shade." Rodgers and Hammerstein unveiled their musical in 1949 in the war's aftermath. What were *you* taught? What are you teaching by example now?

- Janis Ian was taught some harsh truths "At Seventeen." She sings the piercing heartache of an "ugly duckling" lacking social skills and a beauty queen's pretty face. No valentines and never picked when sides are chosen for basketball, she overhears the in-crowd "murmur vague obscenities." She suspects, however, that those who trade on externals acquire "dubious integrity." How can both the ugly duckling and the beauty queen unlearn their roles? Ian lamented being "Society's Child," losing her boyfriend to her mother's taunting admonition, "But honey, he's not our kind." When have you felt the sting of this mind-set? Do you have a nose for those who aren't your kind?

- Frank Sinatra sings a self-satisfied tune written just for him by Paul Anka. As he contemplates a career spanning seven decades nearing its end, "Ol' Blue Eyes" has few regrets in a very full professional life. Although there were blows and tears, he saw things through and he did them "My Way." High school dropout, civil rights activist, and Academy Award winner, he takes pride in expressing himself honestly. "For what is a man? What has he got? / If not himself—Then he has naught." What things have you done that you would call "my way"?

- Days "When I Was a Boy" provide happy memories for Dar Williams, days flying with Peter Pan and riding a bike shirt-free. She longs for times before gender roles dictated appropriate behavior. As she reminisces with a friend, he shares his reverie of days when "I picked flowers everywhere" and "I could cry all the time." Oh, for the simple life when he was a girl. Why do we obey the "rules"? How much misery is evoked by the taunt of "tomboy" and "sissy"? We can do better, Williams sings, as "The Christians and the Pagans" celebrate Christmas and Solstice "together at the table." Quite a holiday with family and friends "lighting trees in darkness, learning new ways from the old, and / making sense of history and drawing warmth out of the cold." Who might gather around your table?

Styling with Sartre

- Bass player, pianist, producer, arranger, band leader, and composer. Bebop, hard bop, classical, gospel, or jazz? Hot-tempered, perfectionist, unconventional Charles Mingus never compromised his sense of musical integrity; it is impossible to classify this major player in twentieth-century song. Mingus abhorred the harsh segregation in Little Rock, Arkansas, enforced by Governor Orval E. Faubus, and raged against it with his instrumental protest "Fables of Faubus." How does Mingus convey wordless outrage? Describe your image of him as you listen to "Self-Portrait in Three Colors." What colors does he use? What are *your* colors? What is "it" that you "Better Get It in Your Soul"? Do you think you have "it"? For an artist with more than one hundred albums, there are relatively few covers of his work. Why would it be difficult to "cover" Charles Mingus?

- Trained as a child in European classical music, Chen Yi was sentenced to forced labor during the "Cultural Revolution," and claims that she learned the importance of individual lives and education in the internment camps. Her compositions are rooted in a blend of both Western and Eastern traditions; Chen tweaks this foundation into *her* music. *Chinese Myths* is a multimedia event in which she combines symphony orchestra, a choir, a Chinese dance troupe, and an instrumental ensemble, all complemented by visual projections onstage. This prominent Chinese-American composer earned her doctorate from Columbia, a long way to travel for a child who practiced fearfully with a muted violin. Listen.

- A tall-haired, steep-booted Texan pipes up that "If I Had a Boat" I could get out on that ocean, "and if I had a pony / I'd ride him on my boat." Like Roy Rogers but without Dale, Lyle Lovett would ride Trigger onto his boat and sail away. Tonto would abandon the Lone Ranger and strike out on his own for a chance to saddle up on this boat. What a funny song! Who is this ranch hand, Hollywood actor, and college student of journalism and German? What kind of music is this? Country or folk or jazz or pop or big-band swing?

- A shy, diminutive cabaret singer boasts that she harbors "No Regrets," not for temporary blindness as a child while boarded in her grandmother's brothel, nor for having to make her way singing on the streets and in the bars of Belleville, and despite a frantic, turbulent personal life . . . "no, nothing at all, I regret nothing at all." Could Édith Piaf, "The Little Sparrow," have foreseen that "this magic spell you cast" in her "La Vie en Rose" still hovers over France? What makes her voice stand alone? How can you live without regret?

Recite and Write

Read aloud and discuss the following poems. After your conversation, jot down ideas as they occur to you in your journals. Take a quiet break and then find a private perch just for you. Write a poem that expresses deep-down you. Tuck it away.

- Who has what it takes to be a hero in fourteenth-century Persia? Who has that rare quality that draws everyone near? Who "always keeps" true to her/his "word"? Why does the penetrating gaze of Sufi master Hafiz find "Integrity" an almost superhuman possession? What does it mean to be true to your word? What "word"? With all the words we speak, how can we honor the words that matter? Do unspoken words count? What about the promises we make to ourselves?
- Life is full of tough, frustrating "Choices" for Nikki Giovanni. Prevented by social pressures from doing as she likes, her only free choice remains how best to avoid

doing what she dislikes. With no chance to realize her dreams today, she chooses to want more for tomorrow. She winces "when I can't express / what I really feel," and she insists that it is this aching repression that teaches humans to cry. Can you express what you really feel? To yourself? To another? In words? In actions? Is this as important to you as it is to Giovanni?

- You earn admiration from e. e. cummings, a poet who toasts individuality in his inimitable style and verse, "because you take life in your stride (instead [sic]" of opting out of the exquisite opportunity to be fully alive. You do not lie to your stout heart and no one should try to fool your resolute mind. Refusing to despise life because it's messy, you peek around every corner hungry for more. Fearlessly immersed in living, you proudly win your self "because you aren't afraid to kiss the dirt." Are you willing to kiss the dirt? Why do you think cummings uses this image? Is it too much work to dig into life and plumb its depth? Will you take cummings's dare and plant a kiss?

- Canada's Cheryl Denise warns us of all "They'll" try to do to stamp any aspiring individual with a Spelman label. With your soul decked out in a suit, blemishes covered with makeup, loans acquired for a dream house just like the Joneses', your life will be as meticulously arranged as a floral bouquet. No crying and no rainy-day tango; the right sneakers and cheerleading pom-poms required. But you defy them at last and "ooze your soul" in the sunlight and "read poems to swaying cornfields." Of course, low voices whisper that you're surely mad. Do you care about the hints of disapproval? Who are the Joneses, anyway?

- Walt Whitman weaves a magical "Song of Myself" that sings for every listener as well. His soaring celebration of the individual comes in fifty-two sections; read the entire poem prior to your meeting and choose one or two segments to read when you gather. I'm going to the beach in #11 and live with the animals in #32. Whitman rejoices in life's infinite splendor and revels in being part of the spectacle. Sea-rocks, kisses, curling grass, quail, biscuits and milk, sunbeams and love-making . . . oh, joy. "There is that in me—I do not know what it is—but I know it is in me." What inner fire moves Whitman to sing of himself? What thrills him so? What is *your* song? "And what is reason? and what is love? and what is life?" He waits for breathless you. When you catch up with him . . .

• Derek Walcott's gift is "Love After Love." His Caribbean promise is that one day you will know yourself through and through, and love again your constant companion. You will say hello to yourself "at your own door, in your own mirror," and smile and be glad. Walcott knows that self-love often comes late, too much time wasted in pleasing others and seeking their approval. Now, no longer a stranger to yourself, you can accept Walcott's oh-so-welcome invitation: "Sit. Feast on your life." Savor a meal only you can prepare.

Read and Talk

• Bring a rake and a hoe and join Henry David Thoreau during his two-year retreat on the shore of Walden Pond. Searching for himself in the Massachusetts woods, Thoreau lives in his homemade hut a mile from any neighbor. Observing that "the mass of men lead lives of quiet desperation," he determines to learn the lessons of simple living and find "*his* own way" and not "his neighbor's instead." Thoreau's quest is to "suck all the marrow out of life" because "to be awake is to be alive." How much of you has been lost in the crowd? "If a man does not keep pace with his companions, perhaps it is because he hears a different drummer. Let him step to the music which he hears." What personal leave of absence can you take to reconnect with yourself? Hearing the beat of your life again, can you turn up the volume and listen to it above the roar of the crowd?

- "Freeing yourself was one thing; claiming ownership of that freed self was another." How can we "own ourselves" in light of and in spite of a hard, hard past? Toni Morrison's characters learn to ask that question and fumble and struggle mightily for their answers in *Beloved*. In her distinctive style, Morrison lures the reader into the marred lives and the long legacy of the African slave trade; the book's dedication page testifies to the death toll: "Sixty Million . . . and more." What is slavery? What are some of the many forms it takes? Does it exist today? Scarred and isolated by her personal history, Sethe travels slowly toward herself. "To Sethe, the future was a matter of keeping the past at bay. The 'better life' she and Denver were living was simply not the other one." Stamp Paid's tribute at book's end proclaims her ultimate victory: "You your best thing, Sethe. You are." How can you be "your best thing"? "Me?" "Me?" Yes.

- Though Steve Martin was *Born Standing Up*, he sat down for good in the early eighties, turning his talent to novels, plays, nonfiction, and screenplays after eighteen years in stand-up comedy. He detoured from early plans for a doctorate in philosophy, weary of abstract discussions "that suggested that philosophy was nonsense," wanting to know for sure if he "could . . . have had a career in performing."

Years pass; he sits with his dying parents, remembering his tough youth in intimate detail, and his reminiscence is written with poignant, painful honesty. "I moved closer and said goodbye to my mother. I put my arms around her and, surprising myself, choked out, 'Mama, Mama, Mama,' a term I hadn't used since childhood." With the multifaceted persona of Steve Martin as a backdrop, enjoy hearty conversation that would restore his faith in philosophy. Is every person more than one thing? Does your career *define* you? Have you found a vocation that suits *you*? If not, is it possible to forge a new way?

- Lee Smith introduces us to twelve-year-old Molly Petree *On Agate Hill*, a Civil War orphan and consistently plucky individual. She expresses herself in an early diary entry: "I am like the ruby-throated hummingbird that comes again and again to Fannie's red rosebush but lights down never for good, and always flying on." We patch together Molly's hummingbird life through journal entries, recipes, poems, newspaper clippings, songs, and our imaginations. Do you agree with B.J.'s assertion that all people want a "kind of life of their own"? What qualities does Molly possess as a child that foster a "life of her own"? Describe her acquired traits that bring this joyful self-confidence: "Now that I have shrunk down as a child, I figure I might as well act like one. I don't care. I like ice cream, Juney does too. We like to put bourbon in it, and make ourselves a milkshake."

- Does "being honest in the only way I know" define integrity? A seventeen-year-old boy, locked away in a Borstal reform school, makes this discovery when he takes to heart *The Loneliness of the Long-Distance Runner*. A talented runner, he can earn special privileges from the uniformed gaolers if he brings the "Blue Ribbon Prize Cup" home to his "school." Can he muster the cunning to win the race? In Alan Sillitoe's short story, his cross-country narrator fervently mutters, "I'm a human being and I've got thoughts and secrets and bloody life inside me . . . I *am* honest." What to do? Can he beat the system and win *his* race? "You should think about nobody and go your own way, not on a course marked out for you." We cheer the breathless runner home, "blubbing like a baby, blubbing now out of gladness that I'd got them beat at last." Can you relate to the Borstal boy's frustration? What does winning the race mean to you?

- Frida Kahlo renders her Jewish, Mexican, Austrian, Spanish face and her complex inner being in impassioned self-portraits chock-full of splashy colors and bold honesty. Born in 1907 during the Mexican Revolution, she endured the effects of childhood polio only to suffer a crippling accident at the age of eighteen. A trolley car left Frida with a short lifetime of emotional and physical pain. This eye-catching original artist flung herself full-throttle into a life unimaginable in *any* day, and she leaps alive in Hayden Herrera's *Frida: A Biography of Frida Kahlo*. "The story of Frida Kahlo begins and ends in the same place . . . the house on the southwestern periphery of Mexico City. . . . Inside is one of the most extraordinary places in Mexico—a woman's home with all her paintings and belongings, turned into a museum." What do you make of untamable Frida and her talking art?

Watch and Reflect

- How many of us can say as convincingly as Elwood P. Dowd that "I always have a wonderful time, wherever I

am, whoever I'm with"? Mary Chase wins the Pulitzer Prize
in 1945 for introducing Elwood to his faithful companion,
Harvey, a rabbit just under six-foot-four. From the moment
that he holds the gate for Harvey with a sweeping "After
you" until he exults in finding him on a swinging glider
with a beaming "There you are," Elwood savors every moment of a life uniquely his (and theirs!) alone. "Harvey
and I warm ourselves in all these golden moments," he
smiles. He had to make his own freedom, admitting that
"I've wrestled with reality for thirty-five years and I'm
happy to say I've finally won out over it." His sister, Veta,
the psychiatrists from Chumley's, and the local judge are
"swizzled" by Dowd's sheer delight in life. Accept one of
Dowd's calling cards and join him and Harvey for dinner.
Sneak a look at their portrait in the sitting room. How can
you bring a bit of Elwood's triumph into your life?

• Photographer Zana Briski falls hard for children *Born into
Brothels* in Calcutta, India, and she uses her ingenuity to
"teach them to see the world through *their* eyes." Her camera captures the individual faces and inner lives of children who warm to her interest; "Zana Auntie" then puts
cameras into their hands and teaches them her craft. Little
girls who heretofore imagine no future other than following "in the line" of their mothers' and grandmothers' work
now realize a bigger world. Boys trying their hands at pho-
tography ponder new ways "to put across the behavior of
a man." What these skilled amateurs allow themselves to
see and choose to photograph creates a reality unique
to each one. Putting daily trauma on hold, Shanti, Suchi-
tra, Manik, Puja, Tapasi, and Gour develop a sense of self
as they develop film. "I wonder what I could become" with
an education, Kochi dreams. Avijit's self-portrait, comple-

mented by his inventive backdrop, identifies this young boy to himself in an intimate way. The children find their own perspectives and frame their visions, unveiling their artwork at a gallery gala in India, beaming as they sign their names on the backs of their photos even though "my hands are shaking." Their "Auntie" arranges scholarships for some to go to boarding school; Kochi is one who stays the course. "I won't fulfill my dreams," Avijit fears, but his face says otherwise. What do Zana and her students teach you about individuality? Grab a camera and slowly compile a series of photographs that speak your name. Enjoy your own group exhibit.

Get Up and Do

- Spend an evening play-reading Sartre's *No Exit*. Take turns "living" in a hell of their own making with Garcin, Inès, and Estelle. The "Valet" makes but a brief appearance; have the host who welcomed you take his part. As they look back on their lives, full of disclaimers and justifications, what insights does each of the characters unintentionally impart about self-knowledge and integrity? Inès forcefully rebukes Garcin, "It's what one does, and nothing else, that shows the stuff one's made of." True? Do you agree with Garcin that "hell is other people"? Be on the lookout for a performance of *No Exit* by a local theater company, and you can check out film versions in many public and college libraries.
- Between meetings, each person hunt for stereotypes lurking in advertising, newspaper coverage, magazine articles—it won't be hard. Be on the alert for generalizations and projections that may have escaped your notice prior to encountering Sartre and Spelman. "Perhaps because we learn

the categories so early and are continually asked to reflect our knowledge of them, they seem unproblematic" (*Inessential Woman*). I surprise myself every time. Watch the news and listen to radio broadcasts. Bring clippings and/or vivid descriptions to share.

- Represent yourself, faithfully, through any artistic medium.
- Knock down (unobtrusively!) one of Spelman's doors by knocking *on* it. Get to know, at least a little, the cafeteria worker, carpooler, co-worker, groundskeeper, employer . . . someone you see quite often but with whom you assumed you had nothing in common.
- Have you gotten to know one another as individuals in your philosophy club? Think of something, however small, that would be interesting and/or fun for people to know about your life. Have you clogged on a tabletop? Are you a whiz with a yo-yo? Do you have the best recipe for watermelon rind pickle?
- Entertain yourselves and two Brazilian individuals at a dinner party. Welcome Paulo Freire (POW-lo freh-EE-reh) with bossa nova sung by his legendary countrywoman Rosa Passos. Perhaps a Brazilian menu . . . mango, papaya, cashews, figs, sautéed collard greens, beans and rice, a spicy stew and cheese bread, fried banana, and maybe a toast with a caipirinha. Freire brings food for thought on the topic of individuality. He was a revolutionary educator determined to bring literacy to the peasant masses laboring under dictatorship in the twentieth century. His advice to those seeking social change comes with a caveat: do not become an unwitting accomplice in the oppression of *any* individual. "What can be said . . . of a man considered to be progressive who, in spite of his talk in favor of the lower

classes, behaves like the lord of his family, whose domi-
neering suffocates his wife and children? What can be said
of the woman who fights for the interests of those of her
gender but who at home rarely thanks the cook for the
cup of water that she brings her and who, in conversations with friends, refers to the cook as one of 'those people'?" (*Teachers as Cultural Workers*). Digest his questions
together.

- Feet up and popcorn out! Four of our prose works/authors
  come alive on the screen. Laugh with Steve Martin in any
  one of his barrier-breaking films; he wrote *Shopgirl*, both
  the novel and the screenplay, and stars in the movie.
  Dance with *Frida*. Run as far and as fast as the Borstal boy
  in *The Loneliness of the Long-Distance Runner*. Do more
  than survive with Sethe in *Beloved*.

Resources

Music
- *The Who: The Ultimate Collection* by The Who: "Eminence
  Front."
- *God Bless the Child: The Very Best of Billie Holiday* by Billie Holiday:
  "God Bless the Child," "Them There Eyes."
- *Eric Dolphy in Europe, Volume 1* by Eric Dolphy: "God Bless the
  Child."
- *Out to Lunch* by Eric Dolphy: "Out to Lunch."
- *Stravinsky Conducts Stravinsky: Petrushka/Le Sacre du Printemps;*
  Columbia Symphony Orchestra.
- *South Pacific* by Richard Rodgers and Oscar Hammerstein II (Orig-
  inal 1949 Broadway Cast): "You've Got to Be Carefully Taught."
- *Rodgers and Hammerstein's South Pacific* (The New Broadway Cast):
  "You've Got to Be Carefully Taught."
- *Live: Working Without a Net* by Janis Ian: "At Seventeen," "Soci-
  ety's Child."
- *My Way* by Frank Sinatra: "My Way."

- *The Honesty Room* by Dar Williams: "When I Was a Boy."
- *Mortal City* by Dar Williams: "The Christians and the Pagans."
- *Mingus Ah Um* by Charles Mingus: "Self-Portrait in Three Colors," "Better Get It in Your Soul," "Fables of Faubus."
- *The Music of Chen Yi: Chinese Myths* (4 Cantatas), performed by The Women's Philharmonic, JoAnn Falletta conducting.
- *Pontiac* by Lyle Lovett: "If I Had a Boat."
- *30th Anniversaire* by Édith Piaf: "Non, Je Ne Regrette Rien," "La Vie en Rose."
- *Rosa* by Rosa Passos: "Sutilezas."

Poetry

- *The Gift* by Hafiz, translated by Daniel Ladinsky: "Integrity."
- *Collected Poetry of Nikki Giovanni: 1968–1998:* "Choices."
- *95 Poems* by e. e. cummings: "Because you take life in your stride (instead [sic]."
- *I Saw God Dancing* by Cheryl Denise: "They'll."
- *The Complete Poems* by Walt Whitman, edited by Francis Murphy: "Song of Myself."
- *Collected Poems, 1948–1984* by Derek Walcott: "Love After Love."

Prose

- *Walden, Civil Disobedience, and Other Writings,* by Henry David Thoreau, edited by William Rossi: *Walden.*
- *Beloved* by Toni Morrison.
- *Born Standing Up* by Steve Martin.
- *On Agate Hill* by Lee Smith.
- *The Loneliness of the Long-Distance Runner* by Alan Sillitoe.
- *Frida: The Biography of Frida Kahlo* by Hayden Herrera.
- *Teachers as Cultural Workers* by Paulo Freire.
- *Inessential Woman* by Elizabeth Spelman.
- *Being and Nothingness* by Jean-Paul Sartre, with Hazel Barnes.
- *The Wall: Intimacy* by Jean-Paul Sartre, with Lloyd Alexander.
- *No Exit and Three Other Plays* by Jean-Paul Sartre.
- *Existentialism Is a Humanism* by Jean-Paul Sartre, translated by Carol Macomber, preface by Arlette Elkaim-Sartre, introduction by Annie Cohen-Solal.
- *Hatred, Bigotry, and Prejudice* edited by Robert M. Baird and Stuart E. Rosenbaum: "Portrait of an Anti-Semite."

Drama

- *Harvey* by Mary Chase, directed by Henry Koster (DVD).
- *Beloved*, directed by Jonathan Demme (DVD).
- *The Loneliness of the Long-Distance Runner*, directed by Tony Richardson (DVD).
- *Frida*, directed by Julie Taymor (DVD).
- *Shopgirl*, directed by Anand Tucker (DVD).
- *Tommy* by The Who, directed by Ken Russell (DVD).

Documentary

- *Born into Brothels*, directed by Ross Kauffman (DVD).

Belonging

~~~

What, in fact, is a great individual if not a man who lends
his face, his words, and his actions to a great civilization?
—Albert Camus, *Camus at Combat*

THE TOPIC

Years ago I "remodeled" my college classroom on the sly, remov-
ing an imposing lectern from the front of the room and rearranging
desks so that my students and I could sit together in a circle. Many
of my colleagues were aghast. How would the students know who
was in charge? "You'll lose your authority! Isn't this sort of radical?"
Their shock demonstrates how conditioned we've become to linear
social structures. With little thought we form lines, sit in rows, and
climb corporate ladders. Yet we learn much of what we know from
one another; face-to-face dialogue wraps us in social bonds. What's
going on?

Sitting in an energized circle during a discussion of human nature
recently, a student abruptly asked how I defined myself. When I
didn't respond, she supplied multiple choices, some more acceptable
than others! Not only didn't I have an answer for her, but the notion

of "defining myself" felt quite new. Suddenly words came to me, almost unsought: "My connections define me. Who I am unfolds in relationship." The room buzzed with off-the-cuff musings about the meaning of relationship, the reality of interdependence, and the value of community. "How could anything be *un*related?" "Everything in the world is co-dependent. Wow, co-dependency is cool!"

Belonging. The feeling when your mechanic asks how your family is doing. When a co-worker takes the time to pass on a compliment. When you return to your hometown and the grocer calls you by name. When your neighbor closes your windows when you're away just as the first raindrops fall. It's the feeling that you matter in a big and busy world. With a sense of belonging, you can rest assured. But how to find the right words for this feeling, this spark lit by connection? What *is* belonging?

Belonging is being emotionally encircled by your relationships with others. The ribbons of belonging tie you to the places that you call home. People belong to us not as possessions but as essential ingredients of our lives. The many ways of belonging gladden our hearts. Connections near and far, known and unknown, plant seeds of trust and security. The personal restoration granted by privacy and solitude complements the fulfillment found only in community. Grateful for all the relationships that ground and center us, we reach out toward the world.

In my discussions with college students and philosophy clubbers, talk of belonging tends to produce both happy tales and a sense of yearning. "I use my grandmother's old ball gown as a tablecloth. I replaced her worn-out bodice with the perfect centerpiece." More examples of kinship pop up: "Kite-flying and the office picnic on the mountaintop," "poker game every Thursday night," "summer concerts in the park," "the annual office party," "the smell of Thanksgiving." Stories of the unexpected joy of reconnecting with childhood friends abound: "Reconnecting with her was like finding a light left on in a window." "I felt like myself again when the old team got together." Still, testimony to the satisfaction of belonging often tapers off, giving way to sighs of deeply rooted frustration at the difficulty of building a sense of belonging in modern society. "I stick with my childhood friends because I'm too busy to make new ones." "No one seems to have the time or inclination to help when you need them most." "I don't get involved because I don't feel needed." So? Is belonging just a matter of luck? Do some belong and others not? How can I enhance my sense of being a part of things?

Talk of belonging invariably leads to an examination of responsibility. I must earn my place in the lives of others—in my biological family, in my extended family however far it stretches, in communities both small and large. An example springs to mind: "I'm in a book club that was founded in 1965 with three charter members still gluing us together," a twenty-year participant offered in tribute to belonging. Our gathering of philosophers agreed that this book club works because its members keep their commitments to one another and to the life of their community. Lifting at a barn raising, answering patiently the repeated questions of an elderly neighbor, retrieving a child's ball, calling a retired colleague out of retirement and into the softball league, even taking the time to give directions while in a hurry—such investments of time link us to the world and nourish our sense of belonging. The world calls our names repeatedly. Will we find that we have *response ability*? No answer spoken, everything deemed a burden, pretending not to hear . . . guarantees our isolation. Answering the call, offering repeated assurances that we can be relied upon, this bouncing in mutual give-and-take . . . carries us all the way home.

Philosophers have always been interested in the ways that human beings relate to one another and to the natural world. Who is of primary importance, the individual or the members of a community? Is there a reason I should look out for you and you for me? Do we owe anything to the world itself? Is isolation possible, and if so, is it desirable? Is everyone really related? Is my life enriched through belonging to community?

Determined circles form as we corral the concept of belonging, talking together, discovering community, and rethinking responsibility. For most, this marks their *first* attempt to grasp the meaning of *response ability*. Albert Camus (ahl-BAIR ka-MOO) extols the demands of responsible living. Every test has the potential to bring out the best in each of us. Rita Manning extends her ethic of care to her students in California, to all life forms, and to the land itself. "Hooray!" for the web of relationship.

THE PHILOSOPHERS

One must not cut oneself off from the world. No one who
lives in the sunlight makes a failure of his life.
—ALBERT CAMUS, *Notebooks 1935–1951*

Algerian-born and -educated, French scholar and citizen of the world Albert Camus sought philosophical clarity and ethical consistency with vigor and purpose. Through his provocative novels, essays, editorials, plays, and introspective notebooks he probed the true nature of human beings. He made a stunningly convincing case that it is only through the achievement of community and fellowship that our earthly salvation can be won. He lived this conviction, stoking the fires of French solidarity by ensuring that his newspaper would not be silenced during the German occupation of France. Fingers clung to their heritage with every secretive reading of an issue of *Combat*. What motivated Camus to sneak off to the newsroom night after night? Perhaps the editor would have answered that "at times I feel myself overtaken by an immense tenderness for these people around me" (*Notebooks 1951–1959*).

Life is hard. Neither the starry, ink-black sky nor the blazing desert sun can answer our questions about life's meaning—human affairs are of no interest to the seas or the mountains. For Camus there was no higher calling than joining forces in a compassionate human fraternity to work for the collective good. "One serves mankind all together or not at all" (*Notebooks 1942–1951*). As we persist in the struggle for social justice and welfare, our accomplishments create an environment increasingly conducive to human happiness. Life can be easier, but only if we organize our collective homecoming. Direction and purpose come to us through working together to improve society. Shared humanity provides the context for personal growth and happiness; we are not alone after all. We give life its meaning through shoulder-to-shoulder unity.

An almost tangible feeling of urgency sparks Camus' philosophical work and social activism. The barbarism of world war showcased for him the human penchant for cruelty and extremism. He knew that "the worm is in the man's heart" (*The Myth of Sisyphus and Other Essays*) and that he and all of us need to resist apathy and "fear and silence and the division of minds and souls" (*Camus at Combat*). He wars against feelings of impotence and futility at the prospect of a peaceful worldwide community. He pleaded, and pleads with us still, to accept his charge: the time to act together is now . . . before it is too late. "If we fail, mankind will be plunged back into darkness. But at least we will have tried" (*Camus at Combat*).

What was Camus thinking? Fragmented populations of every size cry out for reunification; we can defeat the menace of isolation and the wounds of injustice proudly, defiantly. Embracing life's difficulties together takes the sting out of hardship and makes living more than bearable. Beauty, love, and joy await us, from time to time, if we resist the urge to flee from our own suffering and the suffering of others. Refuse to give up, ever. How can each of us rise to full stature? What work must I do on myself so that I can join you? Will I refuse to play the role of victim and choose to stand up to life? Yes? All aboard, then, for a trip to the town of Oran. Camus' novel *The Plague* offers the cure of brotherhood for the affliction of spiritual misery. The townspeople learn life's big lesson the hard way: "it was quite true that men can't do without their fellow men" (*The Plague*).

Taking the Train to Oran

The town gates clank shut at the confirmed outbreak of plague, enclosing an unsuspecting and unprepared populace. Oran is a town like most others, its people taking life for granted in the well-worn tread of comfortable routines. Plague changes everything. What to do with no place to hide and sentries blocking escape? Blaring sirens drown out fearful, distracted conversations. The soccer stadium plays host to quarantine centers while physicians frantically concoct experimental anti-plague vaccines. Volunteers form sanitary squads, choosing to unite against an overpowering enemy. The fight is on; the fight is all. This physical plague attacking Oran possesses all the ingredients of the spiritual plague that threatens to suck the heart out of every human being. The townspeople feel alone, exiled from a world to which they no longer belong. When they can no longer deny the plague's presence, some cower in panicky isolation and refuse to join the fight. Their spirits defeated, they abandon themselves as well as one another. Camus introduces us to one character who retreats from belonging, though others surely lurked in shadows and slunk away from human contact; we meet four individuals, footsteps and hearts beating in unison, who dig deep into their humanity and win the duel with plague. Relationship saves lives and defeats plague. Let's pick up some anti-plague serum and take to heart Camus' rousing invitation to swallow our lives whole. Meet your neighbors:

Dr. Bernard Rieux shapes himself to plague's demands with uncompromising honesty while extending gut-felt sympathy to all. The doctor, Camus' ideal of ethical consistency, holds tight to his best pre-plague self while raising the bar on his own humanity. Oran's physician belongs to his townspeople, "linked to the world by everything I do, to men with all the gratitude I feel" (*Notebooks 1935–1951*). The book's narrator unveils a fully human hero in Joseph Grand, an aging bureaucrat with a tender and generous heart. Spurred on by unaccustomed camaraderie, he hurries resiliently into the fray though deadened by fatigue because "it is not true that the heart wears out" (*Notebooks 1951–1959*). Grand uses the plague as an opportunity to substitute years of loneliness with belonging. Jean Tarrou and Raymond Rambert are newcomers to Oran. Tarrou pitches in with self-assured tenacity and never questions that his mission is to fight suffering. He and Rieux celebrate the joys of friendship through honest communication and unspoken respect, their fierce bond shielding them from plague's killing separation. Rambert wants out of the journalistic assignment that thrust him into Oran, but ditches his desperate escape plan and signs on with the volunteers, realizing that plague is "everybody's business." Cottard, a mysterious, shifty-eyed chap with a shady past, refuses to help. He misses his chance to shake his demons by joining in the fight and thereby finding courage in human fellowship; he exaggerates his torment alone. Cottard presents the symptoms of spiritual plague . . . withdrawn, guilty, spiteful, untrusting, splintered from the human group. Tarrou asks only that he "try at least not to propagate the microbe deliberately" (*The Plague*).

Isolation, like cooperation, spreads quickly.

Victory

Spending time with any group of philosophers in Oran, I admire brave thinkers as they uncover personal truths and also develop a deeper understanding of social responsibility. Many, finding confidence in Camus' assertion that "you can change everything" (*Notebooks, 1935–1951*), call their plagues by name—selfishness, addiction, fear, abuse, insecurity—and opt out of excuses and into the human community. "I have never forgiven myself for what happened to me. My secret kept me apart." "After one bad experience I toyed with relationships. *Every* relationship." "Being sensitive to criticism, I couldn't put myself out there for people to know." "I find yucky ways to get the upper hand and feel superior." "My Oran was jail. That's a hard way to learn the value of the community you blew off." Ah, Camus muses, "Go all the way . . . dissolve in love . . . vanish in fulfillment" (*Notebooks 1951–1959*). These philosophical survivors of plague understand now what Camus knew—that each of us must establish the communities that allow us to make our own way out of Oran.

Yes, life is hard. Oh, but yes, the struggle paves the way for extraordinary riches. I can make something of myself. "I can negate everything . . . except this desire for unity, this need for clarity and cohesion" (*The Myth of Sisyphus and Other Essays*). I want to know the world honestly, to dive into it with gusto, and to strive to meet my own high standards of responsibility. I can stare at apathy without flinching . . . putting one dogged foot in front of the other, Rieux-like; serving without question in a Grand way; treasuring friendship and candor as Tarrou; accepting my weaknesses and resuming my work in the community Rambert-style; acknowledging the Cottard in me and resisting self-defeating isolation. "Everything considered, a determined soul will always manage" (*The Myth of Sisyphus and Other Essays*).

A Letter to the Editor

Would Camus pen under his byline that *our* time is "the century of fear," as he wrote on November 19, 1946? Look at your world; look at our world. Where can you point to the triumph of brotherhood, of sisterhood? What hard-won accomplishments of smaller and larger communities can you toast? Still, the old questions linger. . . . Where is the plague virus festering today? Where has community fractured? Where is self-pity trumping responsibility? Do we ask much of ourselves and often become "better than we are" (*Notebooks 1942–1951*)? Do we turn difficulties into opportunities for combining forces?

Imagine the letter you would write today to the dedicated editor of *Combat*. What about belonging? What about "the beauty of the world and of people's faces" (*Camus at Combat*)? What matters, after all?

> *If I see myself as part of the living body of the earth,*
> *I will see myself as connected to other persons, animals,*
> *and the earth itself.*
> —RITA MANNING, *Speaking from the Heart*

Imagine a patchwork quilt extending endlessly in all directions. Each piece is essential to the whole; if one patch rips away the entire quilt unravels. Despite the vast distance seemingly separating all the many squares, they are inextricably, inevitably linked. For San Jose State University philosophy professor Rita Manning, the earth is much like this quilt. Human caring is the thread that stitches our world together; regardless of the immense physical spaces between us, everything exists in relationship. Manning's focus ranges from social and political philosophy to business and medical ethics. She fortifies her laser-sharp critical analysis with her extensive background in history, law, music, and drama. Whatever issue she tackles, whether corporate destruction of our environment and its tie to poverty, human rights problems in the aftermath of Katrina, or the immediate cry for animal rights, she applies her compassionate feminist ethic of active caring.

According to Manning, human beings are embedded in a network of relationships and "our self-identity is . . . a function of our role in these complex interconnections" (*Speaking from the Heart*). Our welfare depends on sustaining our relationships and belonging to communities of all kinds.

While Camus focuses on the human community and social justice, Manning extends her concern to the earth and all its inhabitants. This global community serves as the parent for all communities; all humans find their common ground beneath their feet. Because we belong to the earth, we must fulfill our responsibilities by caring for it and its creatures; *everything* qualifies for consideration. We *are* wrapped into the fabric of the world, and it is through active engagement that we hang out our shingles and make our home.

Earth First

Philosophers of diverse ages and backgrounds are grabbed immediately by Manning's approach to personal responsibility; they are attracted by her focusing first on the significance of the world as community and second on human connections. Our obligation to care for one another originates in our kinship with *everything*. *All* is interwoven; human attachments are not the only ones. Appreciating the natural world as home to everything makes human relationships obvious in a fresh way for many philosophers. "Who cares about some parts of their body but not others!" "I warmed to human contact only after I started to work at the wildlife sanctuary." "If we experience our connection to everything from rivers to bees, then our connection to humans, too, will be apparent." The most common student description of Manning's "earth first" approach: "nonthreatening." Marine life links to polar ice caps; you link to me. Let's follow Manning's lead, working our way into human communities after locating our individual patches in the earth's quilt.

"An ethic of care is holistic. . . . It assumes an underlying picture of the earth as one body, and of ourselves as part of this body" (*Speak-*

ing from the Heart). Awe sweeps through me at this heart-quickening realization. I have a part in the big show! It's high time I learn my lines by heart and not let the rest of the cast down. Manning calls for a refreshed, eye-opening understanding of "my place as a member of the natural world" in which I "face my fellow creatures with humility" (*Speaking from the Heart*). If I am to experience relationship and to reinforce it when it weakens, it's essential that I get to know my relatives. I ought to *look* at the swan's feathers, *listen* to the creek, *recognize* the hawk's colors, *appreciate* the texture of the leaves. I must "make the attempt to relate honestly with the natural world" (*Speaking from the Heart*). My roots are entangled in the family of all things; the better I understand this interrelation, the more surely I will be moved to care. Environmental activism and personal responsibility spring from the revival of this conscious affinity with all. Since our decisions affect the one body, we must act with care; "we will not be able to continue with our policies of wanton destruction" (*Speaking from the Heart*). Each of us is obligated to honor the world itself and to welcome our place in its tapestry.

Laments of our disconnect from the natural world echo wherever my philosophical travels take me. "I feel no connection between the food I eat and its origins in the earth. It's like it grows on supermarket shelves." "I can go for days and never see a blade of grass." "I was taught that humans are superior and I act that way." "Why would I care about something I know nothing about? My knowledge of nature comes from high school textbooks." We must "find the earth," Manning chides, in order to restore our most fundamental relationship; indeed, alienated from the earth, I lose my home. I am uprooted and adrift, exposed to the plague of separation. Often our disheartening revelations lead us toward a promising, quite unexpected insight: fractured human relationships very likely stem from this earth-human disconnect. Wait! Perhaps if I look more closely at the sky, if I walk along the shore and notice the shells and the rocks in detail, then my sense of belonging will embrace humans, as well. Hmmm . . . Maybe if we appreciate the earth in *all* its aspects, we can gradually slip into treating one another better. Admiring the sunset, our anger cools. Protecting the eagle and the tiger, we look out for our "first" cousins, as well. Manning gives each of us the charge; I now know that I must become more sensitive to all that is. It is my responsibility to cultivate a more caring disposition. "It might, if widely adopted, make the world a better place" (*Speaking from the Heart*). Look at the whiskers on that catfish. The redwood's girth stokes my curiosity. That worm has been crawling all afternoon. Awe. Respect. Gratitude. Care. Look! Look! Opossum. Metal. Pigeon. Morning glories. And soon . . . this person, that person, and me. Reunion.

Community

Yes, my keen awareness of belonging in and to the earth invigorates my appreciation for human connections. I am newly convinced of the inherent value of all relationship; I am cradled in an intricate web that gives me life. Aha. Of course obligation comes with the rewards of relationship. All streets are two-way and I must reorient myself to this interconnected world. Nap time is over. Now the project of making myself a caring person has my full attention. Repeated acts of caring will develop a natural tendency to respond to any situation caringly. As I hone my sense of relationship, my sympathetic identification with others guides me more instinctively. My social interactions feed on the connective tissue that glues us together. Like dominoes falling, caring action leaves more care in its wake; "when we feel loved and cared for we naturally respond with sympathy to presentations of need" (*Speaking from the Heart*). Genuine efforts at compromise and accommodation soften my stance in dealing with others. Unbending, cocksure, often extreme positions divide us into enemy camps. It may not be possible to please all the members of a group, "but a compromise that accommodates everyone is less rare than we think" (*Speaking from the Heart*). Loggers and environmental activists *both* care about the health of the forests. Farmers and consumers *both* care about the soil. Dissenting votes at a school board meeting are cast by *all* those with children's interests at heart.

Everyone faces tough choices and seemingly impossible situations that demand resolution. Manning provides no abstract theory guaranteed to provide yes-or-no answers. Life is complicated. My "solutions" gradually emerge when I ask what my *ideal* caring self would do. The more I toss myself into the world, active and caring, the more obvious my responses appear. All sorts of relationship await my full-bodied tending. Some evolve from certain roles: parent, teacher, employer, animal "owner," lover, neighbor. At times, caring involves me with people and places I will never see: a VA hospital, a rain forest, political protest against military action. Active commitment to the welfare of a community uplifts all its members. And because caring is my compass, I take care of myself with devotion. I indulge in fulfilling activities and I relish my life.

A Home for One . . . A Home for All

For Manning, the harsh reality of homelessness poses an absolutely unacceptable dilemma for *all*. "A sense of place, or belonging, is missing" for some because "our overall undervaluing of community" (*Speaking from the Heart*) goes undetected. Are those human forms I see sleeping in the churchyard over there not part of "our" web of relationship? The desperate need for all humans to belong to community is evidenced in the "tent cities" that spring up among the homeless. Every homeless neighbor proves that we live in a "precaring" world. *Be* care full. Strangling poverty is robbing many in our human family of a place to belong, a home *right now*. Manning proclaims homelessness in this country "a damning indictment of social policy . . . which leaves poor people struggling madly to keep their families afloat" (*Speaking from the Heart*). Look.

Manning leaves us with marvelous opportunities yet real obligations. Students are quick to agree with her that many institutions and practices must be challenged and changed. "This college ought to have a day care center. How can it claim to provide open access unless every parent can attend?" "This is not a 'humane society' unless we mandate that all animal shelters have a 'no kill' policy." "How indecent that those who teach in this city cannot afford to live in it." But, remember, the ethic of care nudges: "The school district cut the funds for the one-on-one reading program, but we can still volunteer as a group." "We used to stock canned goods in a big shed at my church for *anyone* in need in the community. Some carpentry and paint and we can open again in no time."

Can we all bask in the warmth of belonging? Manning's vision requires hard work and humble commitment. Her ethic of care prods and pokes and invites. Life deals each of us a hand. You in?

DISCUSSION QUESTIONS

- What is belonging? What are its essential ingredients?
- Where do you belong? What does "home" mean to you?
- What defines a community? Is community membership valuable to you? Why?
- What is the meaning of responsibility? Do you approach responsibilities as opportunities? Burdens? Give examples.
- Do you think that you must earn your place in the world? What is the price of belonging?

- How do you strike a balance between the need for solitude and privacy and the desire to belong and contribute to community?
- Do you agree with Camus that camaraderie alleviates the difficulties inherent in the human condition?
- What qualities do you have to offer in relationship? What attributes would you like to develop that would enhance your participation in all communities?
- Do you find it natural to compromise? Do you possess extreme views that set you apart in stubborn isolation? How can you relate better to those with whom you disagree?
- What are the rewards of "pitching in" and doing your part? Do you find that shared, shoulder-to-shoulder effort improves your humanity? Yes? How?
- Have you experienced the web of relationship that connects everything? When? Can you think of a person or a thing existing in isolation? Who or what?
- Is Manning's "ethic of care" a sound guide for your decision-making? Would your life and the larger world benefit if this ethic were your daily approach?
- Is it possible to live without affecting others? If so, how? If not, what does this realization mean to you?
- What is your definition of plague? What is your proposed cure?
- What is your definition of caring? Will it create and support community? Do you include yourself among those you envelop in care?
- What one piece of Camus' philosophy now belongs to you? Manning's?

HOMEWORK

Listen and Hum

Enjoy the spirit of community as you listen to music together. Invite Manning and Camus, comment freely, replay favorite pieces, and gain insights into belonging without having to try. Music relies on and fosters relationship, the perfect hostess for our topic.

A Sense of Place

- Bill Frisell's jazz guitar welcomes an intercontinental mix of "Good Old People," and this eclectic group of musicians from Brazil, Mali, Los Angeles, Greece, and New York make music that's at home anywhere. Brazilian vocals meet pedal steel guitar meets bouzouki joins with snare drum and violin. "We Are Everywhere," they play, everyone respectfully and joyfully included in a group without an obvious "star." Listen as the musicians connect through their instruments and form one relationship, one sound improvised from a variety of distinctive world sounds. To what new places does this music take you?

- From her youth in the fifties at the Tropicana Club in Havana through her ongoing international performances, Omara Portuondo carries Cuba's history and heart on perfect pitch. Solo, bolero, duet, or group, her voice conveys the rhythmic beat of music that is distinctly Cuban. "We should not dwell / on love that is past," she sings in "Veinte Años," paying tribute to legendary Cuban composer María Teresa Vera. Portuondo takes us home with her accompanied by the rich array of Cuban musicians in the Buena Vista Social Club. Describe the homeland that is captured by her voice.

- Book a trip to Finland with Jean Sibelius, the perfect tour guide. Hunger for independence from Russia prompted an outpouring of Finnish patriotism at the turn of the twentieth century, and Sibelius celebrates his country's history and landscape and Finns' deeply rooted pride of place in *Finlandia*. Flip through photographs of his homeland as you listen to his music, passing through Helsinki, Oulu, Tampere. What piece of music takes *you* home?

- The members of Phish are at home wherever they go, and welcome home their family of fans, heads bobbing in unison with the beat, at every concert. Most of their recordings are "live," proof that the "Free" interplay between band and audience is part of the music: "Swimming weightless in the womb / bouncing gently round the room." This crew with roots in Vermont joins with Vermont-based Ben & Jerry's and contributes the royalties from the sale of Phish Food ice cream to support environmental protection of "their" Lake Champlain.

- "Will the Circle Be Unbroken / by and by, by and by?" June Carter Cash sings in tribute to her very own "First Family of Country Music." You can picture the Carter family returning from church and gathered for a Sunday afternoon on the back porch, singing the old tunes and picking at the banjo and autoharp, heel-stompin' with the harmonica and tickling the guitar. June always stays true to the traditional folk music and the distinctive twang of Maces Springs, Virginia, whether performing as part of Mother Maybelle and the Carter Sisters or in duet with her husband, Johnny, in Hollywood or onstage at the Grand Ole Opry in Nashville. How does the Carter family welcome you into their circle?

Stepping Out with Camus

- Ben Harper endorses Camus' insistence that each of us must work to improve society, singing that he can make it better, kinder, brighter, and safer "With My Own Two Hands." Harper promises to help the whole human race, one at a time, "but you got to use / use your own two hands" as well. When we have others' assurance of their best efforts and can feed on their confidence, are we more likely to join in? Is activism contagious?

- "If Not Now . . ." then when? Tracy Chapman demands. Procrastination is an unaffordable luxury; this moment, this day is ours to seize. How can we overcome the shrugged shoulders of dormant good intentions? "A love declared for days to come / is as good as none." Name one responsibility that calls to you *now*. What is your answer, *now*?

- Sarah McLachlan understands that "hearts are worn in these dark ages"; huge problems overwhelm our better instincts and leave us feeling powerless. But there is a "World on Fire" and we need to fuel our resolve and hear the call to "bring it to the table / bring what I am able." Do you agree with her that the less we give, the less we are? What do you have to bring to the table? Who can you invite to work alongside you?

- Jazz pianist Keith Jarrett calls on his Nordic friends to explore the meaning of "Belonging," and they chat about it together on drums, saxophone, and bass. Jan, Jon, and Palle plant their Scandinavian roots in a soulful conversation with Jarrett and his piano. What do the members of this quartet accomplish musically that any social group would do well to emulate? Name the ingredients of their cooperative playing. Does this tune earn its title?

Getting Together with Manning

- "People Get Ready"! Aretha Franklin blows a loud whistle because "there's a train a-comin'" and "there's hope for all" who love. Hurry to board this train bound for the promised land; the only ones left behind will be those who live selfishly at others' expense. "I believe," she intones, and Curtis Mayfield's lyrics gain momentum as Aretha encourages a big social movement. In what kind of world do you want to live? Are you working to create it?

- Franz Schubert composed lovely music to the delight of his circle of friends in nineteenth-century Austria. Imagine the composer at the piano playing for a merry social gathering, aptly coined a "Schubertiad" by his cohorts. Much of his music was performed only in these intimate settings during his short life; Schubert relished the bonhomie of his supporters as they accompanied him on various instruments and often sang along. His community sustained him emotionally and financially, and Schubert was devoted to this small and faithful audience. Share apple strudel, cheese Danish, and coffee at your Schubertiad, listening to "Gretchen at the Spinning Wheel" and "The Shepherd on the Rock."

- "It's time to overcome our fears . . . the time has come to be a family." Barbra Streisand reminds us that all our hearts beat "At the Same Time." We could build a world together if we acknowledged our similarities . . . our faces, our hands, our dreams, our loves. Why are we afraid? What scares us out of belonging? What fears can you dispel so that you can sing with her, "saying yes, creating unity" (Camus, *Notebooks 1951–1959*)?

- Giacomo Puccini assembles a community of struggling artists in Paris's Latin Quarter, and his *La Bohème* serves as a revered celebration of the ties of belonging. In his Italian opera we meet robust young bohemians in the chilly garret that always calls them home. Landlord issues threaten to spoil Christmas Eve for the poet Rudolfo, the painter Marcello, the musician Schaunard, and Colline, the resident philosopher; still, no matter what, they belong to one another, and they welcome the ailing Mimì into their family. Luciano Pavarotti singing "Che gelida manina" both stops and thrills the heart, as does Mirella Freni's "Sono andati." Some one hundred years after its premiere in 1896, Puccini's score inspires Jonathan Larson's musical *Rent*, and our bohemians resettle in the East Village of Manhattan. Still facing poverty and the new plague of AIDS, Christmas Eve nevertheless finds them toasting the "Seasons of Love." Despite hard lives, they sing that "We're Okay." Why does relationship supply such comfort? What do you learn from Colline on the Parisian Left Bank and his alter ego, the philosopher Tom, in the back alleys of the Village?

Recite and Write

Read the following poems prior to your meeting. Jot down your immediate responses to each one in your journals. Incorporate the title of one of these works into your own poem of belonging. Take turns reciting the poems and toss your creation into the mix.

- "Unspeakably I have belonged to you, from the first," Rainer Maria Rilke responds to the world in praise and gratitude. What a privilege to be "at one with the earth" that calls to us always to participate in its beauty. Know the essence of things deep in your being, intensely attentive to a bridge, a fruit-bearing tree, a windowpane. Everything matters. Just one spring is enough to convince Rilke of the world's majesty. Can you identify with the sense of belonging conveyed in his mystical swing dance with the earth in the Ninth Duino Elegy?

- Manning suggests that the better we know the world, the more readily we honor its interwoven tapestry. Elizabeth Bishop discovers instant rapport with "The Fish" she catches and pulls alongside her rented boat. "Battered and venerable" with strips of skin "like ancient wallpaper," her captured fish displays five old hooks grown like trophies into his lower jaw. She stares long and hard at her prisoner, looking into his large eyes; the day itself becomes a rainbow and she releases him into the water. Poet and fish are related. How can such intimate discoveries of kinship enhance an ethic of care? When have you experienced a similar and unexpected relationship?

- Marge Piercy seeks "To Be of Use" in the quiet yet fiercely determined way of people who "jump into work head first," throwing their full weight into the things that need doing without hesitation. She professes loving admiration for those who harness their collective energies and patiently inch forward with dedication to humanity's tasks. Such labor "has a shape that satisfies, clean and evident." Piercy insists that our souls cry out for the opportunity to pay our lifetime dues for belonging to the world. Do you agree with her that being of use is fulfilling? Discuss a time that your contribution to community left you clean and gratified.

- Camus has a soulmate in Carl Sandburg, American child of Swedish immigrants, Chicago newspaperman, author of children's stories and political biographies, folk songs and poems, plus a book of commentary on the Second World War. Sandburg rejoices unabashedly in "The People, Yes," his 1936 testimonial to the "vast huddle . . . of the Family of Man." Feel your heart swell with Sandburg's as he extols our capacity to endure, to renew, and to bounce back from all manner of mistakes and difficulties. His poem sings in 107 sections; enjoy it in its entirety and choose two sections to recite at your gathering. Sandburg loves the feeling of belonging that radiates from festive get-togethers and the invigoration and fresh hope that comes from lining up side by side. "The people march," in step, through grief into gradual fulfillment of human promise. Do you join Sandburg in his chorus of "Yes"? Why does he find his anchor in the mass of humanity? Do you take pride in belonging to the "Family"?

- Being alive to cross a sun-streaked, icy stream in September delights Gary Snyder. The music of the creek is also the music of his heart, and his union with the natural world floods his soul. The grateful poet pledges loyalty to the soil and to the one splendid ecosystem so rich "in diversity," and he promises his allegiance "with joyful interpenetration 'For All.'" Can you allow your heart to be penetrated by a mossy bank and stones underfoot? Do such immediate experiences of the natural world awaken responsibility?

- A man wakes from his regular all-night overnight on the subway train, carefully folding his blanket and dressing with dignity in his "antique blazer." "Tell Me" how it comes to this, Anne Pierson Wiese implores, that this man clothes himself in front of a world that has disowned him. Perhaps he is comfortable in his public dressing car because life has unveiled for him its greatest secret, "that all our secrets from one another are imaginary." Respond to the poet's tender regard for her fellow passenger. Does he intuitively know the secret of belonging? Do we know one another better than we think?

Read and Talk

- Ashoke Ganguli settles on a name most dear to him for his firstborn, "Gogol," and his son's struggle to fit into two cultures ripples through each page of Jhumpa Lahiri's novel *The Namesake*. Gogol finds comfort in Bengali culture and traditions while at the same time rejecting them for American cool. On his last return to his childhood home on Pemberton Road, Gogol is touched as never before by his parents' bravery in leaving family and friends behind in Calcutta, while "he had spent years maintaining distance from his origins." At book's end, grown-up Gogol exults at connecting with his father again, bound to him by his inscription in a book given as a birthday present decades ago. "The name he had so detested, here hidden and preserved," now stands as a symbol of his father's many gifts. Can you relate to the complex meaning of home for Gogol? Where does he belong? The taste of his mother's mincemeat croquettes . . .

- An incredible saga unfolds as a nine-year-old girl from Uganda leaves her loving family behind and grows up and away to further her education in Arkansas. Many hands join in support of Beatrice Biira. Members of a community church in Niantic, Connecticut, buy goats for African villages via the long reach of charitable activities sponsored by Heifer International. Milk sales from her family's goat allow Beatrice to go to elementary school. Her hard work was rewarded by scholarships to high schools in Uganda

and Massachusetts, and finally to the site of her undergraduate degree from Connecticut College. Twenty Heifer
International donors finance her living expenses along the
way. In 2008 Beatrice is earning her master's degree from
the Clinton School of Public Service in Little Rock, plan-
ning her eventual return to Africa to assist women in winning financial independence. The young girl has done her
beloved goat Mugisa quite proud in the years since Page
McBrier's and Lori Lohstoeter's 2000 publication of *Beatrice's Goat*. With how many lives worldwide is Beatrice's
interwoven?

- Home is *A Place to Come To* for Jed Tewksbury in Robert
Penn Warren's story of this man's hard-won homecoming.
Despite his academic success and notoriety, Jed founders
in isolation wherever he goes. Returning to Dugton, Ala-
bama, after his mother's death, he enters his childhood
home in a daze, fixing on newly familiar objects such as
"the black and white China bulldog on the mantel . . . the
crocheted antimacassar things . . . the box of cards."
Clutching his suitcase, Jed is struck by the realization that
"I was returning to my final self, my lost self," and "had
the wild impulse to lie on the earth between the two
graves, the old and the new, and stretch out a hand to
each." What does Jed know now? Can we belong to times
and places that are neither happy nor especially loving
and find truth and personal meaning therein? Why does
the world traveler return to Dugton, when Perk dies, to
"try to figure out why things had all turned out the way
they had"?

- "Animal time and human time swirled together" at the
Warsaw Zoo in Poland during the Nazi occupation in
1943. Jan Zabinski, the director of the zoo, and Antonina,

The Zookeeper's Wife, provide refuge for Jews and Polish resisters as well as their beloved animals in Diane Ackerman's passionately written and researched testimonial to the human spirit. She finds her first inspiration in Antonina's diary, the entries filled with evidence of the Zabinskis' unassuming goodwill. They mingled with their Jewish neighbors before the war, and the zookeepers find it natural to turn their villa and the animals' cages into a safe house. Though they shoulder incomprehensible responsibility, Jan states simply: "I don't understand the fuss. If any creature is in danger, you save it, human or animal." What lessons from the Zabinskis can you apply in your daily life? What does Rabbi Shapira preach? Why do the members of Zegota rescue Jews?

- The desperately poor belong to Dr. Paul Farmer and he belongs to them, a relationship fostered as Farmer climbs *Mountains Beyond Mountains* in Tracy Kidder's riveting account. "Healing the World" no longer seems an empty phrase as Farmer turns his specialization in infectious diseases and a doctorate in anthropology into a bustling hospital and medical center in rural Haiti, as well as a fight against tuberculosis in Peru and Siberia. A network of donors sustains his Partners in Health charitable foundation. Kidder recalls: "What struck me . . . was how happy he seemed with his life." Why might Farmer be happy despite his grinding schedule of travel and doctoring? Do you agree with his philosophy that "the only real nation is humanity"? With Camus that "the sight of human pride is unequaled" (*The Myth of Sisyphus and Other Essays*)?

- The phrase "For you, a thousand times over" binds Afghani lives—Hassan, and his best friend, Amir—from start to finish in Khaled Hosseini's story of *The Kite Runner*. Although

Amir betrays their friendship, Hassan's loyalty knows no bounds. As a boy he safeguards their prized kite and endures a brutal beating as a result; as an adult he takes his father's place as caretaker of Amir's family home and thereby suffers the wrath of the Taliban. Now a successful writer in America, Amir seizes the opportunity "to be good again" and to reciprocate Hassan's fidelity. He returns to Afghanistan in a desperate attempt to locate Hassan's son and bring the boy home with him. Amir and his wife cannot break into Sohrab's broken heart until their first kite-flying expedition. As Amir scampers to collect the boy's kite with a familiar look over his shoulder, he cements the unspoken love linking many lives spanning two generations. Why does he agree to Rahim Khan's entreaty to return home? Why does Sohrab belong to Amir?

Watch and Reflect

• "All people belong to a we except me," laments twelve-year-old Frankie, "an unjoined person" in Carson McCullers's *The Member of the Wedding*. She suffers constant rejection from the neighborhood clubhouse, screaming after the in crowd cutting through her yard after a meeting: "Why didn't you elect me? Why can't I be a member?" When her older brother announces his upcoming nuptials, Frankie fantasizes that she will also belong to the union of Jarvis and Janis: "They are the we of me." She overlooks her daily kitchen community; housekeeper Berenice Sadie Brown faithfully keeps "supper on the stove and pie in the icebox," and young John Henry lovingly emulates his much-admired older neighbor. Unable to appreciate her bonded community of three, Frankie longs desperately for world travel with the married couple when they will be "members of the world." She imagines belonging to a world in which "we'll just walk right up to people and know them right away." Only Berenice grieves at the breakup of the kitchen trio. Can you identify with Frankie's longing? Have you overlooked authentic connections that matter? "Why should my heart be lonely?" Frankie wonders. Think of important reasons that you can say "we."

• Israeli filmmaker Danae Elon takes *Another Road Home* to find her roots in Palestinian community. She was reared from infancy for twenty years by Musa, and her search to reconnect with her Palestinian guardian begins with his children in the United States. She traces the path of members of the Obeidallah family, following leads and immersing herself in the Palestinian neighborhoods of Paterson, New Jersey. The warmth of recognition finally lights the faces of Danae and Musa's sons. "You were part of his life," one son recalls, and Danae confirms his central place in her heart. She is introduced at the grand opening of "Prospect Pharmacy," an Obeidallah family enterprise, as "a friend of the family." Danae and Musa's boys struggle together to grasp their youths in the backdrop of the Arab–Israeli conflict, as well as their parents' absence. Amos and Beth, Danae's parents, allowed Musa to become the formative presence in their daughter's life; Musa traded time with his own children for the employment that assured them a prosperous future. Swapping memories and looking for "home," they resolve to bring Musa to the United States; Beth makes the much-anticipated phone call. The Elon and Obeidallah families belong to each other as they welcome him to "family dinner"; gratitude for Musa's love, now and then, creates a new community out of old relationships. After two months Musa longs to return home, and Danae accompanies her seventy-six-year-old relation on his return to his community. Why was she driven to reconnect with him? How many homes does Musa own?

Get Up and Do

- Instead of *Bowling Alone*, "we Americans need to reconnect with one another," Robert Putnam insists in his challenging work published in 2000. He explores in painstaking detail the disintegration of social ties and civic engagement in the latter part of the twentieth century. "Henry Ward Beecher's advice a century ago to 'multiply picnics' is not entirely ridiculous today. We should do this, ironically, not because it will be good for America—though it will be—but because it will be good for us." Spend an evening together, freely discussing the rewards of philosophizing with others on a regular basis. What has this commitment brought to your individual lives? What distinguishes the give-and-take of philosophical dialogue from "philosophizing alone"? Would you recommend multiplying clubs such as yours? Why? What do you foresee?

- Research the history of national and international charitable efforts sponsored by Heifer International. Philosophers of all ages discover ways to contribute to their neighbors near and far. Decide on a project of particular interest to members of your group. Enjoy the connections made through your efforts.

- Check out Paul Farmer's Partners in Health. Consider joining the partnership individually and/or collectively.

- Make art together. Represent the meaning of belonging through collage, a sand castle, a tile mosaic, a rock sculpture.

- Discuss the meaning of responsibility. Have all members

of the group make a list of things for which they are responsible, well balanced by a list of things for which they are not responsible. Be mindful of obligations assumed needlessly; breathe. Be aware of responsibilities overlooked; breathe.

- Think of someone you know who suffers as an outsider. Simply, quietly, lend a sense of belonging.
- "We now live in an age of idolatry of the Self . . . we shouldn't be surprised if civility has suffered." What is your response to this statement by P. M. Forni in *Choosing Civility*? What is civility? Discuss the importance of civil behavior in our interpersonal relationships. How can each of us contribute to "considerate conduct"? Discuss the lack of basic manners so obvious in everyday exchanges. Give simple examples. Work together on a good definition of rudeness. Offer unacceptable examples of this prevalent social illness. Is there ever an excuse for rudeness?
- Devote a special meeting to the topic of belonging. Everyone invite a guest to introduce to your philosophy club. Divide into smaller groups of new acquaintances for a discussion of the meaning and importance of community.
- Reflect on the relationships that reaffirm your sense of being at home on the planet. Tend, especially, to one tie today.

Resources

Music
- *Intercontinentals* by Bill Frisell: "Good Old People," "We Are Everywhere."
- *The Buena Vista Social Club Presents Omara Portuondo* by Omara Portuondo: "Veinte Años."
- *Sibelius: Tone Poems*, Göteborgs Symfoniker, Neeme Järvi conducting: *Finlandia*.
- *Live in Brooklyn* by Phish: "Free" (CD or DVD).

- *Press On* by June Carter Cash: "Will the Circle Be Unbroken."
- *Diamonds on the Inside* by Ben Harper: "With My Own Two Hands."
- *Tracy Chapman* by Tracy Chapman: "If Not Now."
- *Afterglow* by Sarah McLachlan: "World on Fire."
- *Belonging* by Keith Jarrett: "Belonging."
- *Queen of Soul: Atlantic Recordings* by Aretha Franklin: "People Get Ready."
- *Schubert/Schumann—Songs*, Elly Ameling, soprano, Jörg Demus, piano: "Gretchen at the Spinning Wheel" and "The Shepherd on the Rock" by Franz Schubert.
- *Higher Ground* by Barbra Streisand: "At the Same Time."
- *La Bohème* by Giacomo Puccini, Berlin Philharmonic Orchestra, Herbert von Karajan conducting (CD).
- *Puccini: La Bohème* (Live from the Met), the Metropolitan Opera, Nicola Luisotti conducting, Franzo Zeffirelli production (DVD).
- *Rent* by Jonathan Larson (1996 Original Broadway Cast) (CD).
- *Rent* by Jonathan Larson, directed by Chris Columbus (DVD).

Poetry

- *The Selected Poetry of Rainer Maria Rilke*, edited and translated by Stephen Mitchell: "The Ninth Duino Elegy."
- *Elizabeth Bishop: Poems, Prose, and Letters*, edited by Robert Giroux and Lloyd Schwartz: "The Fish."
- *The Art of Blessing the Day: Poems with a Jewish Theme* by Marge Piercy: "To Be of Use."
- *The People, Yes* by Carl Sandburg.
- *No Nature: New and Selected Poems* by Gary Snyder: "For All."
- *Floating City: Poems* by Anne Pierson Wiese: "Tell Me."

Prose

- *The Namesake* by Jhumpa Lahiri.
- *Beatrice's Goat* by Page McBrier, illustrated by Lori Lohstoeter; "The Luckiest Girl" by Nicholas D. Kristof, *New York Times*, September 23, 2008.
- *A Place to Come To* by Robert Penn Warren.
- *The Zookeeper's Wife* by Diane Ackerman.
- *Mountains Beyond Mountains* by Tracy Kidder.
- *The Kite Runner* by Khaled Hosseini.
- *Bowling Alone* by Robert Putnam.
- *Choosing Civility* by P. M. Forni.

- *Camus at Combat* by Albert Camus, edited and annotated by Jacqueline Lévi-Valensi, translated by Arthur Goldhammer.
- *The Plague* by Albert Camus, translated by Stuart Gilbert.
- *The Myth of Sisyphus and Other Essays* by Albert Camus, translated by Justin O'Brien.
- *Albert Camus Notebooks 1935–1951*, translated by Philip Thody.
- *Albert Camus Notebooks 1942–1951*, translated by Justin O'Brien.
- *Albert Camus Notebooks 1951–1959*, translated by Ryan Bloom.
- *Speaking from the Heart* by Rita Manning.

Drama
- *The Member of the Wedding* by Carson McCullers, directed by Fred Zinnemann (VHS).

Documentary
- *Another Road Home*, directed by Danae Elon (DVD).

Serenity

❧

You can't know it, but you can be it, at ease in your own life.

—Lao Tzu, *Tao Te Ching*

THE TOPIC

Heads bow and shake from side to side, the possibility of a serene life denied and dismissed outright by wistful thinkers beginning their exploration of the topic. Talking at the same time, speaking over one another, the disclaimers go something like this: "The world isn't like it used to be. Our lifestyles make serenity impossible. I don't know anyone whom I would call 'serene.' Maybe when I'm older; maybe when I was younger." Their comments echo with assured authority. As conversation slows, however, faces soon wear regret. Why the hasty denial? When has life ever been easy? Where can we point to people lucky enough to enjoy tranquil lives? Certainly not our philosophers on this topic, one having suffered as a Roman slave and the other having lived during China's Period of the Warring States. With all our time-saving products . . . the riding mower, microwave, answering machine, cruise control . . . shouldn't *we* have a better opportunity, now more than ever, for a serene life?

I picture an appliance from yesteryear, the old-fashioned pressure cooker, its handle clasped in my grandmother's hands. Our lives often resemble that cooker, the pressure building and the whistle about to blow. As a teacher I see repeated evidence that this pressure begins in childhood. When I gather with child philosophers for an investigation of the meaning of education, I always ask: "Can you tell me why you are in school? What happens here?" They sit quietly; it seems the harder they think the more quietly they sit. Surely, this is a trick question! "Come on," I encourage, "you wait on the corner for the school bus five days a week and lug those heavy backpacks to your desk. You're here for six hours or so, and then you climb back on the bus with homework to do for the next day. Can't you tell me why?" Children, somewhat puzzled themselves by their eventual answer yet pretty sure that it is correct, offer some variation of this response almost every time: "I go to school so I can get a job." We laugh together when I exclaim: "But you're only in the second grade!" Real pressure hangs on scrunched shoulders, however, and so many children are weary so soon. What is the source of their anxiety? Another example of the early onset of stress: During a discussion of serenity at a PTO meeting, a parent exhaled fatigue as she described the whirlwind of activities that toss her younger daughter and her from place to place. "Swimming and birthday parties, playdates and piano lessons and on and on." It sounded dreadful. Trying to picture them together in the car, I asked, "How old is your daughter?" Pausing, she smiled at her answer and led us in a hearty group laugh. "She's almost three." And it continues as we grow older. I watch as my college students manufacture self-imposed pressure, matching their full-time jobs with full-time coursework. How can they possibly expect to fulfill *either* task well? "Why are you doing this?" I ask, over and over. "So that I won't get more behind than I already am," I hear, day in, day out. "Behind what?" I chide affectionately. We laugh, but my office fills with their subdued panic.

Most of us accept such go-go pressure. We're oblivious to its damage until the harm is done, and though we may question it at times, we remain on the move. Let's stop for (just!) a moment. Philosophy is born in clear minds steeped in serenity, and reflection and respectful dialogue will depend forever upon this mental calm. *Is* a serene life desirable? Can't we enjoy full *and* serene lives? Have we exaggerated the obstacles barring us from tranquil days? Why not pursue serenity? Wait. Pursue serenity? *Where* is it? *What* is serenity?

Serenity is the possession of a steady spirit that provides a consistent way of being in the world no matter what. This steadiness is rooted in an unflappable inner sanctuary that has room for both sadness and joy. Possessing this essentially undisturbed core does not imply a happy or carefree life nor preclude difficulty and heartache. Up in the morning . . . aware . . . steady . . . living . . . steady . . . day's end . . . steady. Disappointment, adventure, surprise all come and go; deep within, all is calm. This serene constancy is not flashy yet its magnetic force is irresistible. Calm is contagious; a tranquil atmosphere is restorative. Serenity is good for the body. It wears well on the face.

Better understanding of each of the philosophical topics we address in this book will contribute to serenity. We have been sneaking up on it, bit by bit, the path to tranquillity clearer and nearer. Simplicity is a prerequisite for the breath of serenity as it slows the spin of busy lives. Self-respect stemming from personal integrity brings peace to the individual just as belonging in community grants comfort. Freedom from self-absorption broadens our perspective and opens possibilities. Greater flexibility prevents stagnation in our intellectual and emotional lives. Better communication establishes ties that create empathy automatically. Simplicity, communication, perspective, flexibility, empathy, individuality, belonging . . . all set the table for serenity's appearance. Joy basks in its presence. Ahh. Pressure slows to a simmer.

Serenity comes naturally—if we let it. Clenched jaws and frozen brows can thaw, darting eyes and tense grips can relax . . . if we let them. Doesn't tranquillity spread within as you take a walk, dig in the garden, or gaze out the window? A friend, the owner of a fish store, continually shares his astonishment at the number of customers who purchase fish tanks "prescribed" by their physicians. "Sit for twenty minutes twice a day and watch the fish." Another friend, the owner of a nursery, packs cars with plants and seedlings to a familiar refrain: "I'm told this will be good therapy." Do we need "experts" to tell us that we are too hard on ourselves? Fish and flowers are medicine. They remind us that we are part of the world—*part* of the world with *one* part to play.

Circumstances vary and serenity may be hard to imagine in some lives. Still, tranquillity and turmoil can coexist, serving as lesson and reminder. Appreciating its value and making the choice to cultivate serenity is the beginning. Far from being a keepsake to have and to hold, tranquillity is won through awareness, good judgment, and practice. It takes work to uncover our quiet haven. Difficulty is real; escape is neither possible nor always desirable. Bedrock calm *despite* hard times is good living.

Epictetus (eh-pic-TEE-tus) in ancient Rome and Lao Tzu (lau-DZU) in more ancient China partner perfectly. They assure us that the path to serenity lies within our reach if we remember that the world is big and that we are tiny. Reason is the tool that we can use to pry loose from *any* difficulty, promises Epictetus. We follow in Lao Tzu's steps by moving our feet to the beat of the world.

THE PHILOSOPHERS

Begin with little things . . . this is the price of a quiet mind.
—EPICTETUS, *Enchiridion*

First in Rome and then in his later years in northern Greece, Epic-tetus taught Stoic philosophy to grateful students. A philosophical approach with the twin goals of inspiring freedom from insecurity and enjoyment of a serene disposition, Stoicism was most popular in the Western world in the centuries before and after the turn of the first millennium. Its appeal eventually extended from Athens to Rome. Epictetus's life is testimony to the strength provided by his training in Stoic theory. A slave freed from years bound in shackles, he was forced to flee from his teaching in Rome due to yet another shift in the political power struggles that marked his times. No writ-ten works survive him beyond the *Enchiridion* (En-kih-RID-e-on), which he dictated to a student. The *Enchiridion* is a guide to conduct consisting of fifty-three short, straightforward sections collected in a pamphlet-sized handbook This manual celebrates the power of rea-son, asserting that serenity emerges from the human capacity to endure *everything* and the ability to persevere in *any* situation. Reason delivers tranquillity. Think.

Epictetus's practical philosophy *never* strayed from his worldview. Reason is the key to the universe itself and therefore it is our ticket to the good life. The cosmos in its entirety is one large rational being. The world spins on an axis of rational natural laws. Our reason reveals this natural cosmic harmony to us, and by being reasonable we can bring this same balance and harmony to our personal lives. Reason should dominate each response and motivate every action. Because we are part of a universe ruled by reason, a tranquil life is in keeping with this reality. We falter and suffer whenever emotion and desire drown out reason's counsel. A rational life is the *only* life that can endure as it is the *one* that carries us *with* life's current. We strug-gle endlessly against the nature of things without a steadfast mind. Imagine running fast in a footrace, as fast as you can . . . in the wrong direction. Whoa! Stop. Be reasonable and get back on track, Epic-tetus reminds us. A situation presents itself. Pause. "All your attention must be given to the mind" (*Enchiridion*). Develop a permanent character that deals with problems calmly and confidently. Find your groove.

Picture Epictetus walking with his pronounced, shackle-induced limp to a porch. He totes a worn satchel with a big handle and a strong shoulder strap to make the burden even lighter. Our handyman/teacher has a tool for any problem; his workmanship carries a lifetime guarantee. Wrench, filter, caulk, a pry bar . . . a philosopher's tools? Rolling his toga sleeves back, Epictetus focuses on his task: repair serenity. A trustworthy student describes the scene and records major points. We eavesdrop appreciatively.

Epictetus's Tool Bag

Before opening his toolbox, he swings it around by its sturdy handle while switching it from left to right hand and back. As we gather around him, he points to the handle and begins his talk. . . . This same handle has borne my baggage all my life. It withstands harsh weather and rough treatment from others. This old grip has never failed me. "Everything has two handles, one by which you can carry it, the other by which you cannot" (*Enchiridion*). Reason lightens all burdens. Control any dilemma through mastery of your response. Facing rejection? Going to the hospital? Hearing hurtful gossip? Too much to do? Needing to move? Losing a job? Ending a relationship? Choose reason's beefy handle to deal with the situation. "Wait a while, and give yourself pause" (*Enchiridion*). Think before you act.

What marvelous tools are hidden inside this sack? Epictetus pulls out each tool, slowly, one at a time.

First, he positions a level on a flat stone banister. The middle mark indicates perfect balance. Epictetus looks from the level to his audience and offers advice. Be careful not to disturb inner balance. A level is useful for distinguishing between events in life that are in our control and the many that are not. Level your life by making this critical distinction. Most of our worry is over things beyond our control. Do not give your serenity away to uncontrollable disturbances. Your mind will calm if you train yourself to be independent of things you can't change. The weather, the late train, the traffic, the forgotten birthday, the cost of a stamp, your employer's mood—our concerns baffle the repairman. Serenity is not a given; it takes practice. Forget what lies beyond your reach, the futile worries that tip your own life out of control. "And if you train yourself in this habit your impressions will not carry you away" (*Enchiridion*). Take note of the little things outside your influence—the neighbor's scraggly hedge, an interrupted conversation—and gradually your life will level as you let go. You can cope better with your powerlessness in the face of big events that you long to control if you practice with the little ones. Focus your energy where change is possible.

Hmmmm. A gauge? Epictetus explains this tool's role. A gauge can take the measure of all things. It is a device for determining the true nature of a thing. He picks up a clay object and asks, "What *is* this thing?" The gauge registers that it is a jug and it is in the nature of clay jugs to break. Understand this potential if you drop it. "What are *you*?" Epictetus points to a student. You are a human being, and dying is part of human nature. Remember this when faced with the hard loss of a loved one. Horses stumble. Wheels turn. Know the nature of each thing in the world. "For when once you go beyond the measure there is no limit" (*Enchiridion*). High winds and huge debts? What is their nature? What happens in crowded markets or on narrow escalators? Bumping and delay? Gauge it. Know it. Epictetus throws the ice water of a reasoned assessment at *every* situation. Stop pretending. See the world as it is.

Clippers poke from the toolbox. Epictetus snaps them in the air and recommends that we snip at our arrogance. Prune the vanity that drives you into unnecessary competition. Stop overreaching your potential. Accept your nature. Find your niche. Be reasonable about your strengths and weaknesses. "Consider first what it is you are undertaking; then look at your own powers and see if you can bear it" (*Enchiridion*). Think of all the frustrated professional athletes and rock stars. Imagine all the disappointed dreamers with envy for the Broadway actor and the moon-walking astronaut. Keep your clippers sharpened. Boasting is boring. Snip.

Next Epictetus peels a strip of masking tape from the box. Here is a sure way to prevent whining, he suggests. Apply the tape across your mouth, corner to corner, and quit complaining about your lot in life. Play the hand you are dealt with reason as your partner. Wishful thinking is useless; indeed, it is unrealistic and unsettling. Stop it. Do you have physical pain and limitation? My mind helps me overcome my chronic leg pain. I don't expect the pain to go away, but I have found a reasonable way to live with it and diminish its power. Why do you begrudge those who reap the fruits of their labors? Were you willing to study hard to earn the scholarship? No? Be quiet. Did you have the discipline to train and forgo all entertainment to make the team? No? Use tape. Mask your resentment. "You will be unjust then and insatiable if you wish to get these privileges for nothing, without paying their price" (*Enchiridion*). Live *your* life without regret.

Out comes a drill for Epictetus to make this crucial point bit by bit. Anger is a huge problem; it is serenity's chief nemesis. Anger saps us mentally and physically. Drill the realization home that anger is one thing that *is* in your control. How you respond to *any* event is completely within your power. It is *not* true that someone or something *made* you angry. Nothing in the world can anger you without your consent. If you give in to this emotion, you can at best say that you *allowed* yourself to become angry. "You trust your mind to the chance comer, and allow it to be disturbed and confounded if he revile you; are you not ashamed to do so?" (*Enchiridion*) Nothing shackles the mind without its permission.

Finally, Epictetus withdraws a hammer. Nails of all sizes tumble from his tote. The hammer's heft resounds as he bangs the first nail. Stabilize your perspective whenever it becomes shaky. Nail every situation with reason's judgment. Let me give you some examples. Epictetus pounds away. People make fun of my vocation as a philosopher? Given these times and priorities, I am not surprised at all; in fact, I expected that reaction. All sorts of gossip at my expense trickles back to me? I'll nail this backbiting by announcing that they must not know me very well if they couldn't think of anything else to say. My Stoic approach isn't always well received? Yes, but at least I am neither exiled nor dead. HA!

The Unshakable Strength of Reason

Reading the *Enchiridion*, it is clear that its author relied exclusively on reason. "When anything happens to you, always remember to turn to yourself and ask what faculty you have to deal with it" (*Enchiridion*). Epictetus's insistence that a strong mind is *the* path to a serene life, however, has both its admirers and its critics. What about the good times? His manual does not invite exuberance nor encourage emotion. One might argue that in Epictetus's approach problems are not so much solved as met head-on. A sense of resignation and caution laces this guide to survival. But Epictetus's philosophy must be viewed in light of his times. His handbook provided tools for his contemporaries to cope with the great adversity facing most people in the Western world. Life was very hard; survival coated in serenity was the goal. His Stoic model was that of a very reserved, modest person, mostly silent and speaking in few, carefully chosen words. No time was wasted on gossip; laughter was rare and controlled. Bare necessities sufficed. The same sober temperament greeted fame or ridicule. Passion was restrained. No show, no big expectations, no fear, full acceptance of the world.

Student testimony over many years confirms what I hear from first-time philosophers, as well—that Epictetus's toolbox is invaluable when confronting difficulty. I admit that while I enjoyed learning about him in college, I did not give Stoicism much thought until . . . life threw a curveball or two. Then I remembered Epictetus with new appreciation for his cool intelligence and calm acceptance of life as it is. He can help any hitter step back in the batter's box . . . awaiting the next pitch with confidence.

As we twist into a third millennium, Epictetus's dictation to his disciple retains its relevance. What a relief to know that our own minds can deliver tranquillity, that we can relax our futile grip on and nagging fear over things beyond our control. Anger is not inevitable; we can live without it. We are not at the mercy of our emotions; we are in charge. Even enormous difficulty can be endured. Serenity rests in reason's safety net.

> *Each separate being in the universe returns to the common source. Returning to the source is serenity.*
>
> —LAO TZU, *Tao Te Ching*

Soften your force, melt into the world, and let serenity wash over your life.

This irresistible invitation comes from a man of retirement age in ancient China. His job as keeper of village records at an end, Lao Tzu sought greater solitude far from the city and was ready to take his leave. Villagers were curious about this mysterious "old boy" whose solitary, "ordinary" life exuded extraordinary poise and strength. What is his secret? What does he know? Will he tell? Who *is* this fellow? Little is known about Lao Tzu yet legends abound. Did you hear that he was conceived by a shooting star? Born an old man with long white hair?

An alert gatekeeper at the town's edge stopped him as he rode away atop his water buffalo. He asked that Lao Tzu leave behind his recipe for life, a request that resulted in one of the most translated works of all time, the Tao Te Ching (dow-de-zhing), The Way and Its Power. This small book of eighty-one verses, composed in three days, hints at the secret of Lao Tzu's intimate relationship with the world. Child philosophers are quick to jump on that buffalo with him; sometimes more seasoned philosophers, searching for hidden meaning, need a leg up. The verses are remarkable yet straightforward and simple. What is the path to serenity? One step out of our own way and the way appears. Easy does it.

As with Epictetus, Lao Tzu's lifestyle reflected his view of the cosmos. The universe is an all-embracing whole with everything wrapped snugly within its folds. The common source of all being is the Tao; all radiates from its eternal center. This invisible flow of energy is the root that gives birth both to the visible and to the empty space that cradles all things. The Tao permeates everything, lying beneath, inside, around, and beyond . . . through, beside, above, and forever. This pure, complete spirit displays itself in an infinite variety of ways while still remaining whole. It is anteater and meteor, air and mastodon, you and me. It is life's opening and the place of return for all, the center of the circle of life. Unknowable intellectually and unutterable in words, this energy saturates existence. Our human intuition can catch only occasional glimpses.

Tuning In to Nature's Rhythm

The natural world is the Tao's greatest showcase. The rhythm of the universe follows the tune of Taoist energy. Nature is perfectly balanced by this uninterrupted energetic flow. Seeming opposites complement each other: yin/yang, female/male, wet/dry, high/low, new/old, stiff/flexible, soft/hard, in/out, life/death, back/forth, reason/ intuition. . . . Nothing is just one thing and that thing only; nothing is separate or isolated from the rest. In the yin/yang symbol, a circle holds one black and one white shape together as they nestle "against" each other, a spot of black in white, a spot of white in black. Black and white, day and night, come and go from each other. Nature is a shimmering reflection of itself, everything in relation, nothing better or worse. All mirrors the Tao in its way, unique yet drawn from the same well. The drumbeat of the universe beats within each thing as the universe repeats its pattern eternally. Bears hibernate and humans nap. Trees serve as templates for human lungs. Lions and oceans roar. Hummingbirds and dolphins dive. Rivers and lava flow. Resemblance reverberates throughout the whole.

At the heart of Taoist philosophy lies the belief that human life should be lived in sync with nature's rhythm. If the Tao is the way of the world, it must be my way, as well. Why fight it? A serene life is swept up in the inevitable, natural flow of the universe. Feel the beat. Watch the slow, imperceptible pivot as night trades places with dawn's first splash. Stare as high tide trades places with low tide, gradually, everything in its time. "In harmony with the Tao, the sky is clear and spacious, the earth is solid and full, all creatures flourish together, content with the way they are, endlessly repeating themselves, endlessly renewed" (*Tao Te Ching*). Swept up by the rhythm, we can sing along.

But can it be this simple? Yes, Lao Tzu would nod, if we did not complicate our lives. We insist that our will be done. Self-importance, self-absorption, self-assertion all serve to trap and block the natural flow of life through me. I rub myself and the world the wrong way. Serenity finds me only if I live life in accord with its energy rather than as I demand. Now that I am aware of my big-footed missteps, what am I to do? How can I be part of the world again? How can I be part of nature and therefore true to my nature?

Just as I prepare to welcome a special visitor, work is needed to make my life suitable for serenity's arrival. Calm flees clutter and confusion. Tranquillity can enter only where there is room. If I can quiet the incessant cries of my ego, the faint beat of the universe within me begins to stir noticeably. Modesty helps. Bow with reverence before nature's unfathomable mystery. The Grand Canyon and the Sahara Desert, the Alps and the Nile, the durability of stone and the sustainability of soil . . . and I am a (*tiny*) part of It! Such incomprehensible magnificence humbles self-effacing me. Tao's growing force inside me creates space that expands as I slow down. Natural energy flows through me and boosts my own. Serenity appears as a deep breath. My life imitates Life.

Living the Tao Te Ching

The *Tao Te Ching* leaves a simple set of directions for walking on serenity's trail. Slow down, relax your busy mind, and loosen the tight reins you pull to no avail. There is time and space in your life. Allow it to find you. Just as water supports the dinghy, the Tao will support you. Welcome the lift. Soften your stance. Adapt to the movement of the world and work *with* it. Become supple. With rhythm tingling your core, life opens. Fall into its arms. "Open yourself to the Tao, then trust your natural responses; and everything will fall into place" (*Tao Te Ching*).

"Wu wei" is the term for this letting go and consequent swooping up. Even the most challenging venture is undertaken somewhat "effortlessly." The energy flow dammed by the ego becomes an open channel, fueling our lives from within and navigating our way in the world. "Less and less do you need to force things" (*Tao Te Ching*), and hard work is done with ease. As the curtains part, we walk out into our lives and follow a path carved by the Tao. Soft, comfortable slippers carry us over any rough roads. Similarly, the ups and downs of our lives merge into each other, flowing back and forth without resistance. Life's force, both gentle and powerful, pulls us in. Joy and sadness are parts of each other and parts of the whole. Moving *with* them we stay "serene in the midst of sorrow" (*Tao Te Ching*).

Listen for Silence

Lao Tzu knew full well that language mars his simple vision of the world's total integrity. "There was something formless and perfect before the universe was born. It is serene. Empty. Solitary. Unchanging. Infinite. Eternally present. It is the mother of the universe. For lack of a better name, I call it the Tao" (*Tao Te Ching*). He left his eighty-one verses with each of us to make of them what we will. He is a favorite for countless students of all ages and backgrounds. As with any philosopher, however, his meaning can be misconstrued and his intent missed altogether . . . if you try. I see this discomfort most especially in students who seek his approval of their chaotic lives, who despise the notion of losing control and hearing that they never had it anyway, who say unabashedly, "I love my collection of video games," and who think that humans control the world. Lao Tzu did not intend to write or "teach" anything, and such furious reactions would amuse him. But he would listen: "He's just telling me to sit in a lawn chair and do nothing." Or "What's the use of trying to improve my life or the environment or anything else if the world will be as it is?" And a perennial: "He is crazy if he thinks I'm going to accept the way things are. The world is messed up." Lao Tzu's buffalo paws at the dirt.

His message is neither passive nor apathetic. Far from it. His *way* is to work *with* the world *as it is*. "It is always present within you. You can use it any way you want" (*Tao Te Ching*). Is there a *way* to protest injustice? Absolutely, he assures us now, and working with the situation as it is, being flexible and letting the best path for activism appear, is the *way*. Is there a *way* to work on a relationship? Yes, and working *with* the relationship and without forcing it against its nature is the *way*. Can a nurse practitioner devote himself to his patients and still keep up with mounting paperwork? "Do you have the patience to wait till your mud settles and the water is clear?" (*Tao Te Ching*) Let the problem present itself fully, and "do your work, then step back. The only path to serenity" (*Tao Te Ching*).

Lao Tzu's unsought legacy is a path to serenity. Fear? Life and death balance each other, come and go from each other, never exclude the other completely. Regret? Even our mistakes and shortcomings are part of life; we can stop berating ourselves and open the way for improvement. "The Tao is always at ease. It overcomes without competing, answers without speaking a word, arrives without being summoned, accomplishes without a plan. Its net covers the whole universe. And though its meshes are wide, it doesn't let a thing slip through" (*Tao Te Ching*). Epictetus and Lao Tzu, separated by five centuries but rooted in a unified cosmos, marveling at the same stars . . . Reason and Tao, reflections of each other, the roots of serenity.

DISCUSSION QUESTIONS

- What is serenity? What are its essential characteristics?
- Describe a life graced by serenity. Does this description match your life?
- What are some of the pitfalls blocking your path to a serene life?
- What changes can you make that will gradually restore calm in everyday activities?
- Has serenity lost its appeal? For you? For others in your life?

- What sources of daily pressure can you identify?
- How much of your worry is directed at things out of your control? List some quite specific preoccupations that you cannot control. Make another list of things that are in your power that deserve your attention.
- Do you agree with Epictetus that everything has a handle by which it can be carried? Think reasonably through anything that seems to defy handling. How would Epictetus's philosophy address these quandaries?
- Is serenity the absence of things? What?
- What provokes whining? What is its purpose?
- Do you think that being rational about situations can bring lasting calm?
- Is it possible for you to accept a problem and still be active and hopeful as you deal with it? Discuss thoroughly and think of specific examples.
- Does everyone experience difficulty? Can you live serenely if you try to avoid problems? How can serenity be the by-product of facing trouble directly, fully?
- When do you experience connection with life's natural flow? How can you foster this connection in trying times?
- What is the relation between humility and serenity? Simplicity and serenity? Communication and serenity?
- Does time spent in the natural world ease pressure for you? Why? Why not?
- How can Lao Tzu's trust in natural harmony lend itself to serenity?
- When has your life felt synchronized with the natural world?
- What will happen if you reduce your tendency to control things? Really?!
- Imagine any seemingly stressful profession. Apply Epictetus

and Lao Tzu to this daily employment—environmental activist, air traffic controller, principal or teacher. How can a day's events remain the same but the teacher or activist gain a measure of serenity? How can this newfound serenity be cultivated so that it does not disappear for the stockbroker or the social worker?

- Do you need the world to make sense to you? Why? Does it? Will it?
- What will you recall, or take to heart right now, from Epictetus's survival kit?
- What aspects of Lao Tzu's "effortless effort" can you use?
- How do you explain the continuing appeal of Epictetus and Lao Tzu?

HOMEWORK

Listen and Hum

Serenity comes on music's notes from all directions. Pick any/all of these tranquil trios and settle in with the musicians. That's all.

Group A

- What better example of endurance and persistence than the musicians who keep the rhythm of New Orleans alive in the aftermath of Hurricane Katrina? Kermit Ruffins's trumpet does indeed "blow da whistle" on his "Treme Second Line." His faithfulness to the music of his roots has ensured the march of parades for generations to come.
- Brazilian Elaine Elias mixes modern jazz and bossa nova in her renderings of the music of her countryman Antonio Carlos Jobim. Her piano is both playful and peaceful, soothing and at times a tad funky. Listen to "Dindi" and

enjoy the calm induced by her touch on the keys amid the welcoming, reliable strum of a bass solo. The classic "Desafinado" pleases in its simple interpretation.

- Pablo Casals was the first to record *The Six Cello Suites of Johann Sebastian Bach*, so it is fitting to ease into Bach's sublime work with him. A single, uninhibited instrument rises and falls with a life of its own . . . and the listener goes along for the ride. Spend some time with the sixth Suite, for example, and experience "Sarabande" flowing into "Gavotte" and winding into "Gigue." You may want to pick a suite of your own in serenity's name.

Group B

- "Get yourself in gear / keep your stride," overcome fear and tune out the bustle. Alicia Keys complements this Stoic and Taoist advice with her earnest, sincere piano. Her playing feels grounded and assured, making it easier to agree with Keys that "Someday We'll All Be Free."
- Brian Eno gives his listeners time and space in his unhurried, thoughtful "ambient" music, a term he is credited with coining. His unique sound supports conversation, meditation, clear thinking . . . without any demands. Slow down on *Thursday Afternoon*. For anyone on "standby," hang around with *Ambient 1: Music for Airports*. "Thus the Master travels all day without leaving home. However splendid the views, she stays serenely in herself" (Lao Tzu, *Tao Te Ching*).
- Seven minutes given to Estonia's Arvo Pärt's *Cantus in Memoriam Benjamin Britten* instills serenity. Strings and one bell, a naturally descending scale reminiscent of a waterfall, the completeness of one single note: Pärt's mini-

malist technique casts a chant-like spell. The sound of *one* note stretches toward silence.

Group C

- Joe Henderson's "Serenity" is a swinging tune with plenty of musical exploration, yet it never loses the steady hub that unites the musicians. His saxophone invites the audience to follow it wherever it may go—and it doesn't leave anyone behind. Imagine naming this tune!
- Led Zeppelin's "Down by the Seaside" ripples with Taoist themes. "Sing loud for the sunshine, pray hard for the rain / And show your love for Lady Nature." Boats and fish gambol in the water while people are "racin'" in the city, busy, busy. How could we have forgotten to do the twist?! The band's instrumental "Bron-Yr-Aur" stops the "racin'" and you can take time to _____.
- The call of one voice followed by the response of the group, repeated, call and response . . . Hildegard of Bingen's twelfth-century compositions bring us composure through the years from her abbey in Germany. "O Ecclesia" never loses its center; serenity sung clearly in Latin.

Group D

- We fly on the wings of the "Blackbird" into "Strawberry Fields Forever" in the contemplative stillness of Gregorian chant. Chant and the Liverpool lyrics make a stunning combination. Peace comes with the first bell. Epictetus appreciates that "There Is a Place" where we can go for refuge and agrees with the Beatles that the mind is this place. Traveling slowly through the chanted tunes, "The Inner Light" of the spirit shines in every verse. "Let It Be."

- "The earth is always singing." Lizz Wright's earthy, enticing voice salutes "Silence" and her contented sound makes you wonder where she might be. "And even the quiet dove— that silence is a song." The earth sings. Lao Tzu joins Wright in duet, humming that *our* lives sing, as well.
- Go with the plaintive pull at your heartstrings as a violin makes your spirit lighten . . . and fly. Vaughan Williams's short flight of "The Lark Ascending" lifts the listener on wings into serenity's rarefied air.

Group E

- Claude Debussy awakens awe in nature with his compositions for piano. If moonlight were to create any audible sound, it would surely be the shimmering warmth of tinkling keys in "Clair de Lune." Look out your window at the moon with this song as your companion. Then, to get a closer look, go outside and hear your "Footsteps in the Snow." Snowbound, lit by the moon, calm inside and out . . .
- Pat Metheny and Charlie Haden, two Missouri boys, trade wordless stories inspired by the vast open spaces of the Midwest. Their acoustic improvisation on bass and guitar anchors the soul and gives it flight, as well. The two musicians are "Two for the Road" and take us along for the ride to see "Tears of Rain" and hear "The Moon Song." Haden and Metheny make emptiness part of each song, resisting any impulse to fill the "sky."
- The Preservation Hall Jazz Band is in its fifth decade, "preserving" and enlivening the music of New Orleans. The beat goes on no matter what. Preservation Hall rocks in the heart of the French Quarter, the uplifting, joyous rhythm spilling into the streets. "Mood Indigo" portrays a

tranquil mood, while "Joe Avery" trots at a quicker pace. A story of survival, yes, and so much more.

Recite and Write

Bring poetry to your gathering to read silently. The sounds of turning pages and occasional sighs of relaxation are welcome. Recite the following poems in several voices when the group is ready. Return to silence again. Sketch, write in your journal, just sit, read from your poetry book(s). Read the poems aloud once again when the mood strikes.

- "I hear lake water lapping with low sounds by the shore . . . I hear it in the deep heart's core." William Butler Yeats instills the peace that drips slowly into his heart upon his return to nature in "The Lake Isle of Innisfree." Yeats's seductive retreat from the busy world secures serenity effortlessly. The cricket's song is enough. Noon and midnight balance each other and Yeats, as well. Write a poem about your own "Innisfree." What place soothes your "deep heart's core"?
- Kelly Cherry expresses yearning and loss, natural beauty and happiness, "hazard and prospect" in a uniquely lyrical voice. The prospect of a "green place," a farm in Virginia, consoles. "In the Field" takes the reader to this special place, casting a lazy day's quiet spell. A fence post is as golden as the church spire, and crab apples and insects complement one another. The world "seems to be an image of itself / a mirrored photograph." How do you "mirror" the world? How are you like catbird and sunrise, similar to creek and to boulder?
- "Cutting Up an Ox" as a lesson in serenity? Absolutely! Chuang Tzu's Taoist classic from the fourth century BCE

enrolls us in cooking school with Prince Wen Hui's chef.
The cook always finds the open spaces for his cleaver by
taking his time, stepping back, breathing, planting his foot
instinctively. His carving follows the nature of the ox; he
neither forces nor hurries his job. The keen blade never
requires sharpening; it glides through openings as they
present themselves. No problem. "This is it! My cook has
shown me / How I ought to live," exclaims the Prince.
How can you cook such a serene life?

- Hildegard of Bingen opens the heavy wood door to her
  abbey. We gaze at her paintings as we listen to a performance of one of her musical compositions. Hildegard then
  recites one of her poems and leaves us to meditate in the
  abbey's cool, stone silence. Her "Holy Spirit" is the beginning of "all movement," so similar to the Tao, the source
  of all being. The Spirit is her healing "balm." Lao Tzu
  agrees wordlessly. What tonic feeds your spirit?

- "The loud voice is famous to silence / which knew it would
  inherit the earth." Naomi Shihab Nye zaps self-importance
  as she gives a delightful twist to the meaning of "Famous."
  She admires the understated and unpretentious little
  things that always remember their calling. Hooray for the
  buttonhole, the pulley, and the boot! How about that cat
  dozing on the fence, watched by the birds? How "famous"
  in a hard life is a stranger's kindness? Why do both Lao Tzu
  and Epictetus warn against the pursuit of fame? "And
  which do you really prefer? Money, or a faithful, modest
  friend?" (Epictetus, *Enchiridion*)

- "Practice resurrection." How can you do as Wendell Berry
  suggests in "Manifesto: The Mad Farmer Liberation Front"?
  Plant trees, call the forest your crop, love the world, cup
  your ear to the carrion's call, and "lie easy in the shade."

Discuss the phrase "practice resurrection." If you make resurrection your practice, then _____ .

Read and Talk

• Shhhhhhhh . . . Tiptoe into the Hemulen's "Park of Silence" in Tove Jansson's enticing world of Finnish trolls
with all their "human" foibles. Her illustrations in "The
Hemulen Who Loved Silence" are part of the fun. Hold
the Hemulen's hand as he finds serenity in his Park. Lie in
a hammock in the garden, but remember that you "may
laugh and possibly even hum a little" but nothing more.
Yes, this is a children's tale, and also a metaphor for anyone seeking respite from the noise and who longs for the
chance to swing in serenity's air. "He was the owner of
the moonlight on the ground, he fell in love with the most
beautiful of the trees, he made wreaths of leaves and strung
them around his neck." Troll with the Hemulen. What is
the price of a ticket to the "Park of Silence"?

• Roman emperor Marcus Aurelius was Epictetus's pupil as
a young boy. Serenity is the goal of slave and ruler, the
philosophy teacher and general. Marcus Aurelius's *Meditations* are studies in Stoic philosophy. "Be like the cliff
against which the waves continually break; but it stands
firm and tames the fury of the water around it." Describe
the quality that "tames the fury" surrounding it. "Today I
have got out of all trouble, or rather I have cast out all
trouble, for it was not outside, but within, in my opinions."
The slave taught the emperor well. Aurelius also echoes
Lao Tzu: "Consider frequently the connection of all things
in the universe and their relation to one another. For
things are somehow implicated with one another, and all
in a way friendly to one another." Why does the percep-

tion of a harmonious, interwoven universe induce serenity in Rome and China? For you, as well?

- Rachel Carson restores and invigorates childhood curiosity and awe at nature's unfathomable mystery. "I think we felt the same spine-tingling response to the vast roaring ocean and the wild night around us." It is her twenty-month-old nephew whom she takes to the ocean in rainy darkness, his tiny body, wrapped in a blanket, that she feels responding instinctively to the grandeur. Carson introduces the reader to the natural world in *The Sense of Wonder*, taking us there as if for the first time so that we can return to our roots with newly sharpened senses. Amazement comes with rediscovery that "a rainy day is the perfect time for a walk in the woods." Take a day's stresses for a stroll in the woods. Does the pressure dissolve in the woods? Does a measure of calm take its place?

- "Field Notes on People, Place, and the Planet" is the subtitle of William Shutkin's *A Republic of Trees*. Shutkin does more than celebrate our undeniable link to all things natural; he lays down a path to follow to make a "green world" a reality. He makes activism attractive, and his positive tone encourages the reader to get going. Human societies, locally and globally, have a best old friend in nature. Shutkin's ideas are bold, yet he offers them in a gentle tone without scolding or blame. Discuss the ways in which Shutkin's plans combine the approaches of both Lao Tzu and Epictetus.

- Imagine that you are a crew member on a ship trapped in the ice pack that will eventually crush your vessel and leave you stranded in the Antarctic. If ever there were a time for Epictetus's philosophy, this is it. Caroline Alexander tells the riveting tale of Sir Ernest Shackleton's legendary 1914 expedition in the ship *Endurance*. Shackleton finds the right handle to carry the crew and its cat through most dire circumstances. His optimism and determination serve as Stoic parables. Lao Tzu's spontaneity creeps into group singsongs, and this camaraderie lends a measure of calm that matches the crew's steely resolve. Frank Hurley's stark photographs taken during the struggle convey frigid temperatures and ongoing trouble. What lessons about endurance can you take from this Antarctic tale and apply in a meaningful way to your life? From ice floe to office?

- The fiery resolve of the human spirit swims through sharks and sewage in Lynne Cox's *Swimming to Antarctica*. Cox recounts many of her long-distance swims and describes the relentless motivation to test her limits. She willingly undertakes the body-numbing cold that Shackleton gives his all to escape. What buoys Cox is not only the successful completion of a swim, but also the connections made every time she comes ashore. Her joy stems from bringing people around the world together, splash by splash. Her steadfast spirit unites people and places through the water that sustains each of us internally and externally. Cox does not overreach, as Epictetus warns; she reaches out. How does she embody Taoist and Stoic traits? What can you learn from Lynne Cox's story? How can you learn to float?

Watch and Reflect

- We are "surrounded by rhythm." This opening statement comes gut-level alive through Taiko drumming in the documentary *Kodo: Live at the Acropolis*. Feel your heart link to the primal beat of the drum, the sound "ma" cradling your spirit in the world's womb. One of the drummers speaks simply and elegantly of this comforting, soothing sound. The largest of the drums, made from the trunk of a huge tree native to Japan, bears the wavy lines of the yin/yang symbol on its skin. Smaller drums come from the tree, as well. The yoga-positioned drummers create sound that resonates from old rocks filled with empty spaces. Even the drummers' shouts are part of the composition, their voices part of the space between audible beats. Note especially the mesmerizing "Zoku" and "Monochrome." Serenity emanating from the universal thunder of a drum . . . Looking at the faces in the crowd, I try to picture the person who *makes* the drum.

- We must "stand to our tackle as best we can . . . if we have the spittle for it." Sir Thomas More models Stoic virtue in Robert Bolt's *A Man for All Seasons*, always true to his convictions with an iron will and quiet confidence. King Henry VIII wants a divorce; More, the chancellor, remains forcefully silent and staunchly withholds his approval. Times are topsy-turvy in sixteenth-century England, the days full of political intrigue and religious uncertainty. The mischievous and playful Thomas More adds spice to Stoic reserve with his sharp, well-considered words. Despite his resignation as chancellor, the king still badgers him for public endorsement of his divorce. More refuses every demand because "it profits a man nothing to give his soul for the whole world." How does a "stand to our tackle" grant serenity? How can you be immune to Epictetus's "externals" with something of More's "spittle"?

Get Up and Do

- Think of people who could use a third handle to lift their burdens. Family members, colleagues, neighbors, strug-

gling survivors, friends near and far—unfortunately, opportunities abound. Add another handle by joining them
in the situation with Lao Tzu's grace and Epictetus's practical judgment.

- Spend some time with water. Listening to rain, watching
melting snow, hearing a splashing fountain, enjoying a
pool of any size, sitting by a pond, looking out the window
at dew on dawn's grass.

- Get your hands in the dirt: a garden, a pot, clearing a small
spot for mint, stopping and seeing a possibility for new
growth in an unexpected place.

- Choose a day with little responsibility and no plans. Notice the times that you fret about things that are out of
your control. This awareness of unnecessary distractions
requires effort, but little by little these serenity-blockers
will lose their power.

- Have a picnic. Go with your philosophy group and talk
about nothing in particular. Go with just one person and
let the rhythm of your time together find itself. Go
alone . . . the back stoop is far enough.

- Divide your members into two groups, one representing
Lao Tzu and the other Epictetus. Both groups list the
strengths you find in your philosopher's path to serenity.
Offer five tips gleaned from the philosopher, each in one
short, crisp sentence. Take a break. Now share any questions you have for either philosopher's group—how to
apply a theory in specific situations, why you think it may
be tricky, etc.

- Prepare to bring two things to your philosophy gathering. One: present a difficulty—yours, fictional, social, or
historical—and together find an approach that promises
tranquillity in the end. Two: bring a pebble, a stone, or a

rock that you noticed while taking a walk or sitting in the yard. How is a stone's feel reminiscent of serenity's sturdy inner core?

* Begin to notice your tight grip on the telephone, the coffee mug, and things in general. Loosen your hold, slowly, paying attention to the tightness and the welcome relief.

* Choose one activity, or non-activity, that always restores serenity. What is it about *your* life and *this* experience that meshes? Repeat as necessary.

* Sketch serenity.

Resources

Music
* *Swing This!* by Kermit Ruffins: "Treme Second Line."
* *Elaine Elias Plays Jobim* by Elaine Elias: "Dindi," "Desafinado."
* *Johann Sebastian Bach: Cello Suites Nos. 1–6*, Pablo Casals, cello: *Sixth Suite:* "Sarabande," "Gavotte," "Gigue."
* *Songs in A Minor* by Alicia Keys: "Some Day We'll All Be Free."
* *Ambient 1: Music for Airports 1978* by Brian Eno.
* *Thursday Afternoon 1985* by Brian Eno.
* *Arvo Pärt: Fratres*, The Orchestra of Flanders, Rudolf Werthen conducting: "Cantus in Memoriam Benjamin Britten."
* *In 'N Out* by Joe Henderson: "Serenity."
* *Physical Graffiti* by Led Zeppelin: "Bron-Yr-Aur," "Down by the Seaside."
* *Gothic Voices:* "O Ecclesia," by Hildegard of Bingen, Emma Kirkby, soprano.
* *The Beatles Gregorian Songbook* by The Beatles, performed by Schola Musica Choir, conducted by Martin Dagenais: "There Is a Place," "Strawberry Fields Forever," "Blackbird," "Let It Be," "The Inner Light."
* *Salt* by Lizz Wright: "Silence."
* *R. Vaughan Williams: Fantasia . . .* , Academy of St. Martin-in-the-Fields, Neville Marriner conducting: "The Lark Ascending," Iona Brown, violin.
* *Debussy: Suite Bergamasque/Images/Préludes/Arabesques:* "Clair de Lune," "Footsteps in the Snow," Klára Körmendi, piano.

- *Beyond the Missouri Sky* by Charlie Haden & Pat Metheny: "Two for the Road," "The Moon Song," "Tears of Rain."
- *The Best of Preservation Hall Jazz Band:* "Mood Indigo," "Joe Avery."

Poetry

- *The Collected Poems of W. B. Yeats*, edited by Richard J. Finneran: "The Lake Isle of Innisfree."
- *Hazard and Prospect: New and Selected Poems* by Kelly Cherry: "In the Field."
- *The Complete Works of Chuang Tzu*, translated by Burton Watson: "Cutting Up an Ox."
- *Meditations with Hildegard of Bingen*, translated by Gabriele Uhlein: "Holy Spirit."
- *Words Under the Words: Selected Poems* by Naomi Shihab Nye: "Famous."
- *Country of Marriage* by Wendell Berry: "Manifesto: The Mad Farmer Liberation Front."

Prose

- *Enchiridion* by Epictetus.
- *Tao Te Ching* by Lao Tzu, presented by Stephen Mitchell.
- *Tales from Moominvalley* by Tove Jansson: "The Hemulen Who Loved Silence."
- *Meditations* by Marcus Aurelius.
- *The Sense of Wonder* by Rachel Carson.
- *A Republic of Trees* by William Shutkin.
- *The Endurance: Shackleton's Legendary Antarctic Expedition* by Caroline Alexander.
- *Swimming to Antarctica: Tales of a Long-Distance Swimmer* by Lynne Cox.

Drama

- *A Man for All Seasons* by Robert Bolt (play and screenplay), directed by Fred Zinnemann (DVD).

Documentary

- *Kodo: Live at the Acropolis*, hosted by Mickey Hart (DVD).

Possibility

~~~~~

Cowardice doesn't pay.
—SIMONE DE BEAUVOIR, *The Ethics of Ambiguity*

THE TOPIC

This is the chapter of the book I most looked forward to writing. The astonished looks of beginning tennis players when they hit the ball over the net for the first time and realize in an instant that it is possible for them to do it *again*—I wish that look on every face. Possibility crooks a beckoning finger your way.

In a child's world anything can happen and everything arouses curiosity. The future calls out with its unknown and unlimited voice, summoning children to yet another adventure. It is this eager anticipation that fades in most adult lives. We hunker down, laid low by previous choices or missed opportunities. Fixated on the fact that there is no turning back, we forget to move forward. Possibilities evaporate, and sagged-shoulder disappointment drains the oomph out of lives standing still.

A few years ago I was talking with a student about her resurgent academic career and new-fashioned optimism. "Your future is full of possibility," I said admiringly. Without hesitation she replied, "Yours is, too." She thought nothing of her remark; I thought a lot about it. In hindsight I know that she was right. The years since that conversation have been filled with unexpected and lovely starts and turns. Why was I taken aback by her endorsement of my future? Did I think possibility was an already-consumed luxury? I can still see my student's self-assured face in my mind's eye, and her lesson stays with me. I must work faithfully to develop my awareness that possibilities *do* lie ahead; recognizing this truth in hindsight is not enough. A sense of possibility, hands thrown high in the air, stirs the soul. But what precisely is this rejuvenating tonic? What *is* possibility?

Possibility epitomizes free-range living. It means building a life on "I might," "It can happen," and "Now what?" and rejecting the defeat of "Oh, I could never do that," and "The opportunity passed me by." As I become increasingly attracted by possibility's wide arch, I am quick to uncover new chances and sniff out surprising alternatives. My compass can point my life in any direction. Standing on the shore looking toward the horizon, I can accept this one, stationary view as my field of play, or I can wade in and expand the realm of the possible. Using a slow and steady breaststroke, my world widens as I pop up for air and deepens as I swim farther out. An island, an outcropping of rock, octopus, surfer, seagull, sea stars below and nighttime stars above, boat, sun, and driftwood. Scampering back to shore, I hold my breath-giving consciousness of life's possibility close to my breast. The world is full.

Life is not easy for anyone. Possibility does not negate difficulty. But the choice of embracing free-range living does mean that if a thing is possible then it *is* within reach and *not* out of the question. Even when my freedom is impinged I can spot the sliver of an opening and wiggle through the crack. Bedridden, I can be dazzled by the moon's faraway beauty. Laden with responsibilities, I can still be smitten by a smile. Despondent, I can be inspired to keep trying. Children are right: anything can happen.

"Yes, but this is no longer true in my life," a good number of unconvinced philosophers have mourned over the years. "I can't change jobs because I'll lose seniority." "I can't end this relationship because it will hurt my family." "No one will want to teach an old man like me to read." Stop! Plenty of examples of my students' seizure of possibility spring to mind. Blindness does not hinder educational pursuits: "I'm not handicapped. Losing my sight forced me to get out in the world and make my way." Severe cerebral palsy does not deter my wheelchair-bound student, who speaks only with her eyes, from volunteering with her mother's help at an elementary school. A full-time hairdresser earns her college degree: "People ask me why I stayed with it for fifteen years. I did it for myself." A high school dropout mopes into the introductory class and now teaches philosophy with a doctorate in his satchel. A single mother sets off with her two children for another town and her four-year degree. A once disgruntled philosopher presently takes well-deserved bows as a stand-up comedian. On and on.

Philosophical controversy over the meaning of freedom fires up in ancient Greece and spills into present-day classrooms, living rooms, and lunch tables. Are we truly free? "I am bound to get in trouble if I ask." Do we always have alternatives from which to choose? "My entire education was programmed by my parents, who were adamant that I attend their alma mater. My future has always been decided for me." When is something truly *impossible*? Can making a single choice inevitably cancel all others? "I left home to find a new life. I can't go back."

How very many times have I heard the worried confession "I have no idea what I want to do with my life"? My heartfelt reply is greeted with laughter and, when fraught philosophers note my sincerity, almost always with relief and hope: "That's great that you don't know exactly what to do with your life. Neither do I!" What if we did, indeed, know? What if our futures were set in stone? What then? Isn't possibility our life support? Its scent entices rookie and veteran philosophers, regardless of background, to take another peek. Maybe, just maybe . . . "If I define success in my own way, then I'll quit working two jobs. I could try songwriting." "It takes imagination to actually *see* that I can apologize and make a fresh start at work." "Opportunity won't drop into my lap. Who but me can start my own business?"

Watching the gradual restoration of a sense of possibility in lives starved for it remains a thrill for me. Hopeful philosophers shake their heads, at once surprised that it's not too late for possibility and also disconcerted that they had lost their faith in it. "I can." What capers await!

Two philosophers lure us back to possibility's promise in freedom's fresh air. Englishman John Stuart Mill opens up endless possibility to those willing to make some tough personal changes. Frenchwoman Simone de Beauvoir (see-MONE duh boh-VWAHR) tempts us to leapfrog from lily pad to lily pad in a pond stocked with free choices.

THE PHILOSOPHERS

He who chooses his plan for himself
employs all his faculties.
—John Stuart Mill, *On Liberty*

Mild-mannered John Stuart Mill brings down the house wherever I take him. "This dude is awesome. Do you think he'll ever give a talk in this area?" Unlikely for a nineteenth-century British philosopher!

"Nineteenth century? It's like he's talking about this country today and looking straight at and right through me."

Perhaps his faith in human potential and the rewards of personal freedom was a product of a childhood during which he learned Greek and Latin while reading volumes of history and playing with math. Mill was active in the bustle of London, a businessman and member of Parliament, and a major figure in Western philosophy then and now. He saw possibility everywhere: in the United States as the test case for democracy; in his work in opposition to *The Subjection of Women* in 1869; in the human ability to change and to improve; and in the sure happiness to be found in framing our lives to suit our personal tastes and temperaments. His dedication to the advancement of freedom was matched only by his unfailing devotion to his wife, the philosopher Harriet Taylor Mill.

Mill determined, by simple observation, that people want to be happy. His brand of happiness combines peace of mind, mental stimulation, and at least a dusting of excitement. But the number-one ingredient of a happy life is possessing the liberty to turn possibility into satisfying reality. Nothing beats the pleasure of dipping into your treasure trove of qualities and talents and building an original life. Dangers lurk, however, and can quash hope if not met head-on; we can strap ourselves into mediocre, copycat lives if we don't guard our freedom.

Mill's Classroom

Join me in Mill's classroom. On the chalkboard he highlights the problems that, if corrected, open a clear path to a free future: unwarranted governmental interference, peer pressure, and character flaws. He hands each of us an eraser, hoping that our philosophizing will give us the confidence to cross off each obstacle, one by one, allowing plenty of space to write but one word: Possibility.

Too Many Laws

Let's look at the law books first. For Mill, the only justification for a law is to protect citizens from *physical* harm. Note upfront that my opinions, interests, and pursuits do not constitute *physical* harm; however much you may disagree with me, I deserve "liberty of conscience in the most comprehensive sense, liberty of thought and feeling, absolute freedom of opinion and sentiment on all subjects, practical or speculative, scientific, moral, or theological" (*On Liberty*). Furthermore, the law cannot have as its intention the protection of me from myself; remaking me in his image of a good person is not the legislator's job. Prohibition rarely if ever works, Mill acknowledges, and as long as I do not harm others physically, my decisions belong to me. Stop banning books. Disapprove of my reading list but do not touch my spectacles. Punish an officer for indulging in "fermented drinks" on the job, but pay no mind to his high-spirited revelry in the privacy of his home. Do not enforce your moral beliefs. Let me be with this proviso: "The liberty of the individual must be thus far limited; he must not make himself a nuisance to other people" (*On Liberty*). Basement gatherings and college classrooms erupt at the chance to vent at the heavy hand of government!

"How about the ban on same-sex marriage and the outcries against civil unions? What, exactly, do the protesters fear?" "Wiretapping! What are they really listening for?" "Why is tequila available in unlimited supply but the purchase of marijuana—a proven pain reliever—illegal?" "Why are stores in certain counties closed by law until early afternoon on Sundays? Does everyone attend Sunday morning worship service?" As thoughtful examples of legislation that fails the "protection from physical harm test" dwindle, I encourage students to look for sound reasons for some laws that they may have (intentionally) overlooked: "Think about the law requiring motorcyclists to wear helmets. Why helmets and not kneepads? Does a motorcyclist's head injury potentially harm others? As always with Mill, anticipate all consequences." A more sober, circumspect conversation ensues, and many students deny an overwhelming governmental presence in their lives. Mill leaves his detectives carefully combing law books for legislation of morality, eraser at the ready. And they can't get enough. Only once in my teaching career have I returned to my car at day's end to find a revved-up student in the passenger seat. Oh, dude. Not in the least uncomfortable, Jacob replied to my direct, unasked question: "I want to know what Mill would say about seat belt laws. How can we hurt anyone but ourselves by not buckling up?" On this day, my passenger unbuckled quickly, the conversation to be continued. . . .

Society (and We) Disapprove (of You)

Next on the board . . . peer pressure. Mill warns that it slithers into our psyches and causes our lives "to degenerate into the mechanical" (*On Liberty*) unless we put up a fight. When we explore how fear of social stigma leads to the loss of possibility, Mill's inquiry alarms students in two distinct and long-lasting ways. Not only does the human predilection to impose our views on others loom large, but our complicity in forking over our own freedom and futures horrifies. Berating the government was easy in comparison to looking within, but we forge ahead with our British guide.

Our penchant for making the monitoring of other lives our first priority embarrasses. "Can you believe she won't watch movies with subtitles?" "I caught those two men holding hands." "An 'academic' reading science fiction 'novels'? I swear!" "Has Miss Barefoot lost her shoes?" Nonsense run amok! If I welcome the chance to make my own way in the world, to let my personality develop like wildfire, then I am obligated to grant this cherished freedom to others. When will I stop inflicting my likes and dislikes on the undeserving? Mill cautions against this inclination throughout his philosophical work, asking if individuals are "claiming nothing for themselves but what they as freely concede to every one else" (*The Subjection of Women*). Praise be eccentricity; give it free rein and let it push the bounds of possibility. Admit it: "I scoff at a colleague who reads technical manuals at lunch." "I snicker at these hippies petitioning management to 'go green.'" "That guy playing a chess match by himself is bound to lose!" Controlling and now self-conscious philosophers promise to relax their tight-fisted oversight of other lives. Yikes, what if everyone *were* like me? "Persons of genius . . . are . . . a small minority; but in order to have them, it is necessary to preserve the soil in which they grow . . . an *atmosphere* of freedom . . .without hurtful compression" (*On Liberty*). Society needs the chess player and the hippies. Here's to encouraging remarks: "What an amazing collection of vinyl albums." "Play that didgeridoo." Yes, "there should be different experiments of living" (*On Liberty*).

But it is our participation in the sacrifice of our own possibility that most depresses queasy yet willing investigators. Allowing ourselves to live "as under the eye of a hostile and dreaded censorship" (*On Liberty*), afraid of societal disapproval, constantly caring what others think, how can we ever know what it is *we* want? Honest examples of giving up personal freedom sit on the tips of tongues: "I cave in to advertising and mass-produced norms of approval. I allow a commercial to tell me what kind of coffee to drink." "I let movie critics, the 'experts,' pick my entertainment for me." "Even in what people do for pleasure, conformity is the first thing thought of" (*On Liberty*). "I don't question the tie snaking around my neck." "I tug on despised panty hose as a morning ritual." "I accept the 'right' invitations for the wrong reasons," neglecting to ask, "[W]hat do I prefer?" (*On Liberty*). "I purchase designer clothes for my kids so that they won't be mocked at school." Good grief!

Mill raises his voice over the gloomy buzz with a reminder that we can reclaim freedom, glimpsing and snatching new options and different choices—in coffee, in lifestyle, in relationship. How? Mill suggests a strategy for changing your character so that you can live in a world that you create. Yo! The mood livens. If I change myself I can win a better life full of appealing possibilities. Pens in hand, students home in on Mill's recipe for self-improvement and a hopeful future. Yes, today my character dictates specific choices based on the person I have become; "while our character is what it is, our actions are necessitated by it" (*An Examination of Sir William Hamilton's Philosophy*). But tomorrow my character can be the cause of different actions if I make some adjustments. The eraser, please.

Deciding to Choose Differently

Mill insists that each of us acts according to our strongest preference, always. This strongest preference—be it to give you a kiss or to go ahead and accept that job—is the single motivation for my behavior: there are no flukes, no accidents, no inexplicable conduct. Just as there are reasons for shifting wind patterns, allergic reactions, and a dog's pacing, there are reasons for my response to adversity, to a gesture of affection, to an angry outburst, to a family crisis. Furthermore, what I prefer stems directly from who I am, from the person I've made of myself. My flight from adversity, withdrawal from affection, voice raised in magnified fury, tears shed at the family dynamic . . . all are rooted firmly in my character. Just as shellfish causes me to break out in hives, fear of rejection causes me to pull back from an embrace.

Mill's pupils often attempt immediately to offer examples of times when they have, indeed, gone against their strongest preference. Tales of sacrifices made and obligations honored prove that we can act outside the stronghold of preference, do they not? Think it through, he responds. "When I say preferred, I of course include with the thing

itself, all that accompanies it" (*An Examination of Sir William Hamilton's Philosophy*). I cannot say that, although I preferred to go on
holiday, I chose instead to help my friend on moving day; I wanted
to help her *and* avoid guilt, win pats on the back, and have the favor
returned. I did not act against my strongest preference when I left the
party and picked up my children; I preferred to avoid an argument,
feel dutiful, and assure future outings with a clear conscience. Mill
never changes his mind. Our character determines our choices here
and now. But can we prefer otherwise? Yes, we can. We can change
who we are, thereby freeing ourselves to choose differently.

A Brand-new Me

Failed relationships, lost jobs, ugly scenes fueled by frustration . . .
all can be reversed. Mill coins the term "moral antecedents" for all of
our desires, aversions, habits, and dispositions—all of the aspects of
our individual characters that cause us to act in predictable ways.
These moral antecedents must be changed to admit new preferences
and allow different outcomes. "Oops! Why do I keep losing my job?"
It is no mystery, Mill would reply: You love a bash followed by a
sleep-in. You're always frazzled. Cut it out. How? Turn off the phone,
clean house, set an early alarm, find pleasure in being reliable. "Dang!
Why do I lose girlfriends so soon and so often?" Your possessiveness
scares people. You're the overbearing dominator. Step back. How?
Train yourself to spot this bossy tendency; dislike and combat it. Back
off. Don't leave home after dark. Spend time alone. "Shoot! People
walk away when I start a conversation. And I'm a lot of fun." No,
you're not—always jockeying to be the center of attention, interrupt-
ing with repetitive, cynical barbs. Turn it around. How? Find pleasure
in listening to others and kick yourself at your first butting-in syllable.
Wait to be invited into a conversation . . . however long it takes.
      This is Mill's way: change the moral antecedents that created

your character; then you can uncover new preferences and win back possibility. Do it! If you want a promising future, you must look at the past that molded your present personality. Poke around in this stash of influences and figure yourself out. Retrain your will and associate pleasure with chipping away at troubling antecedents; link displeasure to repetition of the old ways. Every choice contains some measure of risk, some eventual consequence, but "no one can be a great thinker who does not recognize that as a thinker, it is his first duty to follow his intellect to whatever conclusions it may lead" (*On Liberty*). Keep at it. Think and redo. Understand your past and use this knowledge well. Erase. And, happily, you can solidify the desires and habits that shape beneficial preferences. Go with your bent to make no demands and preserve loving relationships. Make a habit of celebrating the good fortune of others and continue to boost morale at work. Veer and swerve, stretch and drive.

Mill inspires philosophers of all ages with optimism and an often impatient desire to give personal freedom a go. Child philosophers conspire to adjust their attitude and stay out of the principal's office. College students predict that if they alter their habits, they can cultivate discipline and count on its many rewards. Members in animated philosophy clubs foresee countless possibilities opening up: for example, less time spent complaining means more time for reading and picnics and . . .

It's harder for anyone who does not learn until adulthood "to use and interpret experience in his own way" (*On Liberty*). Fighting against this drawback, Mill emphasizes the critical importance of early and ongoing education that encourages imagination and daring. Children force-fed a planned-out future gain a disadvantage that stalks their adult lives. Liberate them from "despotism over the mind," Mill demands, and extend their notion of the possible to reach into grown-up days. The excitement of possibility exists only where it is celebrated; hopeful philosophers party on, convinced along with Mill that our "errors are corrigible" and that each of us "is capable of rectifying his mistakes by discussion and experience" (*On Liberty*). An individual who wipes the board with Mill's eraser can feed a sweet tooth with the fruits of freedom and spontaneity.

> *The fact remains that we are absolutely free today*
> *if we choose to will our existence . . . which is*
> *open on the infinite.*
> —SIMONE DE BEAUVOIR, *The Ethics of Ambiguity*

Reflecting on her childhood, a Frenchwoman recalled her burning admiration for scholars, artists, and writers who "created other worlds . . . in which everything had purpose." This rambunctious, wide-eyed girl decided that "that was where I wished to spend my life . . . to carve out a place for myself in those rarefied spheres. . . . I had to get on in life" (*Memoirs of a Dutiful Daughter*). Simone de Beauvoir "got on" in a big way, fleshing out unparalleled possibility for a woman in her day, leaving a lasting bequest of full-bodied freedom for women especially and for men, as well.

Giving the world six novels, several series of essays and short stories, volumes of memoirs, and twenty full-length books, Simone de Beauvoir's life unfurled at top speed on the wings of her first philosophy course at the Sorbonne. She is perhaps best known for her 1949 achievement, *The Second Sex*, a book that takes everyone in society to task for playing into gender roles that squelch possibility. Her work published in 1947, *The Ethics of Ambiguity*, dances with the promise of forward-thrusting human potential.

Let's start from scratch, on the springboard of early childhood, and trace a life modeled on de Beauvoir's concept of possibility. Pizzazz, play, and audacity mark the process of becoming a free person, the one, lifelong project that gives life meaning.

Games We Should Play

Life is a game to be won, and the zest for playing games that invigorates childhood should be brought intact into adult lives. Play refreshes us physically, emotionally, and mentally. It hurries the appearance of possibility. "What if I kicked this ball past the pitcher?" "What if nobody can find my tree house?" "What if I hold back the ace of hearts? (What if I *am* the ace of hearts?)" De Beauvoir learned the constraints imposed on young children firsthand and gnawed at the adult censure cordoning her from mischievous romps and uninhibited adventures. "The abyss that separates the adolescent boy and girl has been deliberately opened . . . since earliest childhood" (*The Second Sex*). She wanted it all and was quick to spot gender, class, and ethnic divides passed down to children from the grown-up world. Turn the key that unlocks an unlimited future by giving *all* children, gender notwithstanding, the same rearing, education, and opportunities for play.

De Beauvoir stated emphatically that children deserve the experience of freedom. They are natural explorers spurred on by the bang of discovery. Initially: a caterpillar, a kite, a game of checkers, a bicycle, a tall tale, a tadpole, a flute, a peanut butter and banana sandwich. Soon: art, geography, language, poetry, cooking, invention. More: skinning knees, reeling from diving in headfirst, capturing the flag, making sand castles, sleeping over and staying wide awake. They must have faith in possibility and experience it as the juice of life. It is invaluable for adults to model playful spontaneity and readiness for a lark; otherwise, a child watches as possibility disappears with age. How can the adult-to-be consider possibility unless it was taught in word and showcased in human relations? Children acquire the conviction that they can create their futures only in a climate of freedom that includes them. Her free-roaming father and subservient mother showcased inequity and predictability; her father tried to steer her toward a husband rather than an education. A spirited daughter refused to inherit this world.

While she acknowledged children's dependence, de Beauvoir affirmed their full-blown humanity and innate dignity with persuasive conviction. She argued that we should not rush children into the business of growing up: "To treat him as a child is not to bar him from the future but to open it to him" (*The Ethics of Ambiguity*). The simple act of reading a bedtime story can leave the dreamer with wonder and energy to expend tomorrow; otherwise, "our lack of imagination always depopulates the future" (*The Second Sex*). Uncork bottles fizzing with possibility. "Let's play a game of 'Go.'" "Why don't we learn about Mesopotamia?" "What would you like to plant in the garden?" Take a well-spent moment and catch a whiff of their delight.

As adults we know that soon enough it will be time to play grown-up. The maturing child, pushed from behind by spontaneity and pulled forward by curiosity, wakes up to a world that is no longer a hand-me-down. "With astonishment . . . the child little by little asks himself, 'Why must I act that way' . . . he notices the contradictions among adults . . . their hesitations and weakness" (*The Ethics of Ambiguity*). The newly confirmed young adult has a huge job ahead, an entire world to create. Vitality, sensitivity, and intelligence are essential tools for this future-making business. These three "are not ready-made qualities, but a way of casting oneself into the world" (*The Ethics of Ambiguity*). Here you are! de Beauvoir would clap vigorously. Vigor, savvy, and awareness unleash you into an ever-expanding future, one you've anticipated throughout a wonder-fueled childhood. Exercise your potential constantly by living freely and jumping at possibility. Liberty is not a secure possession to have and hold; it is an activity. Move outward through books and music, onward through relationships and projects, even further through travel and experimentation.

Expanding Our Possibilities

This courageous lifestyle requires frequent gut-checks, of course, because "laziness, heedlessness, capriciousness, cowardice, impatience" (*The Ethics of Ambiguity*) can derail anyone's plans for the future. Ignoring possibility's demands and wallowing in negativity, it's tempting merely to take what's given and to give nothing in return. Says de Beauvoir: "Only the future can take the present for its own and keep it alive by surpassing it" (*The Ethics of Ambiguity*). She forces each of us to ask very hard questions. Am I up for the challenge of assessing the circumstances of my life with uncompromising honesty and drawing up my game plan accordingly? Will I win, again and again, a future so that I can be briskly alive in the present? Pratfalls multiply in the race away from possibility into a safe, suffocating cocoon. Why? "If I don't try I can't fail. I'd rather pretend I could have." "I'm a listless sort. Enough is enough even if it's not much!" "I don't want to lose what I have seeking something more." De Beauvoir made her case up front: every individual must transcend limits and sail past the constricting expectations of others. And if I do not? If all my life "does is maintain itself, then living is only not dying, and human existence is indistinguishable from an absurd vegetation" (*The Ethics of Ambiguity*). She paints a frightening picture of such a divorce from possibility. . . . At times the almost silenced inner voice of "what if?" nags at my vegetating soul; I deny it, mostly, sadly. I define fulfillment as "escaping the stress of existence" (*The Ethics of Ambiguity*). Terrified by the specter of defeat, I do nothing. I sentence myself to the worst of all punishments, life in prison, and serve as my own jailer.

The fact is that we *are* free unless we give our freedom away. Making possibilities real provides such joy that she beseeched her students and readers to clutch their free choice with hearty determination. Ah, to "love life on our own account and through others" (*The Eth-*

ics of Ambiguity). What makes possibility real? You do. I do. What gives the present its meaning? Your future. My future. What is the present without the future? "The tomb while . . . alive" (*The Ethics of Ambiguity*). Unforeseen and uncontrollable events do occur, and how we admire those suffering accidental ruin who regain the "upper hand" and preserve their options for later picking. They choose freedom; giving up isn't an option. Strength of will is developed over a lifetime; some days it wins more possibility than others. But every effort is worthwhile, a victory over a benumbing funk; every venture stirs the desire for more.

De Beauvoir works her way under my students' skin and stays there. They agree wholeheartedly with her that "there is hardly a sadder virtue than resignation" (*The Ethics of Ambiguity*). Vigor, sensitivity, intelligence . . . steady now and proceed . . . misstep and climb back up . . . push and propel forward. The opportunity for regaining freedom can never be lost. Philosophers stage a pep rally. "I'm not sure I can still carry a tune but I'll join the chorus and see what happens." "My soccer playing days are over, but I'm excited at the prospects of coaching or perhaps broadcasting." "I can apply to cooking school and work my way into a bistro kitchen. I'll figure out a way to pay for it." Possibility unsettles and excites, uproots and plants. Philosophy clubs of lunching colleagues and picnicking neighbors respond to de Beauvoir's philosophy of hope with hoorays for their current accomplishments. The chiropractor tries his hand at writing a book. The social worker runs for city council (and wins). A singer and a songwriter take their talents and their friends into the public school system, teaching children how to turn their stories into lyrics. The retired accountant thrives in an art history class and takes a job as a full-time gallery docent. An ex-financier bankrolls her organic bagel business. Pow! The "gloomy passivity" so despised by de Beauvoir now long gone for today's philosophers as it was for her: "My plan to be a writer reconciled everything; it gratified all the aspirations" (*Memoirs of a Dutiful Daughter*). And *your* gratification?

Expanding the Possibilities of Others

We are together in the drive forward; we cannot be free if we are surrounded by the imprisoned. The future is open for me only if it is open for all. I extend possibilities for myself when I make a commitment to your freedom, and to advancing possibility for children, for the elderly, for the poor, for the disabled, for the marginalized, for the uneducated. I lose my future without yours; the essence of freedom lies in its universality. Attendees at philosophy gatherings happily realize that they were at work in freedom's name before meeting their new ally from Paris: organizing and stocking a lending library used by inmates studying for their high school diplomas; fostering dogs for women and their children who are housed temporarily in shelters from domestic violence; serving as "puppy raisers" of eventual Seeing Eye dogs; bringing elderly residents from an urban community home to the country for their first mountain picnic. Funding free public transportation with old bicycles. Little big things.

De Beauvoir's emphasis on childhood gives older children pause to remember: how it felt to imagine possibility with hope; when fatigue was the result of a day completely used up; what it was like to come upon a new skill; where there was no end in sight; the triumph of turning the alphabet into words; the feat of learning to tell time while wondering if time was real; trusting instinct and first impulse; following the heart's lead. The child "feels that he can passionately pursue and joyfully attain goals which he has set up for himself" (*The Ethics of Ambiguity*). You can, too. De Beauvoir teaches adults to play again, for sheer fun and to inspire their passion for the future. Play restores vigor, ignores the *im*possible, and kills boredom. Whee! Wistfulness for days gone by slowly twists into eagerness for days to come. "I raised my eyes and looked at the oak tree. . . . That, I decided, is what *I* would be like" (*Memoirs of a Dutiful Daughter*).

What will you be like?

DISCUSSION QUESTIONS

- What is possibility? What are its key components?
- Do you anticipate possibilities? Does your future appear wide open?
- How does it feel to lose your belief in possibility? What does the awareness of possibility bring to your life?
- What does free will mean to you? Do you have options?
- Can we create potential? Is possibility given to us? Must we take it?
- Is it ever too late to change?
- Is Mill correct in his conviction that you always act according to your strongest preference? Do you agree that you can change your preferences by modifying your character?
- Do you shortchange your future by caving in to perceived social pressure? Have you shrunk your possibilities by tossing freedom away? When? Why?
- Are your perceptions of society's expectations real? Imagined? Who is watching?
- Do you curtail others' freedom? How? Do you expect people to live as you do?
- How important is personal freedom to your happiness?
- What were your childhood dreams? What are your hopes now?
- Do you want unlimited possibility? Are you comfortable having a wide-open, up-for-grabs future?

- If you do not create your future, who will?
- What do you think of de Beauvoir's assertion that possibility and freedom require courage and daring? Have you given up on yourself?
- Is it true, as de Beauvoir insists, that your free will depends on an atmosphere of freedom in the society as a whole? Do you work for others' freedom?
- Do you share the faith in human potential that rings loud in the philosophies of Mill and de Beauvoir? In people in general? In you in particular?
- What possible changes and opportunities excite you?
- What previously closed doors has de Beauvoir opened for you?
- What new possibilities appeared through Mill's encouragement?

HOMEWORK

Listen and Hum
Hit the shuffle button and follow the music. Instrumentalists, composers, and vocalists turn a potential combination of notes and space into the reality of song. Roam freely.

Spontaneity
- Miles Davis brings together a talented bunch of musicians, and generations have been anything but *Kind of Blue* since discovering "Flamenco Sketches." The album was recorded in two days, and each song usually in one take. Just hours before the session began, Davis sketched the grounding scales and dropped all chords to free the group's ad-lib. No rehearsal, no notion of doing it right, no concept of a fin-

ished product. Davis assures spontaneity with his "modal" method and a trumpet blowing "So What." Imagine living such improvisation. Take one!

- Rolling on the river aboard the "Proud Mary," there's no end to Tina Turner's delight that she "left a good job in the city." Money and security are no match for the freedom of finding her way without "worrying 'bout the way things might have been." Turner's rollicking version of John Fogerty's tune incites listeners to run after her and catch a ride. "The mere example of nonconformity, the mere refusal to bend the knee to custom, is itself a service" (*On Liberty*). What would you like to leave behind? Can you face forward without looking back?

- Three little birds sitting on her windowsill jump-start a carefree day for British singer/songwriter Corinne Bailey Rae. It's okay to be afraid sometimes, but you can relax into your future if you "do what you want to do." Me? "Put Your Records On," she sings merrily; "you go ahead, let your hair down." Pick a meeting and have everyone bring a "favorite song." Turn up the volume; let down the hair.

- The range of Sarah Vaughan's voice knows no limits. Listening to a "Sassy" tune feels like fingers combing velvet, tracing the depth of her bottomed-out lows to the peak of her operatic highs. Unfortunately for "Poor Butterfly" but happily for Vaughan's fans, "the moments pass into hours / the hours pass into years." Can you stretch your life high and low? Showcasing the joy of spontaneity, she joins her band members and transforms her vocal cords into a bebop instrument in "Shulie A Bop." The band members strike out on their own and her playful voice bops them home. How about some playtime today?

Hope

- "And when your world seems cold, you got to let your spirit take control," The Allman Brothers Band advises. At times everyone gets dragged down and loses that steady forward march, but your soul can "shine till the break of day." "Soulshine" is brighter than sunshine and fortifies even better than moonshine. Don't give up on possibility; tap into the wellspring of your spirit. How can you hold out against the dark days? Can you flip the light on in your soul?

- Germany's Felix Mendelssohn proves that it's never too late. This precocious teenager composed the symphonic "Overture" to his Shakespeare-inspired *A Midsummer Night's Dream* in 1830. Years of performing and conducting ensue, and in 1843 Mendelssohn picks up where the "Overture" ends and completes his masterpiece. Puck, Bottom, and the Fairies cavort in a lighthearted gambol to a score seventeen years in the making. Is there a project or a relationship or a dream that you would like to complete?

- One of Nina Simone's signature tunes gains new momentum in her daughter "Simone's" rendition of "I Wish I Knew How It Would Feel to Be Free." She longs for the invitation to express herself truly and to give "all the love that's in my heart" real freedom that is long overdue. But first she must "remove every doubt." In what specific ways can you encourage possibility in other lives?

- How you decide to "Teach Your Children" makes all the difference for Mill, de Beauvoir, and Crosby, Stills, and Nash. Adults must not pass down the old fears to those "of tender years," but should convince their children to "teach your parents well" with their youthful promise. What can you learn from a child about possibility? How can you "teach your children" to be independent while they are still reliant upon you? How can you let them go and hold them tight?

- In *At 89* (eighty-nine!), Pete Seeger continues to pluck his banjo and use his music in freedom's name. Though "God only knows what the future will be," Seeger hopes that children and teachers can have the confidence that "our school will get the money it needs for smaller classes." He says yes to Mill's faith in human potential, insisting that we must use our brains now "Or Else! (One-a These Days)." Do you share this faith in humanity? Since the urgings of possibility first appear in childhood, what must we do "or else"?

Triumph

- Austrian pianist Paul Wittgenstein lost his right arm in World War I and proved most resolute in fulfilling his musical potential. He commissioned French composer Maurice Ravel to compose his *Piano Concerto for the Left Hand*, and Wittgenstein premiered this piece in 1932 with the Vienna Symphony Orchestra. American pianist Leon Fleisher turned without complaint to the left-handed concerto when he suffered neurological damage to his right hand in 1965, shifting his talents to include conducting, teaching, and rearranging compositions for the left hand. Fleisher gave his next two-handed concert forty years later, his right hand freed by medical innovation. Is it up to you to create possibility as these two pianists invented new chances for themselves? What keeps their music playing?
- Wittgenstein was a bit unnerved at first by the jazz influences in Ravel's composition, a result of the composer's

admiration for American jazz in general and the work of
George Gershwin in particular. What were the odds that
a boy born in Brooklyn in 1898 to Ukrainian parents
would compose the first American opera in 1935 and that
his opera would feature an all-black cast? Gershwin's *Porgy
and Bess* mixes blues and jazz with opera's classical form
and transports us to Catfish Row in Charleston, South
Carolina. Porgy, a crippled beggar, tries valiantly to save his
beloved Bess from life on the streets. "I Loves You, Porgy,"
she responds to his "Bess, You Is My Woman Now." Gershwin unveils new possibilities for opera; Porgy determines
to find Bess in New York with a hopeful "Oh Lawd, I'm on
My Way." Imagine Broadway on this opening night, as Ira
Gershwin's lyrics grace his brother's music and "Summertime" lasts forever.

- Lori McKenna, songwriting mother of five, touts eccentricity in "Lone Star," applauding the success of the "geek"
bullied in high school and the "fat girl" clothed in her
mother's dress at the prom. Those tormenting high-school
big shots, now in dead-end jobs and dismal relationships,
hear his song on the radio and see her on television. Genius rules! That old, never-cool gang gathers for the big
concert that's come to town and McKenna teases them to
"Tell all the pretty girls in the beer line / how you are an
old friend of mine." HAH. Does eccentricity still take a
beating? Does bullying exist in adult company?

- A Cuban father and son ripple their fingers lightly
over the piano keys, Bebo Valdés playing "Suite Cubana"
in seven variations, and his son, Chucho, pointing out
"Los Caminos." Bound by their love of music during Chucho's childhood, Bebo left Cuba with the advent of Cas-
tro's revolution, living for four of his nine decades in

Sweden and most recently in Spain; Chucho returns to his permanent home in Havana from world tours. As liberating as their Latin jazz is for the listener, their relationship teaches another lesson. Father and son talk by phone regularly and often tour together, refusing to let political differences mar their friendship. "We never talk about politics. Ever . . . everyone can think what they want," Chucho affirms. Do you experience such respect for differing viewpoints in your family? What possibilities do Bebo and Chucho give each other?

• Three cheers, at least, for Howard Tate. An influential soul singer until the mid-seventies, Tate disappeared for thirty years, literally, in a homeless fog of drug addiction and consuming despair. He forgot that you've got to "Get It While You Can," that you must be willing to opt for love and "gamble on a little sorrow." Now in his sixties, the resurrected Reverend Tate ministers to those stuck in his former footsteps, using the money from his new recordings for homeless shelters and a rehab center in Philadelphia. Is there always the possibility of a comeback? "Don't Compromise Yourself" because when you "turn around the corner . . . it's yourself you're gonna meet." Have you shortchanged your talent?

Recite and Write

Read the short poems mentioned below before your meeting. Each one exudes promise. When your turn comes, surprise the group and maybe yourself!

• For Joy Harjo, a grateful member of the Creek tribe, prayer consists in opening one's whole being to the infinite swirl of the world's motion, and she is carried away as that endless movement is repeated by a majestic bird on a morning flight in "Eagle Poem." Beyond sun, moon, earth, and sky, there is ever more, always more than it is possible to see and to hear; "we are truly blessed because we / are born." Are you lured as well by this feeling of "more"? How can you splash some of the freedom of the eagle, circling high in the blue sky, into your daily existence?

- Dylan Thomas reminisces about golden heydays spent gallivanting in the fields without a care in his Welsh childhood at "Fern Hill." Chimneys sang, horses whinnied, and "my wishes raced through the house high hay," Thomas exults; nothing dampened the prospects of each day's amazing possibilities. Owls, foxes, daisies, pheasants, streams, and the sun so perfectly round, and "I was young and easy." Is it possible for you to be "young and easy" in spirit? Must age dull the whirling boy's grown-up thrills? Look! Hay fields high as the house!

- Chilean schoolteacher and educational reformer, and the first Latin American female poet to receive the Nobel Prize for literature, Gabriela Mistral helped countless children realize their potential and offers another option to "Those Who Do Not Dance." Mistral invites the crippled child to "let your heart dance" and the invalid to "let your heart sing." Even the withered thistle dances by giving itself to the wind. Are there glimmers of opportunity everywhere? Is it possible to cultivate the kind of optimism that Mistral brings to the dance? Do pessimism and cynicism foreclose on the future?

- Yes, we want more than an "Ordinary Life," Polish poet Adam Zagajewski enthuses. Everything in the world has an element of the unfinished about it. Forests cover once barren places; homes spring up in wilderness. How often we feel that our thoughts are only approximations, that we are working our way toward, forward, onward, stretching. "Ordinary life" pulses with desire. "Black cinemas crave light . . . a golden oriole prays for rain." Is any life "ordinary"? Does a forward thrust come naturally to all things? To you?

- "Hope Is the Thing with Feathers"; Emily Dickinson knows, deep down, that thing that makes a permanent home in the soul "and sings the tune without words / and never stops at all." Hope warms us even in cold despair and unexpected difficulty. Describe the bird of hope that perches in your soul. What colors are its feathers? Why do hope and possibility depend on each other? Do you agree with the poet that nothing can harm this small, quick-winged bird?

- Will you join Phillis Levin in her exuberant plans for a day in spring? "I've decided to waste my life again, / like I used to." She sets out briskly, promising herself that she will spend her time "in a new way." She drinks in the light filtering through the trees and urges on a wispy vine making its way through a tiny crack in a wall. Levin makes a fresh start on this "May Day." How does letting go of the past open her eyes to possibility? Does your past make claims on your future? Is Levin's rediscovered spontaneity appealing to you?

Read and Talk

- A washed-up newspaperman with a perennial "hand clasped over his chin" retreats to the coast of Newfoundland; Quoyle had "stumbled . . . into his thirties learning to separate his feelings from his life, counting on nothing." In *The Shipping News*, Annie Proulx rejoices as Quoyle cracks open the shell of possibility and "a bolt of joy passed through him. For no reason." Quoyle's flooded heart wonders "what else might be possible?" "Mountaintops give off cold fire, forests appear in mid-ocean . . . a crab is caught with the shadow of a hand on its back . . . the wind imprisoned in a bit of knotted string. And it may be that love sometimes occurs without pain or misery." Quoyle counts on everything now. Why not? "What else might be possible" for you? Why not?

- "We stand out in the lane watching the moon disappear behind a round black shadow. Uncle Pa says, That's a very good sign for you going to America, Frankie." Frank McCourt recounts his desperate childhood in Limerick, Ireland, walled in by poverty and adult cruelty, and his memoir paints possibility in a zigzag of colors. Rising from *Angela's Ashes*, the plucky youth with an indomitable sense of humor fulfills his dreams. "I stand on deck with the Wireless Officer looking at the lights of America twinkling. He says, My god, that was a lovely night, Frank. Isn't this a great country altogether?" "'Tis," Frankie concludes. What could you learn as a student in Mr. McCourt's high school classroom? How does his compassion free him to board that ship?

- Soul-sapped by his experience as a soldier and Japanese prisoner of war, Tayo must revisit his past if he is to win back his future. As he gropes for ways to recover his physical and spiritual health, he winds his way back to the rituals celebrated on the New Mexico reservation where Tayo heals in Leslie Marmon Silko's *Ceremony*. "The buzzing of the grasshopper wings . . . made his backbone loose. He lay back in the red dust. . . . The dreams had been terror at loss . . . but nothing was lost; all was retained between the sky and the

earth and within himself." Silko shares her character's La-
guna Pueblo heritage and knows the "vitality locked deep
in blood memory." What possibilities for the future can you
rediscover? What does your "blood memory" reveal?

• It is indeed a *Long Walk to Freedom* that Nelson Mandela
hikes in his unbending determination to defeat apartheid
in South Africa. Much of this autobiography was written
during his twenty-seven years as a prisoner on Robben Island, a life sentence surely anticipated in this description
of his wife: "Seeing my face, she knew that I was about
to embark on a life that neither of us wanted." He sacri-
ficed all those years so that others could be free. Why?
Why couldn't he be happy with a stable family life and a
successful legal practice? If it wasn't the path he would
have chosen for himself, why does Mandela state simply
that "the struggle is my life." Mandela was the first demo-
cratically elected president of South Africa. How many
futures does Mandela ensure?

• A newly minted teacher reared in the socioeconomic
safety of a "gated community," Erin Gruwell dives headfirst
into student lives riddled by gang violence and poverty,
and her courageous achievement is showcased fittingly in
*The Freedom Writers Diary: How a Teacher and 150 Teens
Used Writing to Change Themselves and the World Around
Them.* Clear ideas and good writing are tickets to college
for *all* 150 Wilson High School students, who find their
troubles surprisingly mirrored in Shakespeare's *Romeo and
Juliet:* "I've never read something in school that related to
something that happened in my life." That the diaries are
penned freely by students deemed "unteachable" is a celebration of human potential and of "Ms. G's" creativity
in finding a way to tap into it. Respond on behalf of

de Beauvoir and Mill to Gruwell and her "fighters." If buying a book can substitute for "buying a gun" in Long Beach, then . . .

- The sounds of Beethoven waft toward an LA *Times* reporter and the "Violin Man" with the battered, two-stringed instrument changes Steve Lopez's life. Nathaniel Ayers, a homeless man of "grubby refinement," is *The Soloist* in Lopez's uplifting and sobering tale of *A Lost Dream, an Unlikely Friendship, and the Redemptive Power of Music*. Once a Juilliard student full of promise, Ayers is felled by paranoid schizophrenia and takes up residence on Skid Row. Watching as "the music pushes him free of all distraction," the columnist sets out to reconnect the violinist with his potential. How does the music you love "anchor" and inspire you? "This is a man who at his best has a way about him that could be called self-possessed and charismatic," the reporter says of his friend. What lessons do this duo impart about possibility? Along with Lopez, ask why there are streets named Skid Row in so many American cities. Who lives on the "Row"?

Watch and Reflect

- "How weary, stale, flat and unprofitable / Seem to me all the uses of this world!" wails the Prince of Denmark, William Shakespeare's *Hamlet*. Called home after his father's death, Hamlet regretfully trades his philosophical studies at the University of Wittenberg for a passel of troubles in the castle at Elsinore. His mother, Gertrude, after but two months of mourning, has married his uncle, Claudius. Romance with his ladylove Ophelia knots with confusion. Already grieving and lost in contemplation, Hamlet's agitation soars when his father's ghost appears to him with the news that he died at Claudius's hand and that his son must avenge this deed most foul. Hamlet feigns a break-down, plays for time, hatches plots, and broods, "O, what a rogue and peasant slave am I!"; indeed, "what an ass am I!" Should he suffer his torment silently or exact revenge upon Claudius? "To be, or not to be: that is the question" that racks the would-be philosopher with indecision. "Ay, there's the rub" with *every* possible choice. Join the fray. Do you agree with Mill that Hamlet acts according to his strongest preference? What *is* his preference? Couldn't he go back to the university?! Why does his "noble heart" crack?

- In Room 56 at Hobart Elementary School, Rafe Esquith and his fifth-graders "defy the culture of the neighborhood and the country." This remarkable educator lovingly deliv-ers a future to children who speak English as their second language, dodge gangs and beggars on the streets of down-town Los Angeles, and mix with police as well as their peers in the hallways leading to their magical classroom. *The Hobart Shakespeareans* stage an unabridged production of *Hamlet* before an audience brought to tears and to their feet in delighted applause. Esquith's central, repetitive teaching, "be nice and work hard," pays dividends for stu-dents who literally own their educations. They learn how to use "money" by renting their desks and paying fines for incomplete assignments. True education is countercul-tural; violence, rudeness, and television are traded in for violins, math games, and rafting. "The readiness is all," Esquith knows, and he sends his charges into sixth grade with a tearful and happy farewell. "What are you going to accomplish next year?" he encourages. Despite the many disappointments that come with his vocation, he lives his creed that "good teachers don't give up." What do the young Shakespeareans and their guru teach you about possibility?

Get Up and Do

- Accept John Stuart Mill's invitation to a dinner party honoring his wife, Harriet Taylor Mill, who serves this provocative statement: "For a mind which learns to be satisfied with what it already is—which does not incessantly look forward to a degree of improvement not yet reached—becomes relaxed, self-indulgent, and loses the spring and tension which maintains it even at the point already attained" (Harriet Taylor Mill, "Enfranchisement of Women"). What is your response? Are you alert to possibilities for mental improvement? What does Harriet mean by a "self-indulgent" mind? A visitor from ancient Greece arrives just in time for feta and olives. Aristotle nods in adamant agreement with Harriet's position, adding that each of us is a "product of habit" and "our actions . . . determine our dispositions" (Aristotle, *Nicomachean Ethics*). We are what we do; never underestimate the power of habit, Aristotle concludes. An "incessantly" self-indulgent mind grows stiff and stagnates, and it eventually becomes impossible to restore the "spring and tension." Do you sacrifice mental growth and narrow your notion of the possible? In what ways do you nourish your mind's potential? Can it be said of you and/or those whom you know well that "inferior pleasures are . . . the only ones which they are any longer capable of enjoying" (John Stuart Mill, *Utilitarianism*)? What is the connection between mental stimulation and uncovering possibility?
- Try something new. One thing, however small. What else?

- Do something that you had somehow convinced yourself was impossible.
- Mark the day. Follow your heart.
- Sketch your future.
- Name and describe an invention that amazes you. Discuss the spirit of innovation with these creations as your backdrop. What is the meaning of invention?
- Devote a meeting to a chat about your hopes for the future. Each person expresses one thing that he/she wants to achieve and what he/she needs to do to make it happen.
- Invite two local folks who steered their lives in uncharted directions to your gathering . . . a career change, behavior modification, adventure, pastime. Ask your guests to pose five questions about freedom and possibility to the group.
- Uncontrollable circumstance can obscure possibilities. Sickness, calamity . . . Think of ways that you can provide openings in lives shadowed by trouble.

Resources

Music
- *Bittertown* by Lori McKenna: "Lone Star."
- *Put Your Records On* by Corinne Bailey Rae: "Put Your Records On."
- *Kind of Blue* by Miles Davis: "So What," "Flamenco Sketches."
- *At 89* by Pete Seeger: "Or Else! (One-a These Days)."
- *Ravel, Prokofiev, Britten: Piano Works for the Left Hand*, Boston Symphony Orchestra, Seiji Ozawa conducting, Leon Fleisher, piano: Piano Concerto in D Major by Maurice Ravel.
- *An Evening with the Allman Brothers* by The Allman Brothers Band: "Soulshine."
- *Bebo de Cuba* by Bebo Valdés: "Suite Cubana."
- *Bele Bele en La Habana* by Chucho Valdés: "Los Caminos."
- *Carry On* by Crosby, Stills & Nash: "Teach Your Children."
- *Howard Tate Rediscovered* by Howard Tate: "Get It While You Can," "Don't Compromise Yourself."

- *Simone on Simone* by Simone: "I Wish I Knew How It Would Feel to Be Free."
- *What's Love Got to Do With It* by Tina Turner: "Proud Mary."
- *Sarah Vaughan (Verve Jazz Masters 18)* by Sarah Vaughan: "Poor Butterfly," "Shulie A Bop."
- *A Midsummer Night's Dream* by Felix Mendelssohn, Boston Symphony Orchestra, Seiji Ozawa conducting.
- *George Gershwin's Porgy and Bess*, Houston Grand Opera (CD).
- *Porgy & Bess* by George and Ira Gershwin, Glyndebourne Opera, Sir Simon Rattle conducting, directed by Trevor Nunn (DVD).

Poetry

- *How We Became Human: New and Selected Poems, 1975–2001* by Joy Harjo: "Eagle Poem."
- *Eternal Enemies: Poems* by Adam Zagajewski, translated by Clare Cavanagh: "Ordinary Life."
- *Selected Poems 1934–1952* by Dylan Thomas: "Fern Hill."
- *May Day* by Phillis Levin: "May Day."
- *Gabriela Mistral: A Reader*, edited by Isabel Allende, introduction by Marjorie Agosin: "Those Who Do Not Dance."
- *The Poems of Emily Dickinson*, edited by R. W. Franklin: "Hope Is the Thing with Feathers."

Prose

- *Ceremony* by Leslie Marmon Silko.
- *The Freedom Writers Diary* with Erin Gruwell.
- *The Shipping News* by Annie Proulx.
- *Angela's Ashes* by Frank McCourt.
- *The Soloist: A Lost Dream, an Unlikely Friendship, and the Redemptive Power of Music* by Steve Lopez.
- *Long Walk to Freedom* by Nelson Mandela.
- *Essays on Sex Equality* by John Stuart Mill and Harriet Taylor Mill: "Enfranchisement of Women" by Harriet Taylor Mill.
- *An Examination of Sir William Hamilton's Philosophy and of the Principal Philosophical Questions Discussed in His Writings* by John Stuart Mill.
- *Basic Writing of John Stuart Mill: On Liberty, the Subjection of Women and Utilitarianism* by John Stuart Mill.
- *The Second Sex* by Simone de Beauvoir, translated by H. M. Parshley.
- *The Ethics of Ambiguity* by Simone de Beauvoir, translated by Bernard Frechtman.

- *Memoirs of a Dutiful Daughter* by Simone de Beauvoir, translated by James Kirkup.
- *Nicomachean Ethics* by Aristotle, translated by Joe Sachs.

Drama
- *Hamlet* by William Shakespeare, directed by Kenneth Branagh (DVD).

Documentary
- *The Hobart Shakespeareans*, directed by Mel Stuart (DVD).

Joy

~~~~

We ourselves cannot put any magic spells on this world.
The world is its own magic.

—Shunryu Suzuki, *Zen Mind, Beginner's Mind*

THE TOPIC

Philosophizers nibble at the corners of joy but find it hard to articulate its essence. Is it the experience of "merriment" or simply "feeling your best"? Is joy more than happiness and less than pleasure, or is it the reverse? What's happening? Such an anticipated topic, such a longed-for reality, and we can barely talk about it? Another philosophical prank!

Somewhat defensive students assure me and one another that they know what joy is even if they can't define it. "Everyone knows what joy is." "Really?" I inquire with arched eyebrows. After more fumbling attempts at a definition, it's a relief when a hand goes up and a spokesperson admits for the gang that "maybe we don't know what we're talking about!" Join my students and me as we tiptoe toward joy's meaning. Here's the assignment: "Imagine that joy has sensory qualities and jot down your images. Our descriptions can serve as building blocks for our understanding of joy. What is the look of joy? Taste? Sound? Its touch? Smell?" Thinkers sink into private wanderings. Some sketch and write only an occasional word; others scribble quick phrases and compose paragraphs. But we're on our way at last.

I feign surprise at my companions' difficulty in defining joy, but it's a challenge for me *every* time. I mosey after joy, trying to know it better. . . . To my eyes it appears as hands clasped, my two or mine with another's, as the brightest sun on whitest snow, and in smiling eyes squeezed shut. Its sound is laughter, stringed instruments pitching' ever higher, and dancing feet. It tastes like nothing else, as it combines both the delicacy and strength of crystal clear water. Tingling warmth radiates from the touch of joy, and it has the feel of rich, moist soil crumbling in fingertips. Joy smells like home. My sensory exploration leaves me better equipped to ask: What is joy?

Joy is a heart full and a mind purified by gratitude. It is steady elation with a current of "at last" coursing through it. Joy's fingers lift my heart out of my chest and hold it high so that nothing can touch it. A tincture of bliss, the scent of perfection and completion accompany joy. It has more staying power than happiness with no chance of being diminished by circumstance; I can be happy and still want more. Joy is *it*. This full-blown exhilaration stands in stark contrast to the tired heart and weary soul that often precede it; I know joy as misery's opposite. Joy's tall branches are secured by deep roots; it grows in the wake of trouble and sadness in a life fully lived. Its consuming presence can surface even in the midst of disaster. Joyful experiences pass; memory keeps joy alive. Joy is life's reward.

Now the group is ready; their first responses to my explanation of joy are questions: "Why do I feel joyful so seldom?" "Something always nags at that feeling for me. I wonder 'what next?' or 'maybe it won't last.'" "I know about pleasure but I don't think I've felt pure joy." "It's like I always expect something more." These laments give me an opening.

"Why do you think that joy is such a rare experience?" I ask. "You were so sure of joy's meaning and value at the beginning of our discussion. Remember?" The memory makes them more determined to grasp its meaning and we settle in. . . . "What gets in the way of a full heart?" I inquire. Chins get a rubdown. "I complain about the least thing." "Everyone seems to have an easier life." "I'm always disappointed in the end." We sit, a bit disgruntled but optimistic, and take turns poking at joy. And then this fortunate interruption: "Wait! It's what I said earlier—I always expect something more. That's the problem. I'm never satisfied, never thankful for what I have." Yes, that's it. We lack gratitude. How might I describe . . . ?

Gratitude is in-your-bones appreciation for what comes your way; it answers "yes," come what may. It purifies the mind of the confusion wrought by "me first" and creates plenty of room for joy. Gratitude reverses the attitude that the world owes you something, lots of things, and that you deserve them and much more: the biggest-screen television, gourmet dining, travel and leisure on demand, a partner who is all yours, a baby who never cries. Drowned out by the noise of entitlement, joy hasn't a chance. A grateful person approaches each day with a sincere "thank you" poised on the lips.

Just the thought that the world owes us nothing frees and fires dialogue. I agree to go first in a quick round of "grateful because." I'm grateful to the man who taught me to play tennis for no payment or reason other than love of the game and belief in a kid's promise. I'm thankful for infusions of grace that lighten my way however long the time lapse between injections. Every time love nips me by surprise, my being registers an automatic thanks. And, how fortunate I am that I make a *living* by sharing philosophy. Now encouraged thinkers jump at their chance to answer "grateful because." "My sister raised me." "I survived testicular cancer and have three children." "My boss took a chance hiring me." "I was moping around because I wanted a sweater I couldn't afford with my fifteen-hours-a-week, minimum-wage job. When I plugged my annual salary into a global study, my income ranked in the top eleventh percentile in the world. I shut up." "Pasta is cheap and can be cooked with infinite variety!"

What to do? Can I lean into each day with thanksgiving? Thank full because relationships, levees, and faith hold fast? Will I learn that joy can spring *only* from a grateful heart?

Two grateful philosophers offer us ways of living that invite joy to soak our beings. Zen Master Shunryu Suzuki (shun-REE-oo suh-ZOO-kee), exhaling slowly, tempts us to breathe and laugh big-mindfully. Inhaling at sunrise, Jane Addams enjoys, every day, the immense satisfaction of a job well done. Hello, joy. Here you are.

THE PHILOSOPHERS

When you can laugh at yourself, there is enlightenment.

—SHUNRYU SUZUKI, *Not Always So:*
Practicing the True Spirit of Zen

Japanese Zen Master Shunryu Suzuki spent twelve years with American students hungry for a joyful life of the spirit in the midst of material plenty. The climate of change that rippled through the United States during the sixties struck him as fertile soil for the growth of the Buddhist concept of right mindfulness. The practice of cultivating right mindfulness brings simplicity and joy, and this steady state of mind serves as a faithful daily guide. Suzuki knew that it is not always easy for us to steer our minds straight and true. Appreciating the human talent for complicating life, he gives directions for piloting our lives toward joy, directions that are compellingly straightforward.

Suzuki's students relished their Master's way of teaching. At his Zen Center in California, he specialized in informal, lively talks that encouraged questions. He was famous for his patient, consistent responses, and his humor and compassion endeared him to all who had the privilege of being in his presence as he imparted Buddhist lessons. For today's philosophers, as well, Suzuki instills confidence that the world's magic beams into unclouded minds.

Counting Breaths

My students often share the initial suspicions of Suzuki's pupils, somewhat dubious that the following simple sequence, if observed, will lead to joy. I put myself in his sandals: Inhale slow, belly-deep, rib-expanding breaths. Exhale. Count these breaths with full concentration. Practice just this. Deep breathing provides a sense of well-being while at the same time it increases mental alertness. Discipline your mind, coming to full attention through one-two-three-four breathing. Consciousness sharpens as oxygen delivers. We sit and breathe.

Suzuki and I continue: Enhance your attentiveness with five-six-seven-eight breaths. Be mindful. Appreciate each and every thing with your energized "big mind." Let gratitude swell, nine-ten-eleven-twelve. Laugh. Breathe with mind and lungs full. Inhale the universe; expel fear. Death? The river flows. Joy.

"What kind of philosophy is *this?*" doubters exclaim. "Breathe and pay attention? Isn't he stating the totally obvious?" The doubt solidifies when I tell them that Suzuki's chain reaction is intended to solve major problems. "Like what?" a polite scoffer asks. The number-one problem, that "I lost my mind," is an answer that pleases my philosophizing buddies immensely. "I say that all the time but I don't really mean it," many agree, ready to dismiss the problem. "Well then. Where is your mind right now?" I challenge. They are intrigued. "In how many places? With what thoughts and feelings? What is your focus? Where *is* your mind?" Such questions startle students (and teachers!) of all ages; they make us merry, too. "I am out of touch with my mind." "I can't point to any *one* thing in my mind. I was thinking a lot of things when you asked and can't remember even one." What's going on? Suzuki warns that this divorce from the activity of our minds will cost us plenty. How shocking to realize that I have not been the captain of the ship that is my life. Reclaim your mind, the Master urges, issuing a call for mental discipline. Our minds expand when they stand at attention, observing the whole world with penetrating awareness. A mind full of concentrated energy sails us smoothly, joyfully through life. But until then? Breathe, Suzuki insists.

Breathing *is* essential. Suzuki generously repeats his advice to count breaths and thereby restore the mind's full capacity. This is much more difficult than anticipated. "I say 'one' and my mind wanders before it registers the second breath." "Seems as if something else has my mind as a thing of *its* own!" "It takes every bit of hardheaded concentration to connect a count with a breath." Students of all ages warm to the counted-breaths assignment and, with a bit of practice, discover its rewards. "I wish I could count to infinity!" exclaims a happy child philosopher. "When I count my breaths I actually breathe. I'm not so tired," a grown-up philosopher marvels at this basic truth. "It's a good way to learn to pay attention; my breath is like wind blowing my confusion away." Counting breaths induces mindfulness that carries us more lightly on our way; when we are wrapped up in practiced breathing, this calm stays for longer visits. Suzuki likens breathing to boating, in an image treasured by many of my students: "We should wear this civilization without being bothered by it, without ignoring it, without being caught by it. . . . Be like a boatman. Although he is carried by the boat, he is also handling the boat. This is how we live in this world" (*Not Always So*).

But it is not easy to train the mind to perform these breath-counts. It takes practice, regular and disciplined. Soon, however, the composure found in breathing leeches into daily life. "To count each breath is to breathe with your whole mind and body" (*Not Always So*). Counting awakens mindfulness of breathing; with time and diligence, breaths begin to count themselves. Running for the bus, typing on the laptop, inhaling and exhaling life's juice . . . one hundred percent concentrated.

Dazzled

Now, more alert, more mindful, I observe the world as I did as a child. Without preconceptions or self-imposed limitations, my new/ old "beginner's mind" takes nothing for granted. Color. Wet. Sound. I am smack in the middle of the world, absorbed in it, filled with life unbounded. This beginner's "big mind" swallows the world in one delicious gulp. Fascinated and wowed, my big mind serves as a collection basket for every single thing. Cleansed by breath, I am quietly dazzled. I appreciate everything just as it is. Flower. Ginger. Stick. Water. Me. "That is all, but it is splendid" (*Zen Mind, Beginner's Mind*). Now fully conscious, I'm hooked. I get it! How could I find joy in a world that I was not experiencing? No, the world never lost its luster; yes, I stopped giving it my undivided attention. Noticing nothing, nothing satisfied. "In the beginner's mind there are many possibilities; in the expert's mind there are few" (*Zen Mind, Beginner's Mind*). Joy comes when I give each moment my big-minded all. One. Two. Three. Four.

Suzuki describes mindfulness as a "smooth, free-thinking way of observation . . . without stagnation . . . soft . . . imperturbable . . . stable" (*Zen Mind, Beginner's Mind*). A big mind is on its toes. It opens to the whole world with complete trust, not looking for trouble or expecting to be hurt. This is a mind full of respect for . . . this rock, right here; this conversation right now. Mindfulness is sincere; it is empty of deceit. Its merger with the world is direct. Can this attentive mind be the key to joy? How can it be so simple? My mind was running interference with the world's communication of joy.

After a few weeks of experimenting with breathing and mindfulness, stunned students testify to the merits of Suzuki's way. "My breath was in my throat; I was always slightly panicky and at least a little sad. Now I can be in the world and okay, more than okay, with it and with me." "Honestly, I thought this was a bunch of woo-woo. I concentrated on my breathing to prove it was ridiculous. But it was like going from a black-and-white world to a full-color one." "I'm more interested and involved in the world, feeling that I have something to offer." Suzuki joins the testimonials to breathing: "we are, in actuality, giving out everything. Moment after moment we are creating something, and this is the joy of our life" (Zen Mind, Beginner's Mind). "I was so happy when I realized that I can wake up my childlike thrill and still be a responsible adult. Why not? How neat to be worldly-wise and innocent." This glowing report card comes with an insistent reminder. Practice, students learn, is key. Keep counting your breath or you will lose your mind.

Breathing Gratitude

"When you really experience counting your breath, you will have deep gratitude" (Not Always So). Mindfulness leads ultimately and inevitably to gratitude. Mindful of life's beauty, I naturally express gratitude and with its release experience an increasing upswing of freedom. Big whew. Gratitude takes the sting out of difficulty. "When we forget ourselves . . . we can enjoy our life" (Zen Mind, Beginner's Mind). Gratitude kicks me out of my own way. Thankfulness floods into a mind big enough to behold each piece of the universe. The ordinary is miraculous. Tree bark; dog bark. Bird whistle; my whistle. My problems are no match for the world's magic, and "they are just enough" (Not Always So) to measure and handle with counted breath. Mindfulness harmonizes our lives, equipping us with vigor and humility. Everything we do is infused with a "continuous feeling of pure gratitude" (*Branching Streams Flow in the Darkness*). Nine. Ten. Infinity.

Laughter and Joy

Just laugh! "Maybe we are crazy . . . It's okay" (*Not Always So*). No philosopher has a better appreciation for humor's benefits than Suzuki. His sincere consolation that their problems would last a lifetime caused previously frustrated students to burst out laughing. His straight-faced assertion that hell is having to speak English out loud delighted the audience listening to him search for his words. He lavished humor indiscriminately: he "solved" a woman's dilemma about what to do with a twenty-dollar bill she happened upon by sliding it up his sleeve; he greeted the news of his terminal diagnosis with relief that he and his disciple could nibble from the same plate since his illness was not contagious. Come on! Laugh with beginner's-minded delight. Laughing at ourselves softens the rough edges of our small-minded concerns. And this laughter has the added bonus of taking the harshness out of self-criticism. "You are not kind enough with yourself" (*Not Always So*). Use a light brush to highlight your weaknesses. Be big-hearted with yourself; learn not to "take things too seriously" (*Zen Mind, Beginner's Mind*). Shout it out.

A big hand of applause for the Japanese Master's practice of laughter and command to be kind to yourself! Examples of laughter's rejuvenating properties compete with protests that we fall out of the habit of laughing. "The finish of a big laugh feels like the end of a race. Healthy and light." "But people stare at you when you laugh like something's wrong . . . with you." "I'll trade my frown marks for my laugh lines any day." "I love to *hear* laughter; I'm just not used to *doing* it." Laughter enhances philosophizing, and we do both naturally, I remind them. And how much joy we sap by being hard on ourselves. We *are* crazy. Words rush out breathlessly. "Aren't I part of the world, too? Can't I appreciate myself and feel grateful for my life?"

"How do we become so heavy-handed with ourselves? Is that what it means to be mature?" "You know how relaxing it is to hoot at yourself? It's the way to become better acquainted with you and see your good qualities. I'm so clumsy I would make a great clown." "If I can love myself, look out, world!" "With big mind and with pure sincerity and respect, love can really be love" (*Not Always So*).

Death and Joy (Joy and Death)

Once his lessons in laughter put philosophers at ease, the Zen Master guides his students (and mine, from age five to eighty) past joy's last stumbling block. Suzuki picked up quickly on the American preoccupation with death. Indeed, death's inevitability lurks in the mind's nooks and crannies, never far from consciousness. And, now, with renewed gratitude for all that life offers, it's even worse. . . . Yes, he chuckled, but "if you had a limitless life it would be a real problem for you" (*Zen Mind, Beginner's Mind*). Life would be a run-on sentence, dangling without meaning, without death's assurance of impermanence. Dying is part of the magic; it shapes the contours of our being as it rounds our life. Rely on big mind.

Suzuki invites us to enjoy a new outlook on death. He asks that we imagine our lives to be like drops of water. Originally there was only one whole, flowing river—no separation, a steady stream. Your individual existence is a teeny-tiny splash away from the whole. Living is not easy as a lone drop. Death gives you a lift home again, back to your pain-free participation in the one river. "When we reach this understanding we can see the beauty of human life" (*Zen Mind, Beginner's Mind*). Life and death dissolve into each other in the river. The stream moves on. "Our mind should be soft and open" (*Zen Mind, Beginner's Mind*), graciously including death within gratitude's scope. Grief and emotion come naturally; enter these feelings with a beginner's mind that sees no end to the river. "Because we are so attached to our own feeling, to our individual existence," death looms larger than life. What might death be? "We will have . . . perfect composure" (*Zen Mind, Beginner's Mind*). Snag death with big mind; return it to the water.

Suzuki earns high marks from his early doubters. "Nothing guarantees joy. But just those little things, especially laughter, make it possible." "My beginner's mind has been giving me a field day. I'm happy for no reason. Or for every reason." "It shakes me up! Practicing gratitude is like being on a permanent vacation. No worries, thank you!" Suzuki likely would caution overjoyed philosophers that acquiring and maintaining a mind full is the work of a lifetime. He might counsel them that small wrong-mindedness can dampen joy abruptly. We can miss the magic.

But not today. "At first I didn't recognize the sound echoing in the house. Then I realized it was my laugh." "Sometimes I am in love with nobody in particular." "I'm no Master, but I think that joy is a short word for enlightenment." Today, "there is nothing to attain, so we have a sense of gratitude or joyful mind" (*Not Always So*).

> *I have never been sure I was right. I have often been*
> *doubtful about the next step. We can only feel our way as*
> *we go on from day to day. But I thank you all.*
> —JANE ADDAMS, Honoree, Women's International League,
> 20th Anniversary Celebration, *1935: A Centennial Reader*

Joy came to Jane Addams as she fulfilled the big-minded dreams of her youth. Born in Cedarville, Illinois, in 1860, she was inspired by her father's political activism and public service. Young Jane was a bright student and later a college graduate whose plans for medical school were cut short by back problems. She made two trips to Europe with the inheritance she received at her father's death, and it was on the second trip in 1888 that her life's work called to her demandingly. The downside of industrialization was on vicious display, especially in London's East End, and this misery fueled her youthful intolerance of hunger and the suffering of the poor. After visiting Toynbee Hall, a settlement house for boys, Addams returned to Chicago with a plan. A young, well-heeled girl who envisioned living among the poor grew up to be a settlement dweller, a peace worker, and the first American woman to win the Nobel Peace Prize.

Philosopher and Social Worker

Though her peers described Addams as a social worker, and the moniker persists today, she saw her calling differently. An avid proponent of pragmatic philosophy, she believed that "a man's primary allegiance is to his vision of truth and . . . he is under obligation to affirm it" (*Peace and Bread in Time of War*). Duty called her to give practical, real-life meaning to her ideas; philosophizing is worthless unless one's thinking is applied to everyday living. Ideas take shape and refine and deepen in practice. Two ideals in particular, the concepts of democracy and peace, grounded Addams intellectually and motivated her to act. She labored to make her democratic idealism a reality for Chicago's poorest inhabitants. *All* people must live in keeping with its essential meaning if democracy is to have any relevance: national government on all levels, dinner tables, and international organizations, bound together *by* the people and *for* the people. At democracy's core lies belief in the dignity of each individual, validated by tolerance, and it must be proven in practice. Her dedication to the concept of peace was demonstrated in all facets of her work, most especially in her determination to feed the hungry. As long as hunger stalks the planet, talk of peace is but frivolous chatter. Philosopher Addams strove to put into play her big ideas: democracy and peace. She taught their meaning with her life.

Turning Ideas into Actions

Addams experienced joy daily as she brought her ideas to fruition, especially the concept of public service that she had cherished since childhood. "I had at last finished with the everlasting 'preparation for life'" (*Twenty Years at Hull-House*). She was more than ready, and though opportunities for women to play leading roles in society were few in Addams's day, she forged a prominent niche on the local, national, and international stages. Two organizations delivered her lifelong joy as they also promised Addams certain difficulty: Hull-House, the settlement she opened in 1889 and lived in with her college friend and co-founder, Ellen Starr; and the Women's International League for Peace and Freedom, the organization she founded in 1915 and served as president of for twenty years.

Addams gripped her vision of truth with sure-handed integrity, using her natural gifts for organization, for galvanizing others, for spotting talent, and for finding a way to get the job done. This strong-willed woman translated lingering health problems such as pleurisy and pneumonia into mere nuisances, batting aside "self pity, perhaps the lowest pit into which human nature can sink" (*Peace and Bread in Time of War*). Addams's life stands as vivid testimony to the joy that can come from translating our ideas into action. Such joy can be ours, as well, if we learn how to perfect our follow-through.

"The educational activities of a Settlement, as well as its philanthropic, civic, and social undertakings, are but different manifestations of the attempt to socialize democracy" (*Twenty Years at Hull-House*). Addams funded the lease for Hull-House on Chicago's Halsted Street with her remaining inheritance money (and dedicated *Twenty Years at Hull-House* to her beloved father). Democratic principles came alive, reaching out to immigrants clinging to survival on the streets of a busy city. This residential home for approximately thirty women hummed as a hub of activity and a community gathering spot for thousands of visitors each week. Smells of native cuisines welcomed travelers to a new land, and whiffs of coffee lured those thirsty for companionship. The first rental house grew to thirteen buildings through private donations won by Addams's relentless petitioning. Picture it: children scampered to stimulating kindergarten classes, ran races in the courtyard, and played ball with adults in the gymnasium; she was youth's champion. Clubs provided camaraderie as groups enjoyed theater, music, pottery, and philosophy. Night classes accommodated workers toiling long hours in factories, while a day care center freed time for women's education. A museum devoted to the accomplishments of the laboring classes buoyed fatigued onlookers with pride in their work. A museum honoring those sweating on the assembly line and in the garment district! Addams gave her all to the practice of her democratic philosophy: "We were often bitterly pressed for money and worried by . . . unpaid bills; we cooked the meals and kept the books and washed the windows without a thought of hardship" (*Twenty Years at Hull-House*). Garbage collection, faulty incinerators, smallpox, and easily procured cocaine waited for the chief tenant's immediate attention outside her door. Joy found Addams easily, however, because she got what she wanted, every day, a young girl's longings finally satisfied by "a simple, health-giving activity . . . involving the use of all her faculties" (*Democracy and Social Ethics*). Happiness even slipped through a crack in a door left unlocked in the excitement of the first night at Hull-House; Addams rejoiced at dawn at the "honesty and kindliness of our new neighbors" (*A Centennial Reader*).

Joy and Sadness Intertwined

Two situations in Addams's life serve as perfect examples of how joy rooted in meaningful work can help one stay the course even in the face of sadness or adversity. Imagine her heavy, inconsolable

heart after a "wretched night of internal debate" shortly after the outbreak of what would become world war. Addams gazed at the largest
room at Hull-House, once a welcoming space frequently used as a
voting precinct for overjoyed new citizens. She watched as the room
was transformed into a registration center for the draft. She saw
familiar faces in the long lines, people who came *to* her for a lease on
happiness; many of her regulars in the kitchen and library now turned
on her in angry despair. Had she not promised them a better life?
Didn't she remember that her large immigrant family fled warfare to
find safe haven in America?

After living at Hull-House for twenty years, however, the early
returns on her investment predicted much success. "I see scores of
young people who have established themselves" and they flocked to
her with polite reintroductions, faith that she remembered them, and
hearty expressions of gratitude. Imagine her joy as she stood on a
bustling street corner, chatting with a former club member who now
worked at a newspaper, so heartened by his swift, unrehearsed testimony to the meaning of the Hull-House experience: "It was the first
house . . . where books and magazines just lay around as if there were
plenty of them in the world. Don't you remember how much I used
to read at that little round table . . . ? To have people regard reading
as a reasonable occupation" (*Twenty Years at Hull-House*).

Another major source of heartache that Addams weathered was
the bitter criticism she endured for her unswerving and quite vocal
pacifism. The small and larger triumphs and overall joy of life at
the settlement steeled her against these verbal and printed attacks.
She was taken to task for creating such a visible center catering to
the poor; for her instrumental role in making civil liberties real for
children, women, immigrants, and the laboring masses; and for her
dogged fight for political and legal reforms and against raging police
brutality. But it was her continued international campaign for peace
that particularly riled her opposition. Blasphemy! Bawdy woman!

She was not eligible to vote, after all, and this upstart subversive contrived to give President Wilson advice? Pacifists endured enormous unpopularity during the war, an antagonism which only intensified afterward. Even many of her friends deemed her and her sympathizers unpatriotic for criticizing the war. But her girded stance was the only option for a philosopher dedicated to both the concept *and* the reality of peace. As the war dragged on and the irrational, hate-fueled propaganda escalated, "there were moments when we were actually grateful for every kind of effort we made" (*Peace and Bread in Time of War*). Her abiding joy was rooted in dedication and integrity; the appearance of success or failure, the arrival of opposition or praise—all irrelevant.

Baking Bread, Ending War

No philosopher ever spoke of "bread" more than the Hull-House chef. World hunger feeds war; peace and hunger can never coexist. Nourished stomachs empty gun barrels. In Europe, Asia, and at home on Halsted Street, Addams shouted at the carriage-driven complacency of the economically well-to-do. How embarrassing, how indecent, the candlelit satiation in the midst of aching bellies. Hunger shames us all. "Human nature . . . has never quite fitted its back to the moral strain involved in the knowledge that fellow creatures are starving" (*Peace and Bread in Time of War*). Addams never backed off then and she speaks to us now: How can we resign ourselves to hunger? Making peace with hunger is unthinkable. Hunger causes war. Peace is a prerequisite for joy. Bake bread. Only bread can make the idea of peace a reality. Failure to bake is inexcusable.

For the pragmatist Addams, pleasure derived from matching her life with her ideals through books, travel, meetings, speeches, protest, grocery shopping, and educational reform. Joy came from ethical consistency enhanced by her inborn personal dignity. Neither condescending nor overbearing despite her sharp intellect and vast knowledge, Addams sought consensus with bold humility. Though her life's work pitted her against her culture at every footstep, she was thriving in the thick of things. Addams's description upon the death of Jenny Dow Harvey, a much-loved settlement teacher, sums up her own life. She wrote that Harvey made the best preparation for death, "that of free and joyous right-living" (A Centennial Reader).

Philosophers huddled in community centers and living rooms, in college and elementary classrooms, find lots to consider in Addams's applied philosophy. Addams did not sentimentalize her life nor did she invite a do-gooder reputation. Philosophers uplifted by her tireless labor and boosted by her obvious joy in her calling are sobered by her contention that "each of us can do so little in the great task of regenerating society" (A Centennial Reader). The link between her joy and the lack of self-pity also never goes unnoticed. Students wish for the same gratification from fulfilling youthful stirrings and exhausting inborn talents. All are challenged by her finger-pointing at hunger . . . and at them.

Philosophy in Practice

It is a joy for me to see, year after year, what sticks with staying power to philosophers newly emboldened by Addams: the ways in which Addams proved the validity of her thinking by testing it in the "real" world. Philosophy works! "Addams motivates me to be a philosophical scientist, experimenting with my ideas in the big lab of the world." "She gets credit for my volunteer work at the legal aid center." "Addams makes me question whether or not the 'real' United States is in fact a democracy. Is the idea of democracy achieved in practice?" Conversations about democracy spill into hallways and parking lots. Talk of philosophy's merits goes on forever. . . .

Along with my circles of thinkers, I gain ongoing inspiration from Addams's merger of thought with action, from her discovery of joy through serving her ideals. I can see her goals for Hull-House and its daily activities come alive when . . . I watch my evening students shuffle into class, weary from a day's work yet eager for nighttime philosophizing; when I hear children play loud and long at recess and after school; when I pass volunteers canvassing the neighborhood to register voters; when court-sponsored interpreters make a legal proceeding less intimidating for a non-English speaker; when students volunteer at food banks. When prospects for peace brighten, I know that she did her pacifist part. And sometimes when a former student asks if I remember the day that _____, I picture Addams being approached by generations of grateful former tenants on the streets of Chicago.

I met one of Addams's protégés while visiting children who were graduating from two weeks of philosophizing at summer camp. Eleven-year-old Noah pointed to topics written on the board: friendship, responsibility, happiness, justice, courage, prejudice, nature, and love. Glasses slid down his nose to be nudged upward again as he looked from the board to me and back. "All those words add up to help. That's what they have in common. If we help others, it means we understand all those ideas. Just help." Ah, there's the "joy and beauty of youth" (A Centennial Reader) that Addams extolled. Noah knows instinctively what Addams knew for sure, that philosophical understanding calls for action. Addams examined democracy and peace and set out briskly. Noah will find his way.

And you?

DISCUSSION QUESTIONS

• What is joy? What is its essence?
• Is it any more or less difficult to define joy than it is to unravel other concepts? Do you distinguish between joy and happiness? If so, how?

- What gives you joy? When are you joyful? Does joy come easily?
- If you went looking for joy, where would you go? Can you seek and find it?
- Does joy come and go? Do you find an element of permanence in joy?
- What is gratitude? What is its relationship to the experience of joy?
- Do feelings of gratitude come naturally to you? Do they come frequently?
- What gets in the way of gratitude?
- Do you have a sense of entitlement? Do you feel sorry for yourself a bit? A lot?
- What does the world owe you? Be specific.
- Is your sense of humor healthy? Can you laugh at yourself?
- How do you describe "mindfulness"? What are its essential ingredients?
- Do you agree with Suzuki that deep, attentive breathing is crucial for joy? What happens physically and mentally when you practice counting breaths?
- What is "big mind"? Why does Suzuki dub this "beginner's mind"?
- What is the "world's magic" according to Suzuki? Where is joy?
- Why did Jane Addams choose to live at Hull-House? Why was she happy in her digs?
- Do you agree with Addams that joy dangles forever out of reach without peace?
- How did Addams define joy by the life she lived? Be specific.
- Do you apply your ideas to real-life situations, as Addams

tested the meaning of democracy and peace every day? Do you use your philosophical insights?

- Do you have a rib-expanding capacity for joy? Should you lose it, what one brief tip from Suzuki will set you right again? What one boost can Addams provide?

HOMEWORK

Listen and Hum

Gratitude and exuberance ring out as joy shows off in a festival of musical genres.

Begin your adventure with a short trip to Claude Debussy's "L'Isle Joyeuse" (The Isle of Joy). His music substitutes perfectly for the quiet time that usually opens your gatherings. Listen. Picture hands gracing the piano. Listen again and imagine the joy-infused isle. Then decide together how to share the following three "takes." At the end of your tuneful party, discuss this statement by Chicago's premier landlady: "In the deep tones of the memorial organ . . . we realize that music is perhaps the most potent agent for making the universal appeal . . . to forget . . . differences" (*Twenty Years at Hull-House*). Which *one* work would you take into conflict as a peace offering?

Joy, Take One

- Ah, sunset and summer birdsong, bells tolling in the distance, the smell of fresh-cut grass, "by the river holding hands / roll me up and lay me down." Pink Floyd loves that "Fat Old Sun" as it sings a silvery sound and drops into night. Shhhh. Lie down. Watch. Good night. Early "Echoes" from primeval days reverberate, sparking our imaginations and motioning us toward light. Good day! The band salutes sunrise as "a million bright ambassadors of morning" beam through open windows "inviting and inciting me to rise." Are you up?

- Erykah Badu whips together hip-hop, jazz, and rhythm and blues, blending them in celebration of her joyous transformation into an "Orange Moon." She is mesmerized at suddenly "reflecting the light of the sun" in her moonlit life that shines newly bright. "How good it is," she intones, over and over; indeed, "how god [sic] it is." What transports you almost out of your humanity as the dance of sun and moon elevates Badu?

- Antonio Vivaldi paints *The Four Seasons* in colorful violin concertos in 1720. Each season possesses its distinctive beauty. Listen to "joyful spring" with its flowing brooks, soft breezes, and a dog's barking commentary at the shepherds' dance. A cuckoo trills summer's arrival with its annual thunder, lightning, and pounding hail. Autumn harvest calls for singing, dancing, and a good sleep. Snow signals winter's blasting winds, sending shivering thoughts of cracking ice. The Venetian composer captures a season in three short movements. Which season moves you especially? What joy does each season bring without fail?

- Kate McGarry, with vocal encouragement from Theo Bleckmann, gives away the secret that thrills e. e. cummings, singing the poet's joyous assurance to his darling that "i carry your heart with me (i carry it in my heart)" wherever I go. McGarry's lilting arrangement lifts cummings's words from the page into love's rarefied air, love that soars as "the sky of the sky of a tree called life; which grows / higher than soul can hope or mind can hide) [sic]." Whose heart do you carry in yours? Who takes your heart for a daily ride?

Joy, Take Two

- Would "wild geese that fly with the moon on their wings" be on your list of "My Favorite Things"? John Coltrane's soprano saxophone plays with this Rodgers and Hammerstein tune for thirteen-plus minutes, giving you plenty of time to remember your favorite things to recall on days when you're "feeling sad." Coltrane's free-flying sax evokes a trance-like, meditatively rollicking mood. His final notes wind us happily home with the moon-winged geese.

- How about letting go of some stuff . . . mounds of antibiotics, mouths stuffed too full, clamor for recognition, stupid blame, and "how bout not equating death with stopping," Alanis Morissette pleads. Instead, how about shouting "Thank U" for the harbingers of joy: for clear vision, for the humbling awareness of frailty, for no-holds-barred crying until tears dry up; for grief and forgiveness. Oh, and "how bout me enjoying the moment for once!" And most of all, "thank you thank you silence." Silence and joy? Why does this impassioned singer connect the two?

- What better voice to chant the sheer gratitude that "joy and peace is mine" than Nina Simone's? How her soul has longed for "Consummation," and at last she finds perfect fulfillment in "joy, joy, joy, joy, joy." Listen as she holds and elevates each distinct note in the resonating "we are one." Is this the sound of joy? How do you think this song won its title?

- Mississippi Fred McDowell taught Bonnie Raitt to play the slide guitar, which she totes to Maria Muldaur's living room for their duet of one of his favorite spirituals. Muldaur and Raitt engage in powerful plucking and full-breasted singing that "It's a Blessing" to call on the Savior. In spite of life's plentiful trials, there's "no fret, no worry." What a "blessing just to live, a blessing just to be present." Stick with prayer and fingers for blessing-counting, their voices merge reverently. Counting breaths and counting blessings . . .

Joy, Take Three

- India's beloved Ravi Shankar plays his sitar with visible and audible abandon that has brought pleasure to generations of fans worldwide. He translates his soulful connection with this traditional stringed instrument into hypnotizing improvisational ragas. Shankar's "Song from the Hills" happily recalls an old folk tune, while his passion for his craft in the twenty-minute "Raga Multani" yanks the willing listener into the composition. India's guru of song believes that music is the language of the divine, and he has spread this universal means of communication around the globe for more than half a century. A generous mentor, Shankar counts George Harrison, Philip Glass, and Yehudi Menuhin among his many grateful collaborators. Is music God's language?

- Cooking rice, making soup, rubbing on his three-day stubble with no intention of shaving, reflecting on where he's been and where he's going, these pleasures on a lazy day convince Darrell Scott that "It's a Great Day to Be Alive." The sun shines on a redbird's feathers and keeps right on shining when he closes his eyes. "It's a colorful life that we go through," isn't it? Great day! "Why can't every day be just this good?" Can every day be a great day to be alive? Tell Darrell.

- Composer Libby Larsen cheers *Eleanor Roosevelt* in a dramatic cantata based on the accomplishments of the "first lady of our modern world." Roosevelt's life is reprised in song and spoken word, much of the text taken directly from her writings and speeches. "I wanted to work for peace, for the poor and dispossessed, for the rights of human beings everywhere." Roosevelt speaks through the narrator, and the cast celebrates the Universal Declaration of Human Rights, which she sponsored and pushed to fruition in 1948. The cantata closes with her insistence that there is still "so much to do." Jane Addams lived to see this woman carry on her legacy of service from the White House. Imagine these two travelers together. Where might they be baking bread today?

- Latch on to Ruth Brown's flat-out jubilation as "Miss Rhythm" belts out to her mama that "This Little Girl's Gone Rockin'!" Listen, ooh, now listen to me . . . dishes done, food bought, puppy fed, "and I did a lot more." She promises to be home by midnight and not a second later. Do you believe her? "Well-a, well-a, well-a, well-a," could Ruth be out rockin' still? Is she with you?

Recite and Write

Enjoy a soul-glide with the following expressions of joy and gratitude. Recite and repeat until the poem sings to your satisfaction. Pick up the poet's cadence and ride with it. Share your favorite with someone who is not, for now, in your group.

- "Thank the stars there's a day" every week set aside for the flow of quick and lingering strides—Rita Dove is dancing on "Fox Trot Fridays." So heavenly, the smoothness of "heel-ball-toe," locked with your partner in the sweeping space provided by notes and floor. Thank you, Friday, for such happiness, floating with meshed ribs on sure feet.

What lifts your spirit as the poet's lightens to a fox-trot? Can you practice your personal "dance" once a week?

- Despite difficulty and darkness, we continually repeat an utterly sincere "Thanks." Gratitude is called for no matter where we are, even "back from a series of hospitals back from a mugging . . . in doorways and in the backs of cars and in elevators." Waving, we say thank you whether any-one acknowledges us or not. What's gotten into W. S. Merwin that he appreciates the funeral, the war, and the destruction of forests? Should "thanks" play as our tele-phone greeting? Imagine a life in which a bow of gratitude was the first response . . . to everything.

- Marianne Moore toasts the human courage that rises above the inevitability of death through a frank admission of mortality that is surpassed, over and over, by utter glad-ness in being alive. Like a caged bird who grows taller as he sings a full-throated ballad, we heighten our stature as we look death in the eye and scoff: "What Are Years?" Our lengthening strides match the highest treble of the stretch-necked songbird, and both testify that "satisfaction is a lowly / thing, how pure a thing is joy." Do you agree with Moore's suggestion that it is through embracing our mor-tality that we can hug eternity? Tell all. Explain joy's purity.

- Feel your breath catch at Seamus Heaney's mounting plea-sure as he takes us on an autumn drive into Ireland's County Clare. Wind and light play a game of tag; the ocean glitters on one side of the road while the lake is whitened by a meeting of swans on the other. He answers our unasked question: it's pointless to stop the car and to try to see it all perfectly. We can only drive on "as big soft buffetings come at the car sideways / and catch the heart off guard and blow it open." When has joy blown your heart open as it does in the poet's "Postscript"?

- Anne Sexton uncovers joy in everything as she awakens with a hearty "Welcome Morning." Brushing hair, rubbing dry with a freshly washed towel, eggs and coffee and the waiting mug and dish on the table . . . Morning glory such as this speaks God's name, and she always means to drop to the floor in a prayer of gratitude. She mostly forgets, but not this morning. With laughter and an open palm painted with a thank-you, she begs us to remember that "the Joy that isn't shared, I've heard, / dies young." How does shared joy extend its life? Can communal joy extend everyone's life?

- Not a day passes without Mary Oliver's being bowled over by the world's beauty; indeed, she was born to be enlightened by daily offerings of the most extraordinary ordinariness. The commonplace gives birth to miracles. Look! Listen! Let the ocean and the grass be my teachers, she prays, as I nestle "inside this soft world . . . in joy." Be "Mindful," Oliver instructs herself; cause for untarnished delight abounds. Would you appreciate a mind full of the awareness she preaches? Can the world prop up your being in joy?

Read and Talk

- Laugh out loud with "beginner's minded" glee as you trip through Jon Scieszka's *Knucklehead,* a collection of hilarious stories from his youth in Flint, Michigan. Anointed by the Library of Congress the first national ambassador for children's literature, he feels lucky to have found a receptive audience among "juveniles." Squirm at the desk next to his in fifth grade as he hears Sister Margaret Mary's foreboding question, "What's so funny, Mr. Scieszka?" and giggle with his hysterical classmates at his answer. He uses humor to invite children into the joys of reading. What does he teach you about laughter's therapy? What's so funny that your eyes water? How does it feel to be swept into laughter's grip?

• A Kikuyu woman lives Addams's conviction that feeding the hungry is the key to peace. Wangari Maathai wears youthful joy on her face as she extends her pioneering Green Belt Movement, begun in 1977, from her Kenyan home across Africa. "At the time of my birth, the land around Ihithe was still lush, green, and fertile . . . we lived in a land abundant with shrubs, creepers, ferns, and trees . . . clean drinking water everywhere . . . hunger was virtually unknown. The soil was rich, dark red-brown, and moist," she writes in her autobiographical *Unbound*. She watches deforestation change Kenyan life; abject poverty and killing hunger replace topsoil and watersheds. Maathai's solution: pay women to plant trees. Give them jobs that pay for their education while restoring the forests. Forty million trees have been planted, most fruit-bearing, and the rivers flow again: jobs, food, hope, joy. Linking peace to the health of the ecosystem, Dr. Maathai is the first African woman and the first environmental activist to win the Nobel Peace Prize. Her work cost her plenty: imprisonment and poverty. But her face!

• Shells collected at the shore remind Anne Morrow Lindbergh of her "island-precepts" for a life of joy: "simplicity of living . . . balance of physical, intellectual and spiritual life . . . work without pressure . . . space for significance and beauty . . . time for solitude and sharing . . . closeness to nature." Her "moon shells" serve as tokens of her *Gift from the Sea*, recalling her to the simple truths that she does not want to lose in the everyday hustle far from whelk and oyster beds. Ocean waves teach Lindbergh "the joy in the now, some of the peace in the here." She leaves with "the beach at my back," knowing that "there are more shells to find." Where will you find yours? What "precepts" for a life of joy are yours already? What do you know, and what have you perhaps temporarily forgotten?

- "Though he would never say so himself, he has single-handedly changed the lives of tens of thousands of children," David Relin writes in testimony to Greg Mortenson's transition "from a mountaineer to a humanitarian" in their *Three Cups of Tea*. In 1993, lost and alone from his failed attempt to scale the Himalayan mountain K2, Mortenson straggled into the tiny village of Korphe in Pakistan. The villagers happily took him in and, touched by the children's fierce desire for an education, he promised to build a school. Today some sixty schools flourish in Pakistan and Afghanistan and Mortenson's Central Asia Institute supports many hundreds of teachers. One of his mountaineering buddies pictures Greg "quietly, doggedly heading back into a war zone to do battle with the real causes of terror." Joy? Yes, salutes young Jahan: "After I graduated from the Korphe School, I felt . . . I could go before anybody and discuss anything . . . I can start a hospital . . . I want to be a 'superlady.'" Joy for Mortenson? Oh, yes. Upon hearing Jahan's dreams: "Five hundred and eighty letters . . . and ten years of work was a small price to pay . . . for such a moment." Suzuki meets Addams.

- Almost forty thousand runners take off in a flash in *A Race Like No Other*, and Liz Robbins takes us along for the 26.2

miles of the 2007 New York City Marathon. The pre-race
workers spreading gallons of special blue paint to guide the
way, the runners, the millions of fans lining the streets,
the race officials—all complete a picture of joy. Joy in being
a part of it all for the wheelchaired participant with cerebral palsy racing backward, the cancer survivor, recovering
alcoholic, sixty-seven-year-old grandmother. "How far can
they push their bodies?" How far can *anyone* push life's
boundaries in exhilaration? "Today is, indeed, a brand-new
start," the race announcer promises. "We wish each of you
the race of a lifetime." What training tips for life's race can
you find on the streets of New York? What daily exercises
prepare you to give and get the most?

- Morrie Schwartz is dying, and his former student Mitch
  Albom welcomes laughter-laced *Tuesdays with Morrie* just
  as he did twenty years ago. What lessons remain? "The
  most important thing in life is to learn how to give out
  love, and to let it come in," and for the professor "love is
  when you are as concerned about someone else's situation
  as you are about your own." Albom brushes his hand across
  Morrie's head and sees that "the slightest human contact
  was immediate joy." As Mitch kisses Morrie goodbye, the
  last exchange between these "Tuesday people" is "Okay."
  Why? On several occasions his mentor assures Mitch that
  "death ends a life, not a relationship." Discuss Morrie's
  repeated refrain that "when you learn how to die, you learn
  how to live." Shades of a soul mate? "Will you try to find
  some better expression for death? When you find it, you
  will have quite a new interpretation of your life" (Suzuki,
  Zen Mind, Beginner's Mind). Morrie counsels the student
  he loves that by making peace with death we can do what's
  more difficult, to "make peace with living." Peace.

Watch and Reflect

- A Norwegian family transplants its roots to San Francisco at the turn of the twentieth century and daughter Katrin spins her reminiscence in John Van Druten's *I Remember Mama*. Four children and their father sit every Saturday night at their kitchen table ritual, watching as Mama stretches every scant penny to meet their material needs; she spends her own grace, gratitude, and humor lavishly on everyone. These immigrants are poor in cash and rich in joy. Mama's big mind encounters beauty everywhere: in a bunch of violets for sale in the foggy mist; in watching her children's faces as her boarder, Mr. Hyde, pays his "rent" by reading aloud the works of Dickens and Doyle; in the boat whistles sounding from the Bay; in sneaking into the children's ward of the hospital and singing to the sleeping children; in sharing her brother's happy death with a clinking-glassed "skol." To bolster her daughter's flagging spirit, Mama exchanges a recipe for professional advice for the struggling, would-be author. "You must write about what you know," Miss Moorehead tells Katrin, and soon the celebrating family returns to the kitchen table for Katrin's reading of her first published story titled "Mama in the Hospital." What does she "know best"? Mama's full life of joy. What spiritual heirlooms match the brooch Mama gives her daughter? Discuss the absence of entitlement in Mama's world.

- Joy spilling from tents housing the wounded, displaced victims of civil war's violence rides on the riffs of *Sierra Leone's Refugee All Stars*. Six young men survive a decade's madness as bandmates; led by composer and singer Reuben M. Koroma, Franco, "Black Nature," Mohamed, Efuah, and

Arahim give their music as healing balm to their ravaged country. Their joy in playing music proves contagious; faces transform and spirits revive listening to the singers' somehow joyous chant that they are "refugees just like you people." The band's legend spreads as the group travels from camp to camp, winning a world tour for their music and ultimately drawing UN involvement in their home-land. Their smiles spread as wide as the headphones they don in amazement in a recording studio for the first time. Who can believe their great fortune? Who can believe their story? "Today you settle / tomorrow you pack," they sing to amputees and the grieving, returning home to Sierra Leone from the tour in early 2004, "rolling like a rolling stone." Their West African reggae album plays to global fanfare. How do the boys from Sierra Leone impart lessons from Addams and Suzuki? What do you see on their faces? If you went backstage after an All Stars concert in the U.S., what would you do? Say? Ask? Learn?

Get Up and Do

- Gather for a dinner party and bring one musical and one poetic contribution for a merry evening. Yo-Yo Ma hosts the gathering with a talented guest list of musicians in-vited to join him in playing *Songs of Joy and Peace*. His group project stems from his belief that the comfort of peace is a precondition for joy. Five variations of "Dona Nobis Pacem" ("Give Us Peace") soothe in complemen-tary ways: Ma on cello; Edgar Meyer on bass and Chris Thiele on mandolin; Assads Sérgio and Odair on guitar; Paquito D'Rivera on clarinet and Alon Yavnai on piano; and Chris Botti on trumpet. Gladly accept Diana Krall's many compliments because "You Couldn't Be Cuter" or smarter or nicer or smoother. . . . My musical tonic is an irresistible New Orleans brew heated up by Dr. John: "Let's Make a Better World" and "put some love in the air," oh! sing and "dance, dance, dance." Serve poetry for dessert, each person reciting one poem that speaks of joy. Go around the room; soak in the feeling. Wislawa Szymborska slides "A Note" from Poland in your pocket, reveling among many joys that "life is the only way . . . to follow a spark on the wind with your eyes."

- Make a list of things for which you are grateful. Look at it regularly. Add to it.

- Share thoughts gleaned from your reflections on joy with someone who can benefit.

- Notice the times that you clamp down on your laughter. Bust out.

- Set aside certain times each day for counting breaths. Count on these times.

- Choose the musical instrument that most directly conveys joy to you. Enjoy it in a variety of musical genres. Listen for this sound in nature. Listen.

- What place makes your heart sing? Go. Spend some time there physically, mentally, and/or emotionally.

- Paint joy.

- Reflect on the state of mindfulness. What happens? Sketch the feeling.

- Make one cost-free donation to a cause championed by Addams. Today.

- Host an Addams-style welcome for a new arrival to this country.

- Spend one day in joyful step with Suzuki. Breathe, count, open "big mind," say thank you, laugh. Easy.

- Read German philosopher Friedrich Nietzsche's hymn of joy and respond to these soaring passages from "The Drunken Song": "Was *that* life? . . . Well then! Once more!" Would you live your life again? "For joy, even if woe is deep, *joy is deeper yet than agony.*" Does joy touch you more intimately than pain? "Joy wants the eternity of *all* things, *wants deep, wants deep eternity.*" Why might Nietzsche suggest that joy wants to live forever? What about joy?

Resources

Music
- *Rockin' in Rhythm: The Best of Ruth Brown* by Ruth Brown: "This Little Girl's Gone Rockin'."
- *Eleanor Roosevelt: A Dramatic Cantata Based on Her Life and Words* by Libby Larsen; Camerata Singers, Floyd Farmer conducting.
- *Aloha from Nashville* by Darrell Scott: "It's a Great Day to Be Alive."
- *Portrait of Genius* by Ravi Shankar: "Raga Multani," "Song from the Hills."
- *Richland Woman Blues* by Maria Muldaur with Bonnie Raitt: "It's a Blessing."
- *Silk and Soul* by Nina Simone: "Consummation."
- *Supposed Former Infatuation Junkie* by Alanis Morissette: "Thank U."
- *My Favorite Things* by John Coltrane: "My Favorite Things."
- *Moss* by Moss, Kate McGarry on vocals with Theo Bleckmann: "i carry your heart with me (i carry it in my heart)."
- *Four Seasons* by Antonio Vivaldi; Il Giardino Armonico Orchestra, Giovanni Antonini conducting.
- *Mama's Gun* by Erykah Badu: "Orange Moon."
- *Meddle* by Pink Floyd: "Echoes."
- *Atom Heart Mother* by Pink Floyd: "Fat Old Sun."
- *My Favorite Encores*, Van Cliburn, piano: "L'Isle Joyeuse" (The Isle of Joy) by Claude Debussy.
- *Songs of Joy and Peace* by Yo-Yo Ma & Friends: "Dona Nobis Pacem," "You Couldn't Be Cuter."
- *Mos' Scocious: Anthology* by Dr. John: "Let's Make a Better World."

Poetry

- *Why I Wake Early* by Mary Oliver: "Mindful."
- *The Complete Poems: Anne Sexton*, foreword by Maxine Kumin: "Welcome Morning."
- *The Spirit Level* by Seamus Heaney: "Postscript."
- *Complete Poems* by Marianne Moore: "What Are Years?"
- *The Rain in the Trees* by W. S. Merwin: "Thanks."
- *American Smooth* by Rita Dove: "Fox Trot Fridays."
- *Miracle Fair: Selected Poems of Wislawa Szymborska*, translated by Joanne Trzeciak: "A Note."
- *95 Poems* by e. e. cummings: "i carry your heart with me (i carry it in my heart)."

Prose

- *Tuesdays with Morrie* by Mitch Albom.
- *A Race Like No Other* by Liz Robbins.
- *Three Cups of Tea* by Greg Mortenson and David Oliver Relin.
- *Gift from the Sea* by Anne Morrow Lindbergh.
- *Unbound* by Wangari Maathai.
- *Knucklehead* by Jon Scieszka.
- *Thus Spoke Zarathustra*, "The Drunken Song" by Friedrich Nietzsche, translated by Walter Kaufmann.
- *Zen Mind, Beginner's Mind; Branching Streams Flow in the Darkness* by Shunryu Suzuki.
- *Not Always So: Practicing the True Spirit of Zen* by Shunryu Suzuki, edited by Edward Espe Brown.
- *Twenty Years at Hull-House; Peace and Bread in Time of War; A Centennial Reader; Democracy and Social Ethics* by Jane Addams.

Drama

- *I Remember Mama* by John Van Druten, directed by George Stevens (DVD).

Documentary

- *Sierra Leone's Refugee All Stars*, directed by Banker White and Zach Niles (DVD).

THANKSGIVING

The process of writing a book has much in common with an old-fashioned barn raising. It takes many people willing to lend a hand, some unasked, who see the need for the barn and who believe in the book. In the end, nothing can compare to the roof's soaring spire or the shelf's bound treasure.

This barn-raising author wraps grateful arms around:

Joel Fotinos, Sara Carder, and Andrew Yackira at Tarcher/Penguin: Joel, for enticing me to write a book begging to be written; Sara, for savvy editing with her uncommon touch; Andrew, for his expertise laced with welcome humor.

Patty Moosbrugger: trusted agent and friend.

Trey Corrin: my student and entire staff, a gentle man who gives humanity a good name.

Paige Turner, Jan Panzer Kilfeather, and Rachel Gerny: Paige, for her table-pounding insistence to begin writing immediately; Jan, for heartfelt cheerleading from afar, all along the way; Rachel, for gently convincing me the circle was complete, the job done.

Kay Bethea and Brian Keena: Kay, for her ongoing portrayal of a Renaissance woman; Brian, for his bluesy role as the messenger of jazz.

Crystal Newell, Lisa Stockwell, Charlotte Self, and Kristen Brooking: expert sleuths.

Amy Gillespie, Benjamin Sloan, Irina Timchenko, and Beryl Solla: talented and lovely colleagues.

Ace, Betsy, and Jay Dalgleish: providers of wooded walks and kitchen warmth.

John Zunka: a nimble-footed gent who keeps me on his dance card.

Grace Carpenter: a sage advisor who lives up to her name.

And bellowed-from-the-mountaintop gratitude for:

June, my mother, quite simply a star.

Mac, my father, on whose knee I was introduced to the world of ideas and in whose company I saw the beauty of the human heart.

Maria, my cousin, who always cares.

Mel, my dog, who sniffed and pawed until he found my words.

And, of course, every single one of you with whom I have sat in a philosophizing circle . . . and happily become your student.